Make Products That N

A Practical Guide to Understanding Customer and User Needs

Dr Chloe Sharp

C000101685

BIS Publishers

BIS Publishers
Borneostraat 80-A
1094 CP Amsterdam
The Netherlands
T +31 (0)20 515 02 30
bis@bispublishers.com
www.bispublishers.com

ISBN 978 90 636 9684 9

Designed by Studio Chehade
Illustrations by Silwat Wisansak

Contents

Introduction: Understand the Problem Before Building A Product

"The most important thing is knowing what we can't know." (Marc Andreesen)

One of the biggest causes of start-up failure is building something the market doesn't need. CB Insights (2021) evaluated over 100 failed start-ups and found that 42% of businesses made a product that no one required because they didn't prioritise validating the problem or the market. As an entrepreneur, Innovation Lead or Product Owner, it may feel exciting to start building a product or service immediately to create something tangible to demonstrate progress. However, making a product and service this way means that entrepreneurs and product teams focus on the technical aspects and the question, 'Can we build this?' rather than 'Should we build this?'

Not understanding and validating the problem the business is trying to solve means building a solution that no one needs, which has real-life consequences for businesses. Having a product or service no one buys can lead to the company failing as it runs out of money, is in the wrong market and has ineffective marketing.

Start-up Genome (2019), an innovation policy advisory and research firm, found that 90% of start-ups fail, with similar leading causes. The top reason was a lack of Product-Market Fit (34%), and the second was marketing problems (22%). A poor product can lead to difficulties entering the market, reaching profitable sales volume, and communicating its benefits to customers through marketing. As Andy Rachleff's Law of Start-up Success states: *"The #1 company-killer is lack of market. When a great team meets a lousy market, the market wins. When a lousy team meets a great market, the market wins."*

Not meeting market needs isn't a challenge unique to start-ups. Accenture (2010) found across 630 US and UK Executives that, 57% reported the 'inability to meet customer needs', resulting in low uptake of new products and services. Fifty per cent blamed product failure on 'lack of a new or unique customer-perceived value proposition'.

Understanding the market and customer needs takes time. An excellent place to start is understanding and validating the problem, creating ideas for the solution, testing the problem-solution fit as early as possible, and then building the product.

Entrepreneurs and product teams guessing what the market is, what customers and users need can be a more time-consuming, expensive, and resource-intensive approach in the long-term than starting with researching the problem. Starting with small steps by getting feedback early on and throughout the product development process can pay dividends later.

"If you hustle together $50k to start your business and spend all $50k on your first idea only to see it fail, that's bad. On the other hand, if you have $50k and spend $5k to learn you're running down a dead end, that's awesome. You can use the rest to find a viable path to your goal." (Rob Fitzpatrick)

This book walks through the development of new products and services from idea through to launch into the market and how and when to research to make data-driven and evidence-led decisions.

Who this book is for

This book helps entrepreneurs with early ideas or have a highly innovative idea in development and are looking to do the research themselves to understand customer and user needs or understand how it works so this could be outsourced. Read the book from the start to get a comprehensive overview of the product development process and what types of research, tests and experiments are needed at different points.

This book is also for early career UX Designers, Researchers, Product Managers, and Innovation Consultants looking to understand how to do research when developing a product from an idea to the product entering the market through to its continuous improvement. Project or Programme Leads in SMEs or large organisations seeking to develop new products and services and wanting to understand the process can benefit from this book. This book will help you understand how research can keep your business in touch with the customer to stay innovative. Keep in mind the business case and stakeholder management to showcase the benefits of research, prioritise outcomes and stay flexible over focusing heavily on delivering milestones.

Academics and students who may be considering being an entrepreneur or building a start-up or spin-out university venture who understands a new or upcoming innovation or technology but needs support in evaluating customer and user needs. This book can help you navigate how to start the research process in line with the development of the technology you're building to understand not only the technical feasibility but its viability as a business and the market demand.

Key terms

Before we get started, there are some terms you will need to know, in case you are entirely new to product development and research.

— **Product:** A tangible or intangible offering that fulfils customer needs by providing a solution or experience.
— **Service:** An intangible offering that delivers value through actions, expertise, or support to address specific customer needs or requirements.
— **Problem:** A human-centred challenge or opportunity that requires creative problem-solving, empathy and understanding of the user needs to develop innovative solutions.
— **Solution:** An innovative and user-centric response or approach that effectively addresses the identified problem, providing value, impact, and meaningful outcomes for the intended users or stakeholders.
— **Value Proposition:** A concise statement articulating a product or service's unique value, benefits, and competitive advantage to target customers, addressing their specific needs and differentiating the business from competitors.
— **User:** Users are the people who will be using the product. They're also known as end users.
— **Customer:** Customers are those who will be buying the product. Sometimes users and customers are the same person, sometimes not.
— **Validation:** A process to systematically test and gather evidence to confirm or disprove the accuracy and reliability of assumptions made about users, needs, behaviours or market conditions.

Structure of the chapters

The remainder of the introduction will provide an overview of the key ideas in product development, User Experience (UX), innovation and design, which explains major thought leadership across these fields to help you ask critical questions about building products.

Chapter 1 explains innovation, how it has evolved since the 1950s, and what this means for creating innovative products and services today.

Chapter 2 explores where ideas come from that may have inspired the concept for the product or service. Then, we move on to Chapter 3 to learn about Design Thinking in more detail to understand how that approach evaluates the problem and takes a problem-solving approach.

Chapters 4 through 6 provide you with strategies to identify who your users and customers are at the outset, identify your assumptions and prioritise the customers or users you want to learn more about and hypotheses you want to validate. We explore how to use interviews, focus groups, observations, and surveys to understand customer and user needs. Plus, how to analyse the market and competition to evaluate the context of the customer and user. Chapter 6 helps you to plan your research project and can be used for experiments too.

Chapter 7 outlines data collection of interview data and survey data to show you how to ask questions to understand user and customer needs. Chapter 8 covers the analysis of interview and focus group data to inform the generation of ideas with key stakeholders and product teams to set up your ideation sessions discussed in Chapter 9. Chapters 10 to 12 move on to prototyping to learn what solutions could fit the problems that customers and users have and outline different types of MVPs and ways to test these using experimental approaches.

Chapter 13 explores how to move from MVP to the release of the product into the market. Chapters 14 and 15 detail how to continue testing products when they're in the market. Chapters 16 and 17 provide tools for stakeholder management if you're in an environment that doesn't encourage research and how to build a business case and consider business models for the product. Chapter 18 summarises all the research methods and briefly considers the role of AI in research and product development in the future.

Learning from big ideas

Over the last three decades, there have been considerable strides in how entrepreneurs, product teams and innovators approach developing products and services. Lessons can be learned from some of the greats in the fields of product, User Experience (UX), innovation and design to help you ask better questions throughout the product development process, such as: 'Are we building the right product?' and 'Do customers want this product?'

In the early 2000s, organisations were becoming more collaborative, customer-focused, and network-based leading to the popularity of Open Innovation. This was the case, particularly for larger-sized organisations that wanted internal and external influences on innovation.

Through technological advancements and the rise of the internet, software development became more accessible, and people could create their businesses more quickly. In the early 1990s, the idea of the start-up began, and this was when there was a rise of approaches that have the flexibility of Agile but the mindset of a start-up, such as Jobs-To-Be-Done, Product-Market Fit and Lean Start-up.

Today, we need to be sustainable and environmentally conscious when developing product and services and can see the rise of Planet-Centred Design. This enables design and software development teams to consider the impact technology and ways of working may have on the environment, animals, and people.

Each key idea will be expanded from The Agile Manifesto to Planet-Centred Design to explain each concept in more detail.

1980s	User-Centred Design and Human-Computer Interaction
2001	The Agile Manifesto
2003	Open Innovation
2003	Jobs-To-Be-Done
2007	Product-Market Fit
2009	Design Thinking
2010	Lean Start-up
2010	Business Model Canvas
2012	Marmer Stages
2014	Value Proposition Canvas
2016	Design Sprints
2018	Objectivies and Key Results
2021	Continuous Discovery
2023	Planet-Centred Design

The 1980s: Start of User-Centred Design and Human-Computer Interaction
Don Norman, a design theorist, developed User-Centred Design in the 1980s. User-Centred Design focuses on the users and their needs throughout the design process. User-Centred Design (UCD) has evolved through four waves, coinciding with Human-Computer Interaction (HCI) development. Human-Computer Interaction is a multidisciplinary field that brings together engineers and designers to understand how the user, software and hardware interact and HCI has evolved over three waves.

The first wave of HCI focused on engineering and aimed to build systems that are easy to use. The first wave of UCD was where there was external support for users to use software such as training to help people use products. The second wave of HCI was cognitive science and psychology, where the idea of decision-making processes influenced design as minds were seen as information processors. The second wave of UCD was where designers became advocates for users and were more involved in product design. During this time, usability became popular, and the movement toward grouping people started through personas.

The third wave of HCI was inclusivity and the social environment, meaning that users are not just end users but can be part of the co-creation process. The third wave of UCD arose from an evolution of mobile phone technology and the internet. User experience was popularised, as it could help a business to improve its brand position. Accessibility and understanding cross-cultural requirements also became important.

The fourth wave of UCD is the cross-over of UX and innovation. For UX researchers, this means not just meeting unmet needs but continuing to find them through on going product innovation.

2001: The Agile Manifesto

In 2001, seventeen people with a wide range of programming and software development specialisations met in a ski resort in Utah. They were looking for an alternative to the heavy technical documentation that was common at the time. They felt strongly that this type of documentation needed to be changed for software development. The group named themselves 'The Agile Alliance' and created the 'Manifesto for Agile Software Development', the Agile Manifesto.

The manifesto is as follows: *"We are uncovering better ways of developing software by doing it and helping others do it. Through this work, we have come to value:*

— *Individuals and interactions over processes and tools*
— *Working software over comprehensive documentation*
— *Customer collaboration over contract negotiation*
— *Responding to change, over following a plan*
  That is, while there is value in the items on the right, we value the items on the left more." (Agile Manifesto)

This Manifesto is still relevant today. Agile means that team members communicate regularly, incrementally update products, and include users in the process. Agile is relevant for research because product teams need regular and continuous feedback to understand what improvements to make, how it's meeting their needs and what may not be working well.

2003: Open Innovation

Open Innovation was coined by Chesbrough (2003) as a decentralised approach to innovation. Businesses may use it to benefit from wider networks and communities as it allows a broader range of people to be involved in problem-solving and product development rather than all being done in-house, which is called Closed Innovation.

Different types of Open Innovation exist: 'Outside-In' and 'Inside-Out'. Outside-In is when a wide range of people are involved in problem-solving and product development. There are significant benefits to 'Outside-In' Open Innovation, such as having a wider pool of talent to draw from. However, there are limitations to this approach, such as Intellectual Property challenges. Outside-In examples include hackathons, in-licensing IP, funding start-up companies in one's industry and crowdsourcing.

Inside-Out Open Innovation is where a business places activities and assets outside itself. Chesbrough and Garman (2009) show the steps to getting innovation moving from the inside out.

1. Become a customer or supplier of your internal projects.
2. Let others develop your non-strategic initiatives.
3. Make your IP work harder for you and others.
4. Grow your ecosystem even if you're not growing.
5. Create open domains to reduce costs and expand participation.

Inside-Out examples include out-licensing IP, donating IP and technology, incubators, spin-offs, and spinouts.

A mix of both Outside-In and Inside Out Open Innovation approaches is possible, and is called Coupled Open Innovation and examples of this approach include joint ventures, strategic alliances, and networks.

When innovating and developing products, Open Innovation is an approach that is still relevant today and start-ups, and larger organisations use activities such as licensing IP, hackathons, and crowdsourcing.

2003: Jobs-To-Be-Done

Clayton Christensen (2003) outlined 'Jobs-To-Be-Done' (JTBD) in his book *The Innovator Solution* and he later wrote *The Innovator's Dilemma*. Christensen argued that understanding what causes customers to make their choices and helping them fix something they struggle with is crucial to innovation. The core question in JTBD is: 'What job would customers want to hire a product to do?'.

Anthony Ulwick (2017) popularised the idea and developed the JTBD application and Outcome-Driven Innovation (ODI). The JTBD framework has steps by which you look for ways to help your customers.

2007: Product-Market Fit

Marc Andreessen defined the idea of 'Product-Market Fit' (PMF) in 2007 as *"finding a good market with a product capable of satisfying that market"*. Product-Market Fit is a goal that start-ups strive for.

2009: IDEO's Design Thinking Model

The step before Product-Market Fit is identifying Problem-Solution Fit and can be identified by product teams through Design Thinking.

Design Thinking has a long history, from the 1970s when the principles emerged. Design Thinking is a human-centred approach to innovation. The designer can consider how to integrate the users' needs, what's possible through technology and the requirements for business' success.

There are three core models of Design Thinking. First, in 2004, the Design Council released the Double Diamond, which was updated in 2019 and renamed the Framework for Innovation. Second, in 2009, Tim Brown wrote a book on Design Thinking and raised its profile among start-ups and larger organisations. Third, in 2012, Stanford d.school streamlined the design process, since it has updated pedagogies: Design Abilities (Jason Munn) and This is Design Work (Carissa Carter).

There are three main elements of Design Thinking. These are the 'Three Lenses of Innovation': desirability, viability, and feasibility. Desirability: 'Do customers want it?' Viability: 'What is it worth?' and Feasibility: 'Can we deliver it?' (IDEO). Marty Cagan (2019), a product expert from Silicon Valley, adds to these three questions: 'Is it usable?' 'Is it ethical?'.

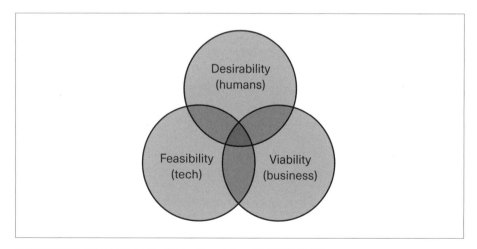

2010: Lean Start-up

Lean Start-up is a book by Eric Ries based on the simple cycle: Build, Learn and Measure to identify what makes a repeatable, scalable business model for a business.

The Lean Start-up advocates continuous improvement, starting with a hypothesis and using experiments to learn. The core of the Lean Start-up is the Minimal Viable Product (MVP) and using this minimal version of the product is a basis for running experiments to test hypotheses. The MVPs are used to run through the cycle as many times as needed to get to a business model which leads to growth.

2010: Business Model Canvas

In 2010, the Business Model Canvas was created by Alex Osterwalder, a business theorist and entrepreneur and Yves Pigeur, a computer scientist and professor. It has nine building blocks based on the three main areas of business overlapping with Design Thinking: desirability, viability, and feasibility. The Desirability blocks cover the value proposition (the product or service), customer segments, channels, and customer relationships. The Viability blocks focus on revenue streams and cost structure. The Feasibility blocks cover essential resources, key activities, and key partnerships.

2012: Marmer Stages for Business Evolution

In 2012, Start-up Genome, an innovation policy advisory and research firm, evaluated how start-ups evolve to become successful businesses through Marmer Stages.

There are six Marmer Stages: discovery, validation, efficiency, scale, profit maximisation and renewal. Marmer Stages are one way of looking at business growth that can be driven by product development and innovation and assesses start-ups and their milestones for growth. It is helpful to consider alongside the other frameworks for product development and innovation.

Start-up Genome looked at entrepreneurial learning and found that those that could listen to customer feedback through tracking metrics had an average monthly growth rate of 7x compared to those not tracking metrics. Start-ups were also 60% more likely to raise funding than companies that didn't track metrics. Start-up Genome found that as well as listening to customer feedback, entrepreneurs need to act on the input. Companies that failed to listen and act on feedback had to change the direction of their business, known as a pivot, multiple times before scaling and growing to scale as they hadn't validated the size or interest of the market. The same companies found it harder to raise money and grow the team.

2014: Value Proposition Canvas

The inventor of the Business Model Canvas, Alex Osterwalder alongside Yves Pigneur later created the Value Proposition Canvas as a companion to the Business Model Canvas. Value Proposition Canvas aims to provide a framework to demonstrate Product-Market Fit as the canvas outlines customer needs and how the product or service can help meet them.

The Value Proposition Canvas outlines the value proposition, or the product or service, and the customer to understand how the two fit together. The value proposition must benefit the customer and relieve pain, problem or challenge, and the customer's jobs (a reference to JTBD), pain and what they're looking to gain are outlined. This simplifies and visually represents the customer needs and what the product or service aims to achieve to help people think about the Product-Market Fit.

2016: Design Sprint

Jake Knapp popularised the Design Sprint in the book *Sprint* (2016) written with co-authors Kowitz and Zeratsky based on the ways of working at Google Ventures. The Design Sprint lasts five days, and within this period, the problem is indentified out, solutions are sketched and voted on as to which one to move forward with, and a prototype is built and tested with potential users or customers. IDEO's Design Thinking approach inspired the Design Sprint, a rapid process that aims to *"solve big problems and validate ideas in 5 days"*.

2018: Objectives and Key Results (OKRs)

In his book *Measure What Matters*, John Doerr (2018) focuses Objectives and Key Results (OKR), a goal-setting framework used to measure quantifiable goals by individuals, teams, and organisations. Andrew Grove introduced the idea of OKRs at Intel; however, when John Doerr used OKRs at Google, the main differences were the frequency of the outcomes being set and evaluated and whom they were shared with. John Doerr set OKRs every three months, ensuring transparency across the organisation as every employee could see each other's OKRs. There was an emphasis on 'stretch' goals that were intentionally difficult to achieve. OKRs can help products aim towards being outcome-led rather than focus on features.

2021: Continuous Discovery and Lean Experimentation

Teresa Torres is a Product Coach who has worked with many product teams. Torres argues that product teams should interview users to identify opportunities, use the Opportunity Solution Tree to map out the findings and use assumption tests to evaluate solutions. It's an approach that fits within Agile, which has an interative process. Torres suggests that small but regular research happens throughout the product development life cycle rather than focusing on one research activity at the start. She argues that there needs to be continuous research in product development rather than project-based research.

2023: Emerging Ideas: Planet-Centred Design, Life-Centred Design
Climate change is a global challenge that is faced by all of humanity. Life-Centred Design is an emerging approach which expands Design Thinking beyond the business and aims to incorporate social, environmental and sustainability. At its early stage, it is also called Planet-Centred Design, DesignX, 21st-century design and ecological design.

It has values like 'Doughnut Economics', identified by Kate Raworth (2018), an Oxford academic, where humanity should respect the planetary boundaries within our resources when creating products and services.

Designers, product teams and entrepreneurs in the product development process may have ethical and moral dilemmas about the power of design and their responsibility. Design has a real-life impact on our ways of working and living and how we use our planetary natural resources.

What lessons can we learn?

As innovation, User Experience and product and service design and development have evolved, more people collaborate and cooperate in product development, a continuous, ongoing process. There are a lot of shared ideas across the approaches listed above, meaning that they inspire and build on one another. There isn't a specific approach that is a one-size-fits-all to product development. In a talk, Teresa Torres (2016) identifies the critical questions that some models listed above ask and how they can be used together rather than in competition.

— **The Agile Manifesto**: Are we building what our business wants?
— **User Experience Design**: Are we building products our customers know how to use?
— **Lean Start-up**: Are we building things our customers want?
— **Jobs-To-Be-Done Framework**: Are we solving the right problems for our customers?

Entrepreneurs often want to know which model or approach to use and when, which can be influenced by the need to learn fast, leading to using the tool to help understand the quickest. However, sometimes slow, project-based research is necessary. The models and ideas outlined here can answer the critical questions about your business and customers earlier in the process rather than after the product is 'shipped' or in the market. For start-ups and product teams, answering these key questions early in the product development process shifts focus from outputs and features to the impact on customers, outcomes, and value to the business. Each of these frameworks encourages customer input from the beginning. The evolution of innovation and Open Innovation has led to the promotion of including outside perspectives to the product team when developing a product alongside customers, including suppliers, users, experts, and employees. Outside views can add value to the product development process.

The most challenging and sometimes confusing parts of some frameworks, particularly Design Thinking, is their application to product development, as they seem theoretical and vague. This book will guide you through the different models and tools available to help you decide which tool could be a good fit for what you're trying to achieve. In essence, to know that you're using the right tool, at the right time, for the right job, speaking with the right people.

Start with customer and user feedback

"Building is often the most expensive way to learn." (David Bland)

Sometimes we see a problem and want to solve it by building a product or service immediately. By doing this, we can fall into the trap of being solution-led, separating us from the problem itself. Being removed from the problem may mean we're closed off from receiving feedback, or it comes late in the process.

Customer and user feedback near the end of the product development process can occur across start-ups and large organisations. The typical 'Build Order', the sequence of steps to create a product for start-ups, is: *"Have an idea, create a prototype, raise capital and launch."* (Chang, 2017).

For larger organisations, the Build Order outlined by Marty Cagan (2018), founder of Silicon Valley Product Group, in his talk about Product Failure, explained that customer and user feedback is too late in the process, as the sequence for developing products is:

— Create the business case
— Outline the roadmap
— Develop the requirements
— Design the product
— Build the product
— Test with customers
— Deploy into the market

Cagan explains that this Build Order means prioritised product features are built, and project management of developing these features leads to a focus on delivering the roadmap. The project management style for delivering the roadmap is generally Waterfall Project Management, a step-by-step, sequential linear approach. Waterfall Project Management leads to the significant issue of customer feedback happening at the end, which is too late. If it's a bad product, no matter how good the marketing and sales are, it's unlikely to succeed if it doesn't serve the needs of people using it or buying it.

Product teams and entrepreneurs that use this approach with customer feedback at the end mean there can be a fixation on delivering the build. Melissa Perri (2018) highlights issues with focusing on the delivery of the product in her book *The Build Trap*:

"The build trap is when organisations become stuck measuring their success by outputs rather than outcomes. It's when they focus more on shipping and developing features than the value they produce. When companies stop producing real value for the users, they begin to lose market share, allowing them to be disrupted. Companies can get out of the build trap by setting themselves up to develop intentional and robust product management practices. At that point, product managers can find the opportunities to maximise business and customer value." (Perri, 2018)

Perri explains value produced through the 'value exchange system' concept, where there needs to be an exchange of value between the customer and the business. Customers recognise value when their problems, needs and wants are met, and they provide money. The company realises value when products or services are monetised and delivered to the customers.

Cagan (2017), in his book *Inspired*, suggests that to create successful products and realise the value between the customer and the business, there needs to be a product development process that has the following steps:

1. Prioritise discovery to collect evidence, to uncover value for the customer, development/engineering team and the business.
2. Help customers understand what is possible by thinking about the problems the solution can solve and what customers will want.
3. Test ideas on real customers; this could be through prototypes.
4. Validate the feasibility for the business – the customers want it, but can it be created, and does it work for the company?
5. Create a clear product vision.

From this point, Cagan explains the importance of the right people, the right product and the right culture for a product to be a sucess.

The product development process

First, what is a product development process? This is the process of developing new products and services and upgrading or improving existing products or services. There are many versions; however, in this book, this process is as follows:

— Idea creation and development
— Explore the market potential and user needs
— Define and test concepts and generate ideas
— Prototype to visually represent the idea and test with users
— Create designs and requirements for MVP
— Validate and test viability, feasibility and desirability for product and business cases using MVP
— Deploy and launch the product
— Commercialise through distribution and marketing
— Continuous improvements and testing

The start of the product development process is messy, as visualised by the Design Squiggle by Damien Newman. The beginning of the Research and Synthesis stage is chaotic and confusing. As time passes, more insights are gathered through research, tests, and experiments to iterate an idea and prototypes. Subsequently, there is clarity as to what is designed and built.

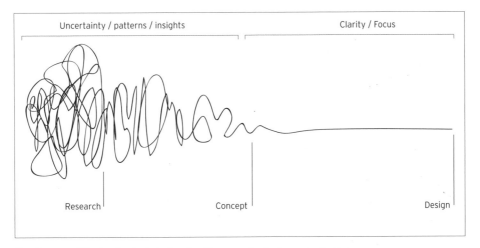

The Process of Design Squiggle by Damien Newman, thedesignsquiggle.com

This book generally follows Design Thinking, Lean Start-up and Agile approaches and shows you where and how research is relevant for understanding your customers and users. Design Thinking prioritises Problem-Solution Fit by exploring the problem in detail and generating solutions tested with users to understand how problems could be solved. Lean Start-up prioritises Product-Market Fit by testing and experimenting with MVPs to assess how the market responds to the product. Agile focuses on the building of the product and its continued improvements. Combining these frameworks across these three phases, is influenced by Gartner's (2016) "Combine Design Thinking, Lean Start-up and Agile" diagram.

From slow research to fast research

Slow research begins with Design Thinking, a problem-focused and in-depth approach to understanding customer and user needs. The problem space or an idea for building a product or service may be abstract, early-stage and hypothetical at the start. The aim is to explore the Problem-Solution Fit and make strategic decisions on the level of risk and investment into the product idea. There is information at this starting point from a mix of qualitative research, such as interviews and quantitative research, for example, surveys. The feedback loops are more extended and slower as it can take time to collect and analyse the data to refine the problem and generate ideas for solutions.

Fast research begins with prototypes or a Minimal Viable Product (MVP), depending on the product or service in development the idea is matured, and the problem and needs the solution seeks to solve is known as there is Problem-Solution Fit. The prototypes and MVP provide a concrete and tangible way of showing the product or service. The aim is to seek Product-Market Fit by having shorter feedback loops between the business and the customer. The approaches to learning about the customer and user needs vary more broadly to learn fast. Feedback is more focused, and experiments can test specific assumptions. Iterations and updates made to the products happen quickly to develop the product or service that fits market needs. Research is ongoing, and feedback loops become quicker as the product development process progresses toward Lean UX and Agile, where user feedback is core to Sprints, which are short and focused periods of activity.

Abstract ⟶ Problem-Solution Fit			Concrete ⟶ Product-Market Fit			
Slow research and in-depth feedback			Fast research, feedback and iterations			
Idea development	Explore problem and the context	Define the problem and ideate solutions	Test prototypes of solutions	Validate feasibility, validity and desirability of MVP	Deploy and launch product	Commercialise and continuously test
-Assess the risk -Create assumptions -Identify knowns and unknowns	-Collect data on users and customers to identify needs -Market and competition analysis	-Analysis and synthesis -Define problem -Generate ideas for solutions -Test concepts	-Create prototypes -Run experiments -Refine solution -Test usability -Prioritise core features	-Run experiments -Test usability -Validate the product and market -Identify business model	-Create final product -Test in real-life settings -Product vision and strategy -Product launch	-Continuous discovery -Metrics to measure engagement and uptake -Impact evaluation
Design Thinking			**Lean Start-Up**		**Agile**	

Slow Research to Fast Research, Sharp, C. (2023)

Introducing

THE LEMONADE VAN

Throughout this book, we'll use The Lemonade Van as a case study to illustrate the practical application of various concepts and ideas. The Lemonade Van is a mobile lemonade stand. Sam and The Lemonade Van are entirely fictional and for illustrative case studies to put theory into practice.

As she embarks on this journey, Sam will explore strategies for product development, market research, and customer engagement to ensure The Lemonade Van becomes a cherished staple in her community.

1

Understanding Innovation

"Ideas come cheap, execution is everything." (John Doerr)

Introduction

This chapter will provide an overview of innovation to contextualise product development. When products are being developed, how innovative they are can influence the investment's risk, the time needed for development, and the research required.

Entrepreneurs and businesses developing highly innovative products initially benefit from market and user research to gauge uptake. A completely new innovation, where the technology is unique and its applications are theoretical, will require a deeper understanding of the need it could solve and how it will do this.

Where there is minimal innovation, small changes are being made to a product to improve it, and it will likely need shorter and regular feedback from existing users and potential users. Continuous feedback from users could highlight new and innovative solutions for customers and users by identifying gaps that need to be filled by existing products or products.

Overview of innovation

First, how is innovation different from an invention? An invention is creating something completely new. Innovation is how the idea can be used. An invention may be a 'thing'. An innovation is how that invention causes a change in behaviour or interactions (Walker, 2015).

Innovation doesn't have a shared definition, but it is generally to 'do something better than what's currently available'. Sociologist Roy Rothwell (1994) tracked how innovation had evolved since the 1950s and how markets and technologies interacted and influenced one another. From the 1950s to the mid-1960s, fast economic growth led to technology-driving innovation, with market insights coming in late in the process. From the mid-1960s to the early 1970s, more competition drove a push toward market-driven innovation.

From the mid-1970s to the mid-1980s, learning from the technology drive in the 1950s-60s and the strong market drive in the 1960s-70s, technology innovation came from combining market needs and technology opportunities. In the early 1980s-90s there was a shift toward integrating business processes to shorten product life cycles. Innovation occurred at every level of the corporate structure and encouraged cross-functional collaboration, with key suppliers and leading customers providing feedback.

From the 1990s, resources were highly constrained, meaning businesses had to adapt again. To overcome these challenges, the focus was on integrating systems and automating processes, and advanced strategic partnerships meant that marketing and research functions could be carried out through 'Open Innovation'. Networking was needed to stay flexible and enable product development to be fast. Innovating quickly was seen as essential to competitiveness when technology change happened fast and often, and product development cycles were short. In the early 2020s, we're moving into the Fifth Industrial Revolution, where there is the 'innovation milieu', the social, economic, and environmental context for innovation and creativity. Various elements need to interact with one another to create favourable conditions for innovation and creativity, such as resources, knowledge, culture, policies, and networks. The innovation milieu is an essential part of regional and national innovation systems, as it can influence the development and diffusion of new technologies, products, and services. Today, this is relevant as it shows how knowledge is transferred and how societies and systems can grow and generate innovation. Start-ups and SMEs may benefit from this through programmes such as government funding that encourage collaboration, in addition to the availability of accelerators, and incubators. These programmes enable a business to develop its knowledge and ability to innovate and collaborate with universities and other companies to create innovative products and services.

Different levels of innovation

"Brilliant thinking is rare, but courage is in even shorter supply than genius."
(Peter Theil)

Innovation can generally come in four forms: **Disruptive**, **Radical**, **Incremental** or **Sustaining**. The higher-risk forms of innovation, **Disruptive and Radical**, usually need much investment and are more likely to require significant research at the start. For innovators considering Disruptive and Radical innovation, Christensen's (2000) *Innovator's Dilemma* shows their conundrum. Product development is time-consuming and requires multiple iterations, with the risk of the value to the customer being minimal. **Incremental and Sustaining innovation** aims to improve existing products and services and help to maintain a market position.

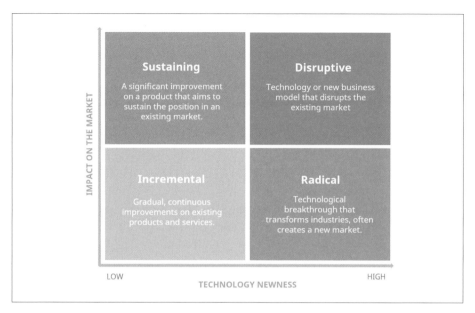

The matrix has four quadrants. The vertical axis is labeled "IMPACT ON THE MARKET" and the horizontal axis is labeled "TECHNOLOGY NEWNESS" (LOW to HIGH).

Sustaining
A significant improvement on a product that aims to sustain the position in an existing market.

Disruptive
Technology or new business model that disrupts the existing market

Incremental
Gradual, continuous improvements on existing products and services.

Radical
Technological breakthrough that transforms industries, often creates a new market.

Kylliäinen, J. (2019), Innovation Matrix, Viima: https://www.viima.com/blog/types-of-innovation

Peter Theil (2014), entrepreneur, venture capitalist, and political activist, explains in his book *Zero to One* about the two fundamental types of innovation. If something new is created, this 'vertical innovation' is called Zero to One (0-to-1), like the previously explained Disruptive and Radical kinds of innovation. If something exists but it's improved upon, this is 'horizontal innovation', where the progress is from One to N (1-to-n). The most common type of innovation is 1-to-n, like the Incremental or Sustaining innovation types.

Zero to One innovation is a giant leap based on asking big questions about the present to meet futures that don't exist yet. For 0-to-1 innovation, there are many unknowns, but having one vision can focus efforts, and this vision should be high enough to *"Shoot for the moon, even if you'll miss, you'll be among the stars."*

Theil believes monopolies drive innovation. A business with a monopoly on the market means that as it provides something so popular, the competition can't survive. No one else can copy the product or service; as many people use it, it benefits consumers. A monopoly has a broad customer base with economies of scale; its customers have strong bonds with the product, can invest in technological advantages, and has network effects that lead to more people using it within the same network. Theil argues that being a monopoly is a goal start-up and small businesses should aim for as it benefits everyone.

For entrepreneurs and product teams, understanding which type of innovation is being developed will influence the approach taken to the research, the product build, and the business model. To summarise, Radical and Disruptive Innovation will require slow research to understand the problem being solved and the risks deeply. Incremental and Sustaining innovation is likely to need fast research as the iterations to the product will be minor but enable a strong and competitive position in the market.

Types of innovation within an organisation

So far, innovation levels have been identified. They can be new and significant changes for the business and market or improvements to an existing product or service. Internally in an organisation, there are different types of innovation.

Hamel (1996, 2000) outlines four different types of innovation, which are 1) **Operational**: Change management, knowledge management and organisational learning; 2) **Product/Service**: From minor changes made to improve features and functionality through incremental innovation to radical innovation to create new products and services; 3) **Strategic (business model)**: Improve a business strategy using radical business innovation to redefine the market space and preconceive products and services and 4) **Organisational/Managerial**: It's challenging to replicate management strategies.

Alongside these four types by Hamel is Doblin's ten types of innovation model. Doblin is a global innovation agency, and the model was created in 1997. In 2013, Kelley, one of the co-founders of Doblin, co-wrote *Ten Types of Innovation: The Discipline of Building Breakthroughs*. The main categories for innovation are as follows:

— **Configuration: Your business model:** New revenue streams and competitive advantage.
— **Offering: Technology:** Using technology, expertise, or knowledge to develop a new solution to a real or perceived need and then transform this solution into a viable, sustainable entity
— **Experience: Marketing:** An existing product that can be repurposed to offer a unique value to a different group of people.

Generally, innovation can be an organisation's business model, operations, marketing, managerial and technological.

Cutting-edge and innovative solutions

National Aeronautics and Space Administration (NASA) developed the Technology Readiness Level (TRL) scale, showing how new technology matures through product development. Gartner, a management consultancy company, created the Hype Cycle that visualises upcoming, new, and existing technology. Suppose you're seeking to develop a product at the very early stage of the Hype Cycle. In that case, you'll likely move through the TRL relatively slowly as you'll be one of the first companies innovating in the emerging market. In turn, we'll explain the TRL and Hype Cycle and then explore how it relates to innovation and product development and the required level of investment and research.

The Technology Readiness Level (TRL) scale was developed by NASA in 1979 and showed the development from concept to the product operating in a real-world environment. The TRL scale can be applied to the product development process to demonstrate how ideas mature and how we move from an early concept to a full product operating in real-world environments.

— **TRL 1 - Basic principles observed:** The basic scientific principles and concepts have been identified through fundamental research and theoretical studies on the technical feasibility at this early conceptual stage. Fundamental research is 'pure research' as it is a scientific investigation to advance understanding and typically takes place in academic institutions and research organisations.
— **TRL 2 - Technology concept formulated:** The focus shifts toward technology development through conducting experiments and laboratory-scale research to explore the feasibility and potential of the concept. There is initial evidence of technological viability.
— **TRL 3 - Experimental proof of concept:** Prototypes can demonstrate the concept's technical feasibility. At this stage, critical assumptions are validated, and the concept's potential is assessed, from a commercial perspective and application as a solution to user or customer needs.
— **TRL 4 - Technology validation in a laboratory environment:** The focus here is on validating the technology's performance and functionality. It involves testing the technology in a controlled environment to ensure it meets specific requirements, standards, and specifications. The aim is to clearly understand the technology's capabilities and limitations.
— **TRL 5 - Technology validated in a relevant environment:** The technology is tested in a realistic or simulated environment. Users are involved in testing the product to see whether it solves their needs.

- **TRL 6 - Technology demonstrated in a relevant environment:** A model or prototype of the technology is tested in a relevant environment to test its functionality, feasibility, and potential impact. The focus is on gathering user feedback to further refine the prototype.
- **TRL 7 - System prototype demonstration in an operational environment:** Building on the validated prototype, the technology is deployed and tested in an operational environment. This stage involves evaluating the technology's performance, reliability, and integration within the intended operational context to assess its suitability for real-world applications and identify any potential operational challenges.
- **TRL 8 - System complete and qualified**: The technology has reached completion as it has undergone comprehensive testing and demonstration activities to validate its performance, reliability, and functionality. It is ready for further deployment and commercialisation.
- **TRL 9 - Actual system is proven in an operational environment:** The technology is successfully implemented and deployed in real-world operations. It will be continuously monitored, maintained, and improved.

Considering the early stages of the TRL and early-stage technology, Gartner, regularly plot on a graph known as the 'Hype Cycle' new and maturing innovative technologies and has five phases to show their application and how attitudes change as they mature. First, the **Innovation Trigger**: A potential technology breakthrough is a catalyst. No usable products exist using that technology, and the commercial viability is still being determined. Second, **Peak of Inflated Expectations**: Early publicity shows several success stories alongside many failures. Third, **Trough of Disillusionment**: Interest decreases as experiments and implementations don't deliver. Investments continue if the surviving providers improve products for early adopters. Fourth, the **Slope of Enlightenment**: Technology can benefit enterprises, and its benefits become widely understood. More enterprises fund pilots, but conservative companies are cautious. Finally, **Plateau of Productivity**: Mainstream adoption takes off. The criteria for assessing provider viability are clear, and the technology's broad market applicability and relevance are known.

The TRLs can demonstrate the internal process from developing and applying new technology, to having a fully operational product in the market. The rate of moving through the TRLs may depend on how new the technology is and how straightforward it is to develop. If a technology is very new, it will more widely be moving through the Hype Cycle as businesses try to develop it for different applications. The level of innovation (Radical or Disruptive) and technical risk in the development of the technology and how it can be used by users and customers will influence the level of research needed to understand how this technology can be applied to solve user and customer problems.

This chapter described the different levels of innovation from minor, incremental changes to radical, highly impactful innovations and types of innovation one may see in an organisation. We outlined the TRL and Hype Cycle to show how innovative products and services develop and how attitudes to new technologies can change over time.

Product development can sometimes start with a seed of an idea. In the next chapter, we will explore where ideas come from if they don't come from ideation sessions after doing research. It's vital to have good ideas as a strong foundation for product development, and the next chapter outlines what a 'good' idea is and what this means in the context of innovation and product development.

2

Where Good Ideas Come From

"Today's most popular approaches to innovation fall into one of two types: those that begin with a focus on solutions (or ideas) and those that begin with a focus on customer needs." (Anthony Ulwick)

Introduction

Innovation can start with an idea. Wherever the idea came from, the quality of the concept and the context of its conception may influence whether it's a 'great idea'. This chapter will discuss where 'good ideas' can come from and how some organisations capture and store ideas for product development.

Discovering innovative ideas

"Chance favours the connected mind." (Steve Johnson)

In this section, the source of 'good ideas' will describe where people can find inspiration for ideas. New environments, outside influences, or serendipitous moments can spark new ideas. Innovation management involves having a system for storing and evaluating ideas. This allows businesses to refer to a pool of ideas that can be assessed and potentially implemented.

Steve Johnson (2010), author of *Where Good Ideas Come From* and co-host of the podcast American Innovations, concluded that 'good ideas' come from talking to others and being around a wide variety of people. In the Industrial Revolution, gatherings would occur in coffee houses or organised by a host at a 'salon' where ideas are shared and discussed prompting intellectual discussion and networking for poets, politicians and factory workers. A theoretical biologist, Stuart Kauffman (2002), believed in the 'adjacent possible' for ideas, meaning that great things for tomorrow come from what's available today.

Exposing ourselves to new surroundings and remaining receptive to fresh perspectives increases the likelihood of discovering innovative ideas. Important ideas take a long time to evolve and have two to three or even ten years to mature due to a collision of smaller hunches, as they need time to incubate.

"The patterns are simple but followed together, and they make for a whole that is wiser than the sum of its parts. Go for a walk; cultivate hunches; write everything down, but keep your folders messy; embrace serendipity; make generative mistakes; take on multiple hobbies; frequent coffeehouses and other liquid networks; follow the links; let others build on your ideas; borrow, recycle, re-invent." (Steve Johnson)

Ideas can come from a plethora of places:

— **Interaction with existing solutions:** There are different ways to address problems when something is not functioning properly. Ideas can come from personal experience, or addressing customer dissatisfaction with current options. It involves finding a solution even when one does not seem readily available.
— **The wider environment:** The market is constantly evolving with competitors adapting their approach, changes in legislation and regulation, new competition, emerging market opportunities, economic environment, and technological advancements.
— **Internal processes for capturing information:** Companies can gather customer feedback on products and use innovative techniques to generate ideas from positive and negative experiences. Business directors and employees also share their ideas internally.
— **Speaking to others:** Individuals can network outside the organisation or have 'water cooler' moments within a business.

To summarise, 'good' ideas come from many different places, but being open to identifying them and having the ability to process them within an organisation is vital for innovation. Brainstorming is not always the most effective way to generate ideas as they tend to be limited to those within the same organisation and environment, lacking outside influence from research findings or other sources.

Sparking ideas

Academics have found that good ideas can come from serendipity, chance events, observation, and curiosity (Koller, 1988; Peterson, 1988; Reynolds, 2005). Serendipity can play an essential role in innovation, as it can lead to discovering new and potentially valuable ideas. For example, a company may stumble upon a new product idea while working on a different project or through a chance encounter with a customer or supplier.

If you're an Innovation Lead or in a product team in a larger organisation, Strategic Knowledge Arbitrage is useful. This is a process where a business seeks opportunities to use knowledge from different markets or industries to gain a competitive edge. Leveraging the firm's existing knowledge and expertise can create new products, services, or business models in a new area. The key idea behind Strategic Knowledge Arbitrage is that knowledge is a valuable resource that can be used to create innovative products or services, and different industries and markets may have unique knowledge bases and expertise. By identifying and using these differences, businesses can develop unique value propositions and outperform their competitors (Carayannis et al., 2017).

For example, a technology company with expertise in Artificial Intelligence (AI) may identify an opportunity to apply its knowledge to the healthcare industry, developing new products or services that leverage AI to improve patient outcomes. By leveraging their expertise in a new market, the company can create a unique value proposition that sets them apart from traditional healthcare providers and technology companies lacking this expertise.

Customers can sometimes prompt innovative ideas through feedback. As a Product Manager, Marketing Lead, UX Researcher or entrepreneur, you may see that customer needs are changing and evolving, creating opportunities for new products, or improving existing ones. There may be a gap in the market, or you are seeing future trends that your business could capitalise on. Maybe an idea was sparked from observing competitors launching new products, adopting new technologies or using novel business strategies that are strengthening their market position. Keeping an eye on the competition and industry changes can help spark ideas about where to innovate.

Disruptive technological advancements can create opportunities for new ideas, as there is pressure to stay up to date with emerging technologies and explore the applications in the industry also within the business. Changes in laws and regulations can create new market opportunities or necessitate the need for innovating existing products. Staying up to date by monitoring environmental changes will help generate ideas on how to adapt.

By reducing business costs and improving efficiencies, innovation can be sparked in processes, product design, and supply chain management. This can lead to ideas for improving ways of working and reducing waste. Employees with expertise and skills can drive change, and fostering a culture of continuous learning and collaboration can lead to new ideas. UX Researchers may conduct Ideation sessions from research work that has been done, which can spur innovative ideas. Amazon, the e-commerce, cloud computing, advertising, streaming and AI business, has the 'Institutional Yes' which is where managers must say 'yes' to ideas that employees have and if the manager says 'no', they have to write a two-page document explaining why.

Collaborating with competitors, suppliers, or research organisations can help generate ideas and drive innovation, as these partnerships can help provide access to new technologies, expertise, and resources. Innovative ideas may come from businesses that adopt Open Innovation, where ideas and knowledge flow externally from the company and processes are in place to capitalise on ideas.

From working with many innovative start-ups and SMEs, I've seen that personal experience of a problem can lead some people to want to make changes and, in some cases, create products and services to solve this problem, which may turn into a business. Tomer Sharon (2016) found that most product ideas come from personal experience. For entrepreneurs, this could be a good starting point.

Managing ideas

In his book (2022a) *Connect the Dots,* Dr Christian Busch advocated serendipity, curiosity, and the ability to listen and do something about the ideas. This is vital for innovation, but executing and implementing these ideas takes grit and tenacity. Busch (2022b) highlighted that Pixar has an informal 'brain trust' (Catmull, 2014). When Pixar innovates, it does something with the ideas and feedback, meaning people feel listened to, and there is a place to store ideas in a 'parking lot' that will be considered in the future.

Nesta, an Innovation Foundation charity, has a similar mechanism called 'distributed discoveries', where innovation is part of the culture at all levels and across the business. It recognised that there are multiple formal opportunities for the organisation to understand itself better, such as in performance reviews and when someone is promoted, to ask employees what has surprised them recently.

Small and large companies can benefit from innovative ideas from outside sources such as customers, competitors, and suppliers. Companies should develop 'absorptive capacity' through research to successfully utilise this external knowledge. Absorptive capacity is a valuable skill in knowledge-based industries that allows businesses to turn new ideas into products and promote organisational innovation. Companies with a higher absorptive capacity can implement new technologies, strategies, and product ideas, giving them a competitive advantage and promoting innovation. For UX Researchers and Innovation Leads, implementing systems that can capture external feedback and turn it into innovative products and services can help businesses stay competitive.

Maturing ideas

Through the book, moving from Design Thinking to Lean Start-up to Agile shows how the product development process develops the maturity of the ideas. Gochermann, J. and Nee, I. (2019) show how ideas mature through the product development process through the Idea Maturity Level (ILM) scale. The phases are:

— **Initial Idea:** Basic assumptions about the idea and its technical feasibility exist.
— **Awareness:** Research is needed better to understand the idea and its feasibility and market need.
— **Appraisability:** The users who will use the application of the idea are known and there is an analysis of the market potential and technical feasibility.
— **Valuation:** The market potential and technical feasibility are known, and its application and users are evaluated, competitiveness can be measured, and the value of the idea is known.
— **Realisability:** The strategic case to the business is known and there are resources available to develop it. The implementation costs and potential return on investment is estimated.

This Idea Maturity Level scale draws on the work of Crosby's maturity grid, the CMM. The CMM shows at the start the chaotic nature of processes. The idea's success is based on the competence of the organisation's people or those who created the idea. As the idea matures, the processes become more controlled and planned. As the idea becomes a product, there are quantitative targets for quality control and the processes for execution are defined. At the last stage of optimising, continuous process improvements are in place.

Wherever the idea may come from, develop your early-stage ideas by understanding the problem in more detail, which is the focus of the next chapter. Storing and managing ideas, executing ideas effectively and leveraging absorptive capacity to internalise knowledge to use it for innovation are all impactful ways of building on great ideas and having a place for ideas within the business.

Start With The Problem or Challenge

"Well-defined problems lead to breakthrough solutions." (Dywane Spradlin)

Introduction

Building products or creating services is usually a solution to a problem as a need is identified. For entrepreneurs and innovators, starting with the problem will lead to a problem-solving approach to generating ideas for the solution. This chapter outlines Design Thinking, which can be a powerful approach to product development when implemented effectively. It also explains Jobs-To-Be-Done framework in more detail as an alternative or complementary approach to Design Thinking.

Begin by exploring the problem

Design Thinking is a problem-solving method that starts with empathising with people to discover and define their needs and challenges. Design Thinking has various established models that highlight the importance of early discovery of customer and user needs in the design and development of products.

Netflix used Design Thinking to reinvent itself:

> *"In general, we use qualitative research methods to generate and refine product ideas, and then A/B test those ideas with real customers to help decide what should be rolled out. The qualitative and quantitative methods complement each other and help validate ideas at different design stages.*
>
> *On the qualitative side, we're continually running surveys, focus groups, and ethnographic research. In the latter case, these more in-depth conversations with people help us understand their wants, needs, and the motivations behind their behaviour. The things we learn may not always be representative of the larger population, but they give us insights into new ideas we may want to test in the future."* (Navin Iyengar)

Design Council, a UK charity that acts as the national strategic advisor for design (2004), developed the Double Diamond. This has four phases: Discovery, Define, Develop and Deliver. The first diamond, Discovery and Define, focuses on the problem and research and the second diamond, Develop and Deliver, aims to create the solution through design.

— **Discovery:** The first step in problem-solving is to gain a comprehensive understanding of the user, their environment, behaviour, tools, and decision-making processes by the designer or researcher. This can be achieved through various methods such as surveys, user diaries, observations, or immersion. The goal is empathising with the user, putting oneself in their shoes, and considering the bigger picture.
— **Define:** During this phase, the designer or researcher focuses on refining ideas and analysing the main challenge.
— **Develop:** The designer or researcher tests design concepts to determine which ones are effective and which ones are not. This involves using and testing user scenarios, service blueprints, and physical prototyping with actual users.
— **Deliver:** The wider product team and developers build and deploy the product or service at this stage. The business launches the product or service with a clear plan for future development. Researchers and designers utilise evaluation and final testing techniques during this phase.

The Design Council updated the Double Diamond in 2019, and it is now the Framework for Innovation. The Design Council shows the role of stakeholder engagement, leadership, design and methods in product development and innovation. The Framework for Innovation shows innovators, entrepreneurs, researchers, and product teams that in product development, they start with the challenge and end with the outcome.

The principles of the Design Council's Framework for Innovation are as follows:

— User-centred design: *"Be people-centred."*
— Visual thinking: *"Communicate visually."*
— Co-creation: *"Collaborate and co-create."*
— Agile/lean start-up: *"Iterate, iterate, iterate."*

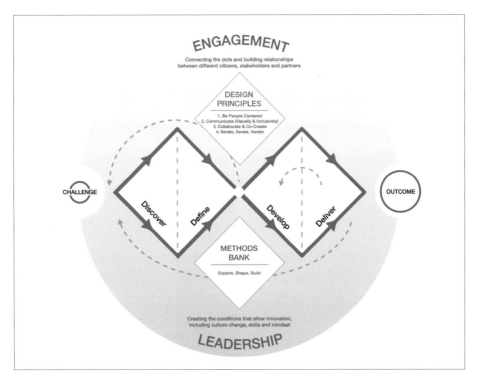

ENGAGEMENT

Connecting the dots and building relationships
between different citizens, stakeholders and partners

DESIGN
PRINCIPLES

1. Be People Centered
2. Communicate (Visually & Inclusively)
3. Collaborate & Co-Create
4. Iterate, Iterate, Iterate

CHALLENGE

Discover Define Develop Deliver

OUTCOME

METHODS
BANK

Explore, Shape, Build

Creating the conditions that allow innovation,
including culture change, skills and mindset

LEADERSHIP

Design Council, Framework for Innovation. Licensed under CC BY 4.0 license: https://www.
designcouncil.org.uk/our-resources/framework-for-innovation/

Stanford Design School: This is Design Work
Stanford Design School created the Stanford Design School streamlined design
process (Legacy, circa 2012) to encourage an experimental, iterative, user-centred
design process. Providing a hands-on approach to problem-solving makes the
Design Thinking methodology more accessible, nurturing creative confidence in
individuals and teams.

— **Empathise:** Understand the user and problems faced by listening to their
  stories and observing existing behaviour.
— **Define:** Organise and analyse research findings to define a concise problem
  statement or possible solution.
— **Ideate:** Identify possible solutions for the problem and evaluate each.
— **Prototype:** Create a visual representation of the solution that could solve
  the user's problem and starting with low-fidelity (low detail and complexity)
  through to high-fidelity (greater detail and more complex design) when testing
  and iterating.
— **Testing:** The user tests the prototype to understand if the product solves the
  user's problem.

Design School has evolved away from the hexagon graphic that represents these five elements. Design School uses 'Design Abilities', a pedagogical framework to empower students. Design Abilities (Jason Munn) has eight elements: 1) Navigating ambiguity, 2) Learn from others, 3) Synthesize information, 4) Experiment rapidly, 5) Concrete and abstract, 6) Craft intentionally, 7) Communicate deliberately and 8) Design work. Design School also uses 'This Design Work' (created by Carissa Carter), which shows the different layers that must be considered when designing work today.

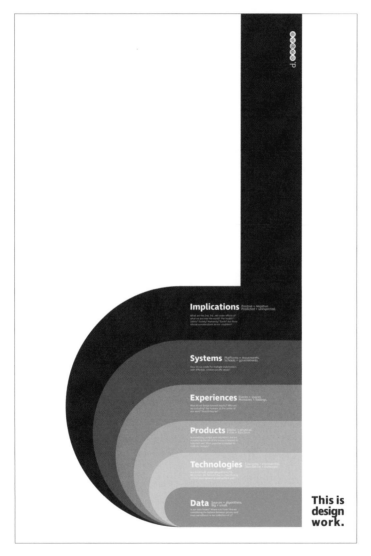

Carter, C, This is Design Work, d.school:
https://dschool.stanford.edu/resources/this-is-design-work

The human-centred design approach by IDEO
IDEO is a design and consulting firm. Their Human-Centred Design (HCD) approach places humans at the core of all design processes, which stresses the importance of empathising with the end user, testing prototypes, and iterating solutions, ensuring the products or services created genuinely meet the needs and wants of the people using them.

— **Observation:** Learn about the end user.
— **Ideation:** Brainstorm many ideas.
— **Rapid Prototyping:** Quickly build a low-fidelity prototype.
— **User Feedback:** Input from your end user.
— **Iteration:** Continue to iterate and fine-tune the product and its design.
— **Implementation:** Test the idea out in the real world.

The three models share the focus on understanding human needs and fostering creative solutions to meet these needs. However, the Design Thinking approach could more explicitly show how user and business needs align. This is where User-Centred Design (UCD) can be helpful. Don Norman popularised the User-Centred Design (UCD) concept in 1988 with the book *The Design of Everyday Things*. The approach begins with identifying needs from user research, reviewing the context of how the customer would use the product or service, understanding business requirements and user goals to align these in partnership with stakeholders and users, designing solutions, and evaluating the designs with user feedback. The critical differences between Design Thinking and UCD are that UCD is action-based and considers the business requirements more explicitly. Both approaches can be used together.

ValTech, a global business transformation company, outlines the Design Thinking mindset that encourages creativity, collaboration, and adaptability.

— **Human-Centricity:** To understand why people behave a certain way, it's essential to approach the situation with curiosity and an open mind.
— **Diverse Collaboration:** Collaboration among varied and cross-functional teams is fundamental to the success of Design Thinking. By bringing together different perspectives, Design Thinking can create order and logic out of chaos.
— **An Explorer's or Researcher's Spirit:** To properly use Design Thinking, thoroughly researching the problem space is essential. This forms the foundation of the approach.
— **Learning Through Experimentation:** Design Thinking is a method that emphasises hands-on learning, primarily through experimentation. For instance, Sir James Dyson famously made over 5,000 prototypes before developing the modern vacuum cleaner we use today.

- **Embracing Uncertainty:** Embarking on Design Thinking can be compared to exploring uncharted waters. It requires comfort with ambiguity and unpredictability.
- **Openness to Possibilities:** Design Thinking encourages an open, curious, and non-judgmental mindset to explore available options.

Case study: Google Glasses

Where there are successes, there are failures, and it's good to learn from when things don't go as planned. In 2013, Google Glass entered the market, but the idea failed because people did not want to give voice instructions in public spaces. Also, the camera on the glasses led to privacy concerns.

What can we learn from a Design Thinking perspective?
First, we could learn if Google had built empathy with users by having early-stage prototypes. In testing prototypes, Google may have learned that users did not want to speak to their Google Glasses publicly.

Second, Google didn't validate the idea that people would be open to wearing cameras on their faces in public environments.

Third, the business case needed to be clarified, and the problem needed to be adequately defined. They decided their first market was the public consumer; however, it may have been better suited to other markets, such as truck drivers or pilots needing directions and reports.

Fourth, the design had quality issues and never became a final product. It was uncomfortable, had short battery life, and was challenging to develop the applications.

Jobs-To-Be-Done framework to identify customer needs

Anthony Ulwick (2016) published a book on the Jobs-To-Be-Done (JTBD) framework, *Jobs-To-Be-Done: Theory to Practice,* a form of Outcome-Driven Innovation (ODI). ODI is a form of innovation that uses multiple research methods to make innovation measurable.

JTBD is an approach to developing products and services based on understanding customer goals or 'jobs' that need to be done that would lead the customer to 'hire' the product for the 'job'. This could be an alternative framework for Product

Managers, entrepreneurs and Innovation Leads to use instead of or in addition to User-Centred Design and Design Thinking to start understanding customer needs.

Ulwick emphasises the customer's job and what they are looking to achieve rather than the focus on the product itself. JTBD can aid a better understanding of their market and create an engaging user experience. To define a customer job, the phrase is used:

"When... [context] I want to... [specific task] so that I... [expected outcome]."

There are fundamental principles to the JTBD approach:

— **Customer Job:** Instead of concentrating on product features or demographics, the JTBD framework prioritises understanding the fundamental problem or need the customer is attempting to solve. To gain a more in-depth understanding of the job, interviews can be conducted.
— **Context:** The customer's job can be influenced by factors such as their environment, emotions, or social context.
— **Job Steps:** Breaking down the job into a series of steps can identify potential areas for improvement and innovation.
— **Functional, Emotional and Social Dimensions:** JTBD doesn't only look at a job's functional, practical aspects and the emotional and social aspects that may influence customer decisions.
— **Competing Solutions:** Customers can choose from various competing solutions to get the job done, which encourages considering alternatives when designing products.

The framework evaluates jobs through eight steps, which are as follows:

1. Define your customers' goals and resources.
2. Locate what information is needed to do the job.
3. Prepare the environment where the job will be done.
4. Confirm that your customer is ready to get the job done.
5. Execute the job.
6. Monitor the job so that it's successfully executed.
7. Modify and make alterations to improve execution.
8. Conclude the job or repeat.

When using the JTBD approach to understand customer needs as jobs. A Job Maps interview method can be applied to break down the customer goals and resources into jobs. This is a very specific approach and one that you may wish to read about further.

THE LEMONADE VAN
USING JOBS-TO-BE-DONE TO UNDERSTAND CUSTOMER NEEDS

The Lemonade Van is a fictional business. Sam is the company's founder, and it's at an early stage. It's currently an idea that Sam has, she has enjoyed drinking fresh, homemade lemonade for years. She used to sell it on a homemade stand outside her house when she was younger.

Sam has grand plans for The Lemonade Van. She can use an electric-powered food truck for local events. She would like to deliver lemonade to local houses and develop an app for customers to order and subscribe to her lemonade. She will deliver it in her truck. Sam wants to use organic ingredients and will use a recipe from her grandmother. Sam wants a premium feel for her brand, as she will use good quality ingredients.

This is the first time we see Sam use one of the theories we cover. To illustrate how to apply the Jobs-To-Be-Done approach, Sam will use this framework to identify the jobs customers have for the event value proposition.

Customer Jobs
Here is a breakdown of the tasks and jobs that customers need to complete for The Lemonade Van serving lemonade to customers at a local event:

1. Quenching thirst
   - Task: Customers attending the event need a refreshing drink to satisfy their thirst
   - Job: The Lemonade Van must provide various delicious and cold lemonade options to quench customers' thirst.
2. Cooling down
   - Task: Customers want to cool down and combat the hot weather during the event
   - Job: The Lemonade Van must offer icy, refreshing choices that help customers beat the heat and stay comfortable.
3. Enjoyment and indulgence
   - Task: Customers seek a delightful experience during the event
   - Job: The Lemonade Van must create a pleasant atmosphere and offer flavourful, high-quality lemonade options that customers can enjoy

4. Quick and convenient service
   - Task: Customers don't want to waste time waiting for their drinks
   - Job: The Lemonade Van must provide efficient and speedy service, ensuring that customers can get their lemonades quickly and conveniently
5. Catering to taste preferences
   - Task: Customers have diverse taste preferences and dietary requirements
   - Job: The Lemonade Van should offer a range of lemonade flavours and variations, including options for different sweeteners, fruit additions, or even sugar-free alternatives, to cater to various taste preferences and dietary needs
6. Providing a fun experience
   - Task: Customers seek unique and exciting experiences at the event
   - Job: The Lemonade Van could offer speciality lemonade recipes, creative garnishes, or interactive elements (e.g., customisable flavours or mix-ins) to provide a sense of novelty and fun for customers
7. Supporting local businesses
   - Task: Customers appreciate supporting local vendors and businesses
   - Job: The Lemonade Van can emphasise its locally sourced ingredients or partnerships with nearby farmers or suppliers, highlighting its commitment to the community and supporting local businesses
8. Refreshments for children
   - Task: Parents attending the event want to keep their children hydrated and satisfied
   - Job: The Lemonade Van should have kid-friendly lemonade options, potentially including reduced-sugar or natural fruit-based lemonades, to provide refreshment options specifically designed for children

By understanding these customer tasks and jobs, The Lemonade Van can tailor its offerings and marketing efforts to meet the needs and expectations of its target customers at local events.

Sam's Conclusions

After analysing the customer jobs using the JTBD framework, Sam has concluded that she needs to understand customer goals, preferences, and resources to cater to their needs, particularly in attracting customers to her stand at events. She's also reflected that information needs to be clear when offering lemonade to help customers make informed decisions. She must select the right location, maintain cleanliness, and ensure a friendly environment when customers approach. The Lemonade Van. Sam has concluded that she needs to get regular customer feedback and be open to change, such as offering new flavours to differentiate from other lemonade vans. She needs to reflect on how she'll create a memorable experience and how they can share this on social media. Having excellent customer experience and satisfaction will help set her apart from competitors.

Design Thinking vs Lean Start-up as your starting point

Knowing where to start to do research and which approach to take can depend on several factors. The table below adapts Sullivan's (2023), founder of User Research and Service Design Consultancy, outline of the differences between project-based UX research and Product Discovery for learning fast through rounds of quick feedback.

	Slow research (Design Thinking, Project-based approach)	Fast Research (Lean Start-Up approaches)
Maturity of your idea	New and immature ILM1 – 2: Initial and Awareness	Maturing idea ILM3 – 5: Appraisability, Valuation and Realisability
Artefacts available	Abstract and hypothetical overview of the product or service.	Early prototype Technical and user requirements Minimal Viable Product
Existing insights	No existing insights with trustworthy insights needed.	Existing insights into the customer or market
Business risk of the project	Strategic decisions to be made. Need to make significant business decisions about investment and risk. High stakes such as resources and business risk particularly if using new technology	Keep the product team focused on the relevant features. Product teams need to stay close to the customer. High uncertainty and risk
Depth of insights needed	Deep understanding of market, customer, and user needs.	Regular, quick feedback is needed.
Technical feasibility	Early stage or unknown	Technical feasibility and market opportunity is defined. Smaller, iterative changes are needed

If you do not have robust existing insights late into the development process, you could go back to slow research and Design Thinking before continuing in the book to the fast research, quick learning, and rapid feedback methods. Later, we'll be looking at Product Discovery and Lean UX, which can be used to understand the customer and users in the later stages of product development.

Project-based research: UX Research and Design Thinking

UX research can be project-based as it is explorative and deeply understands user and customer needs. User (UX) research focuses on user needs, motivations, and behaviours through interviews, focus groups and observations. Later, user research uses techniques, including usability testing, to understand if a product or service is easy to use. In the following chapters, we'll consider market, user and design research to understand customer and market needs.

Fast research: Lean Start-Up, Product Discovery and Lean UX

Lean Start-up is an approach designed to gather information to learn quickly. It's an approach used when there is a high degree of uncertainty. It aims to test assumptions with Lean Experiments. Lean Experiments enable product teams to test risky assumptions, variations of new features and the value proposition.

Product Discovery is product refinement based on a deep understanding of the user and finding the best solution. Product Discovery is *"used to describe the work that we do to make decisions about what to build, while product delivery is the work we do to build, ship, and maintain a production quality product."* (Teresa Torres).

UX research can also be more Agile and overlap with Product Discovery when gathering feedback regularly and testing usability to evaluate how easy a product is to use. Lean UX is *"focused on the experience under design and is less focused on deliverables than traditional UX"* (Interaction Design Foundation).

This chapter explained the starting point as the problem which is Design Thinking and we considered Jobs-To-Be-Done as an alternative. We explored how to decide which type of research to start with for a project depending on what insights are available and the maturity of the idea.

In the next chapter, we'll identify and categorise users and customers to consider whom to include in the research. Then, we'll move on to research methods to give you depth and breadth on the user and customers' problems. Then, we'll look to analyse the data with stakeholders through synthesis workshops and ideation workshops. Following this, we'll look at prototyping and the different levels of prototyping and how to test prototypes. We'll then move on to Minimal Viable Prototypes and how to test these before building the product or service.

How to Identify Assumptions

Introduction

There are two ways to use assumptions depending on whether the research is project-based or using Lean Experiments.

For project-based research, it is helpful to consider what your levels of knowledge are for your customer or user base, define any unknowns before formulating assumptions and define the riskiest assumption that become hypotheses to test. The assumptions may be quite broad as your idea of the market or user need is early stage.

The assumptions are likely to be more specific and targeted for Lean Start-Up approaches to testing and experimentation. The user groups and customer needs are potentially defined at this point. However, if they are not defined, consider using 'slow research' tools to explore user and customer needs in-depth as part of the lean experimentation approach.

Defining user and customer groups

User groups are *"a collection of users who perform a similar task"* (IBM). They share the same motivations, needs and goals. Customers are the buyers and are sometimes different from users. The user is typically the person using the product or service itself, whereas the customer makes the purchasing decision.

The first task I usually do when there are no insights into customer and user needs, and little is understood about the problem and market, is to find the people I want to talk to by writing all the possibilities: the potential markets, customers, and users. Then, consider grouping customers and users based on shared motivations, needs, or behaviours instead of demographics alone. When you do this exercise, be specific when describing these motivations, needs and behaviours and avoid broadly defining user groups, such as 'Millennials who like listening to music', as these become meaningless quickly. Be aware of your own cognitive biases and assumptions about groups of people and their behaviours to avoid stereotyping people.

To refine your user groups, assess the extremes within user groups. These users need less or more of their problems solved, and they can provide insights into their workarounds and unique needs. The people at the end of each spectrum are the extremes of those who would not use it and those who would be 'power users'. This can be useful in considering accessibility needs. See the diagram on the next page.

Another strategy for refining user groups is Lead Users from the Open Innovation framework. Lead Users love the product and frequently use similar products. Prof. Eric von Hippel at MIT developed the idea of Lead Users as a group of progressive users or customers selected at a very early stage in the innovation process.

To help you prioritise which user groups to include in the research, evaluate the user or customer group with the most significant market opportunities, or which one may be the 'beachhead market', a primary niche (small) market. For the prioritised user and customer groups, you can bring them to life through the product development process using personas.

Prioritise user groups to develop into personas for research

A proto-persona is a persona based on assumptions and early-stage research; it brings a typical person from the user group to life. Personas can be refined and iterated as more primary research is done. Sharon (2016) called these 'Bullshit personas' because they are based on guesses and assumptions and not research, meaning they are likely to change as more insights are generated to validate and refine them.

On the next page is a table that can be used to articulate customer (buyer or user) personas at the start of a project to identify who would be a good fit for the research. User personas and customer personas serve different purposes. User personas focus on the user's problem and how the business can address their needs, while customer personas aim to identify buying behaviours, communication channels, and budgets.

Generally, we identify 3-5 user personas and prioritise them to involve the top 1–2 personas in the research process. The proto-persona is a starting point and will be refined and validated through research and insights. The other user groups may be returned to in the future to explore different user group needs and market opportunities.

Name, age, and description	
What are their needs? What is their problem?	
How are these needs currently being met? What are the solutions?	
What are they motivated by?	
What are they looking for? How could their needs be better met?	
Challenges and pain points	
How will your product meet their needs?	
Where will you find this user to talk to them? How would you reach this particular customer (if looking at buyers)?	

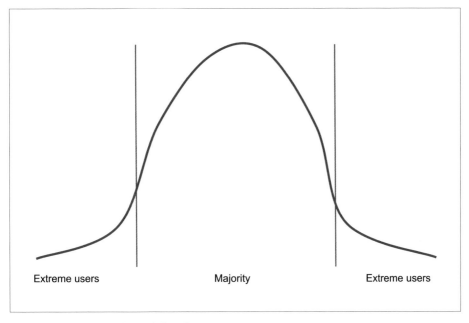

Extreme users   Majority   Extreme users

Extreme Users Sketch by Sharp, C. (2023)

THE LEMONADE VAN

CUSTOMER PERSONA: DELIVERY AND SUBSCRIPTION MODEL

Name, age, and description	Sarah, 28-year-old working professional, married with no children, lives in an apartment in the city.
What are their needs? What is their problem?	Sarah needs a convenient and healthy beverage option that fits her busy lifestyle and provides unique flavour options. She is willing to pay a premium for organic and high-quality ingredients, and values personalised service.
How are these needs currently being met? What are the solutions?	Sarah is always on the go and values convenience in all aspects of her life. She often orders food and drinks through apps to save time and prefers healthy and natural options.
What are they motivated by?	Staying healthy, trying new things, and being productive in her job. Using food and drink vendors that are environmentally friendly.
What are they looking for? How could their needs be better met?	Sarah is looking for a convenient and healthy drink option. Sarah could have drinks delivered to her door.
Challenges and pain points	She has trouble finding healthy drink choices while out and about, doesn't have enough time to make her own, and struggles to find unique flavours in her location. She doesn't have the option for drinks to be delivered to her door.
How will your product meet their needs?	Sarah will be able to order fresh, organic lemonade through the app and it will be delivered to her home.
Where will you find this customer?	This customer can be found in the local area. She can be reached through different distribution channels, such as flyers, social media advertisements and word-of-mouth.

Assess what you know and don't know about the problem

Evaluating what you know and do not know about the challenges, context, behaviours, dynamics and other aspects of the customers and users in the market you're about to enter, or the product you're thinking of building can help you understand what you're guessing, or assuming to be true.

In their book *Lean Analytics,* Alistair Croll and Benjamin Yoskovitz (2013) outlined how to identify Knowns and Unknowns. There are four different ways of looking at data to categorise knowledge and understanding about a particular subject or problem.

— **Known Knowns (Facts):** We know and understand a problem or situation. They are facts or information that we are aware of and have a good understanding of.
— **Known Unknowns (Hypotheses):** We know we don't know about a problem or situation. We know there are gaps in our knowledge and understanding, and we need to fill them to make informed decisions.
— **Unknown Knowns (Our Intuitions and Prejudices):** These are things that we don't realise we know about a problem or situation. It refers to the tacit knowledge, assumptions, or biases we may hold without realising it.
— **Unknown Unknowns (Anything is possible!):** These are things that we don't even know we don't know about a problem or situation. They are the hidden factors we are unaware of and may only discover through research and exploration.

By understanding these different categories of knowledge, we can better identify and address assumptions and biases, ask more informed questions, and design more effective research and problem-solving strategies.

THE LEMONADE VAN
KNOWNS AND UNKNOWNS

Sam has many assumptions about what she thinks will and won't work for her business, The Lemonade Van, at this early stage in her journey. She evaluates her level of knowledge using the Known and Unknowns approach below.

Known Knowns (Facts)
Lemonade sales are growing.
The biggest market is in the US.
The cost of ingredients, the price of cups, recipes, locations where the stand has previously operated, flavours offered.

Known Unknowns (Hypotheses)
There is demand for organic lemonade provided by an ethical and eco-friendly business.
Having strong values will build a good brand.
Target market for the stand.
Ideal locations to operate.
The most effective marketing strategies.
The level of demand for certain flavours.

Unknown Knowns (Intuitions and Prejudices)
May not appeal to children and teens.
The stand may lose customers due to a lack of variety.

Unknown Unknowns (Anything is possible!)
May not be aware of competitors in the area.
May not realise that certain ingredients or supplies could be purchased at a lower cost.

Turning unknowns into assumptions to test as hypotheses

Assumptions are core to Lean Start-Up and Product Discovery but can be used in project-based research to take a hypothesis-based approach. In his book *Lean UX,* Jeff Gothelf advocates:

"Each design is a proposed business solution – a hypothesis. Your goal is to validate the proposed solution as efficiently as possible using customer feedback."

"Starting with a clear and shared understanding of the assumptions you are making is a useful approach. Allowing you to move quickly to clearly defined research hypotheses, which can then act as an anchor for discovery research and learning." (Ben Holliday)

The following sentence structure can be used to frame assumptions (Holliday, 2017):

— **Problem:** We think X is true, OR We think X will happen
— **Solution:** Which is why we believe X is happening OR which we feel creates X opportunity
— **Users:** We can learn more about this assumption by speaking to users in scenarios

If you have many assumptions (more than 10), review them to see if there are any themes where you can start to bring them together. Turning assumptions into hypotheses can help structure how to validate them, as MacCarthy (2018) explains:

> *"A proposed solution with a prediction is a hypothesis. That's if you plan to test it, of course. If not, then it's an assumption. Framing an assumption as a hypothesis helps you prove or disprove it. But it can help the design process in other ways too."* (Oliver MacCarthy)

The Known Unknowns exercise identified knowledge gaps, and now, we want to understand more about our assumptions, some of which may be 'Unknown Knowns' and 'Known Unknowns'. Assumptions using known and unknown plus what's important and unimportant can plot assumptions across four quadrants. Bland (2017) refers to this as 'Assumptions Mapping':

"Assumptions mapping is the practice of identifying the risky assumptions being made about a new product or service. The idea is to inform better products by understanding the assumptions being made about the desirability, feasibility, and viability of a new idea." (David Bland)

The Assumptions Map below has colour-coded Post-it notes based on the Three Lenses of Innovation: Feasibility, Desirability and Viability. Orange signifies Desirable Assumptions; green indicates Viable Assumptions and blue shows Feasible Assumptions. Value proposition and lean experiments focus on 'Unknown and Important'. 'Known and Important' can be assessed against the product roadmap. 'Unknown and Unimportant' can be investigated using user interviews and tests. Finally, 'Known and Unimportant' should be deferred.

Teresa Torres suggested that Assumptions Mapping identifies the riskiest assumptions and can be validated or invalidated in the product development cycle as early as possible. The Riskiest Assumption Test starts with testable assumptions, devising experiments to validate or invalidate these assumptions and measuring the results to gain insights and make informed decisions about the product or idea. Assumption testing helps to reduce uncertainty, minimise waste, and increase the chances of success by focusing on the most critical assumptions and testing them with real users or customers.

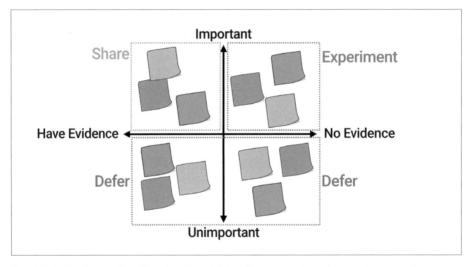

Bland, D. (2017), Assumptions Mapping, Precoil: https://www.precoil.com/assumptions-mapping

THE LEMONADE VAN
ASSUMPTION MAPPING

Here, Sam is focusing on the subscription and delivery value proposition for her Assumption Mapping.

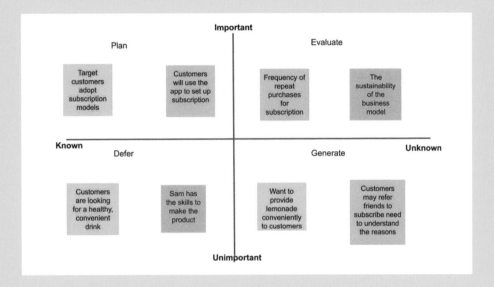

Sam will do this exercise again for the events value proposition, which has a different market and user group.

Riskiest Assumption Test

The Riskiest Assumption Test (RAT) is based on the idea that many start-up failures can be traced back to assumptions that turned out to be false. Therefore, identifying and testing the riskiest assumptions early in the development process can increase the chances of success and reduce the likelihood of wasting time and resources on unlikely ideas.

RAT involves identifying the assumptions most critical to the business idea's success, testing these assumptions through rapid experimentation and customer feedback, and then iterating and refining the concept based on the results of these tests. The goal is to validate or invalidate the assumptions quickly and cheaply to save time and resources on an idea that may not work.

The test can be carried out using various methods, including customer interviews, surveys, prototypes, and experiments. The key is to design simple and low-cost experiments focused on the specific assumption being tested. The test results should be used to refine the idea, pivot to a new direction, or abandon the idea altogether and move on to a new one.

You can use the Riskiest Assumption Finder to identify the riskiest assumption that carries the most significance if proven false. This tool was developed by Ash Maurya (2012), an entrepreneur and author of *Running Lean: Iterate from Plan A to a Plan That Works*.

The Riskiest Assumption Finder is used to identify the most critical assumptions underlying a business idea, product, or business model and to prioritise them for testing and validation. It can help identify and test the riskiest assumptions. The steps are:

— **Identify your critical assumptions:** The most significant assumptions underlying your business model or project. These should be the assumptions that, if proven false, would make your project or business model unworkable.
— **List the assumptions:** Write each in the centre of a sticky note or box. Be as specific and concise as possible.
— **Assess the level of risk:** Next, assess the level of risk associated with each assumption. How certain are you that this assumption is true? Rate the risk level as high, medium, or low.
— **Identify potential tests:** Brainstorm likely tests or experiments for each assumption to help you validate or invalidate the assumption. These tests should be specific and measurable.

- **Prioritise tests:** Prioritise the tests based on their potential impact and the level of risk associated with the assumption.
- **Execute the tests:** Start executing the tests in order of priority. Be prepared to pivot or adjust your business model if the tests indicate one or more false assumptions.
- **Repeat the process:** As you learn from your tests, update the canvas with new assumptions and potential tests. Repeat the process until you have validated your critical assumptions and have a viable business model or project plan.

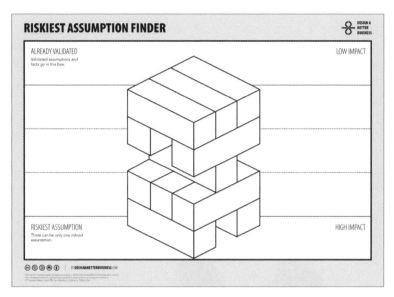

Riskiest Assumption Canvas, DesignBetterBusiness.com. Licensed under a Creative Commons Attribution-Share Alike 4.0 International Licence.: https://www.designabetterbusiness.tools/tools/riskiest-assumption-canvas

Defining assumptions, identifying the riskiest assumption, and using hypotheses provide a foundation for research and experiments. Assumptions and hypotheses narrow the focus of the data collection, meaning that learnings and making conclusions can be targeted. This targeted approach can help understand what is validated, not validated and a new, potentially unexpected opportunity.

This chapter has explained how to approach assumptions to get a comprehensive overview as to what should and shouldn't be tested in research or experiments. Identifying the riskiest assumption is important for testing will help to de-risk the idea if these are prioritised and the key focus of explorative research or tests with users and customers. The next chapter is going to provide an overview on market and competition analysis to better understand the context of the user and customer and can be a good starting point for testing assumptions.

How to Analyse the Market and Competition

Introduction

Gathering information on the competition and market trends and dynamics, as well as looking at the broader picture for potential threats and opportunities, can be a helpful way to provide context to customer and user needs and contribute toward critical strategic decisions on the commercial viability of a product or service. Having a complete picture of the market you may be entering based on the prioritised user and customer groups; will indicate who the buyers are and the markets where the problem lives, and if it is a problem in a growing market.

This chapter will outline desk research and secondary analysis as two strategies for understanding the competition and the market. Desk research is reviewing and assessing existing information such as reports. Secondary analysis evaluates existing company information or databases to understand user behaviours and needs, such as sales or customer databases. We will go through how to do market analysis and industry analysis to identify trends and big players in the market. Also, competition analysis will be covered to determine what similar products and services are currently available and how the product may compete in this market.

Reasons for doing desk research

Desk research or secondary research is learning from existing resources and can be used to understand more about the problem to be solved. Desk research is the review and analysis of existing data and information, which can be online research or printed sources.

Desk research can help to understand the problem better, and it's helpful to read social media posts, reviews, and forums where customers discuss the problem you're looking to explore. Plus, identify existing solutions as we can learn from what already exists and review academic papers for similar programmes or approaches. Additionally, researching how people use workarounds to solve their problems and considering alternative solutions to the problem can be beneficial. Analysing competitor websites can provide insight into potential improvements for your solution or idea and what your unique seeling point is.

Through desk research, we can evaluate the competition. To gain insight into the competition, perusing their websites and examining customer feedback to identify strengths and weaknesses are helpful. As well as staying informed about market conditions, it's essential to read industry and market reports. These reports can provide insight into current market trends, customer behaviours, and potential future market impacts. Additionally, technology advancements should also be considered when examining the market.

How to do desk research to understand the market

Below are the steps that you can follow to undertake effective desk research.

1. **Define your research objective**: Outline the specific research questions you want to answer and the purpose of the analysis.
2. **Gather information**: Conduct research using various sources such as industry reports, news articles, government publications, market research reports, and company websites.
3. **Organise your findings**: Create a system for organising your findings, such as a spreadsheet or a mind map. Organise the information based on the relevant factors for the analysis.
4. **Analyse the information**: Look for patterns, connections, and trends in your collected data.
5. **Identify opportunities and threats**: Based on your analysis, identify your business's opportunities and threats. These may include changes in the market, new competitors, or shifts in consumer behaviour.
6. **Develop an action plan**: Use your analysis to develop an action plan that addresses your identified opportunities and threats. This plan should include specific strategies and tactics for achieving your goals and objectives.
7. **Review and update regularly**: Regularly review and update your analysis to ensure it remains relevant and valuable for your business.

When reading material, you can use many credible sources for reliable findings and assess material through critical reading.

Before you start reading, it's crucial to have a clear goal in mind. Ask yourself what you want to gain from the material and keep an open mind as you approach it. Determine why the author wrote the piece - whether to inform, persuade, or entertain. Understanding their purpose can help you better comprehend their perspective and assess the strength of their arguments.

When examining the material, it is essential to evaluate the evidence provided and determine if it is trustworthy and relevant to the author's argument. Look for any weaknesses or flaws in the evidence and consider the historical, social, cultural, and political context in which it was created. This will help evaluate how the author's perspective and arguments may have been influenced.

Before believing information, it's important to check the author's credibility and the publication's integrity and reliability. Additionally, analyse the logical structure of the argument to assess its validity.

When judging, evaluating the evidence presented and considering alternative perspectives and arguments is essential. By weighing all the evidence, you can make an informed conclusion.

To organise your thoughts and findings, you may want to use visual aids such as a mind map to evaluate some of the patterns and relationships you're seeing. Additionally, use a spreadsheet or database, such as Notion, to keep track of your references to the sources of information you're reading, critical findings and conclusions.

Markets

Before exploring market research and analysis, let's define what a market is. A market is a specific environment where buyers and sellers interact to exchange goods, services, or resources. Buyers express their demand for products or services, while sellers offer them to fulfil the demand.

Markets can have different characteristics, which helps to categorise the market. Markets can specialise by product or service type, for example, technology markets. Depending on the reach and extent of the buyers and sellers, they can have a small or broad geographical scope. Markets can have different structures, including competitive markets with multiple buyers and sellers, monopolistic markets with limited competition or oligopolistic markets with few dominant players. Markets can be segmented based on customer demographics, preferences, or behaviour allowing businesses to target specific customer groups effectively. Markets can have various dynamics, such as supply and demand fluctuations, pricing trends, competition levels and regulatory influences.

Understanding the dynamics of a market is crucial for businesses to identify their target customers, assess the competition, determine pricing strategies, and develop marketing and sales plans. There are several different market types, as listed below:

— **Consumer markets:** Individuals or households who buy goods and services for their use or consumption.
— **Business markets:** Organisations that buy goods and services for use in their operations or to resell to others.
— **Government markets:** Federal/government, state, and local government agencies that buy goods and services to support their operations and the services they provide to citizens.
— **Global markets:** Buyers and sellers in different countries and regions worldwide who engage in trade.
— **Niche markets:** Specialised segments of consumers or businesses with unique needs and preferences that are not adequately served by mainstream products or services. The approach is typically long-term.
— **Beachhead market:** Small market with specific attributes that may buy a new product or service.
— **Mass markets:** Large groups of consumers with similar needs and preferences.
— **Emerging markets:** Markets that have some characteristics of developed markets. It is experiencing rapid growth and increasing consumer demand for goods and services. It may also relate to the economy of a developing nation.

The timing and maturity of the market can influence how to enter the market, the level of competition and market demand. Markets change over time, impacting the level of risk and types of opportunities or barriers experienced when entering the market. To gauge the maturity of the market, they typically follow this lifecycle:

— **Introduction:** This is when new products are launched. It is a time of high risk, uncertainty, and experimentation, and businesses typically invest heavily in research and development and marketing to raise awareness and generate demand for their product.
— **Growth:** During this stage, the market experiences rapid growth in sales and revenue as the product gains broader acceptance and adoption by consumers. In this stage, businesses expand their market share and build brand loyalty.
— **Maturity:** This stage is characterised by slowing growth and increasing competition as the market becomes saturated with similar products. During this stage, businesses focus on cost-cutting measures, process efficiencies, and diversification to maintain profitability and market share.

— **Decline:** The final stage of the market life cycle is marked by declining sales and revenue, as the product becomes outdated, obsolete, or replaced by newer, more innovative products. During this stage, businesses may choose to exit the market, reposition their product, or diversify into new markets to remain viable.

The analysis of this information will impact the development of go-to-market strategies and determine if the idea is a viable business opportunity. It will also significantly impact sales forecasts, considering market trends, business growth, and other factors that can affect revenue, such as economies of scale.

How to do market analysis

Market analysis helps businesses make informed decisions, adapt to changing market conditions and seize growth opportunities. Understanding how industries behave, market trends, and what drives them to grow, competitive analysis of what is blocking entry, and identifying key players will shape a broader understanding of the market context.

Market analysis is qualitatively and quantitatively evaluating an industry to determine whether it suits your business.

— **Drivers:** This could be regulation, technological change, and buying behaviours. These are usually a positive force, providing your business with good conditions to succeed.
— **Blockers:** These would be factors hurting the product or business idea's success.
— **Barriers to entry:** There are likely to be barriers to entry for newcomers in any given market or industry. These should be included in the market analysis and can include regulation, competition, and cost of capital to enter the market.

Top-down market sizing
Market sizing can be determined through a top-down approach, which involves calculating the total market and estimating market share. Utilising Total Available Market (TAM), Serviceable Available Market (SAM), and Serviceable Obtainable Market (SOM) can assist businesses in identifying and evaluating market opportunities. Assessing the size and growth of the market, as well as its drivers, including the Compound Annual Growth Rate (CAGR), can help businesses make informed decisions.

- **Total Available Market (TAM):** The total demand for a product or service in a specific market. TAM represents the maximum revenue opportunity available for a business if it were to capture 100% market share. It is the broadest and largest market size estimation and includes all potential customers in a given market.
- **Serviceable Available Market (SAM):** The portion of the TAM that a business can realistically reach and serve based on its business model, capabilities, and resources. SAM is a subset of TAM and represents the specific market segment a business will target.
- **Serviceable Obtainable Market (SOM):** The portion of the SAM that a business can realistically capture or obtain. It considers the competition, market share, and other factors affecting a business's ability to capture a specific market segment. SOM represents the actual revenue potential for a business.

Once the product is built, the SOM would be determined over a set period and heavily influenced by the extent of marketing plans and budget.

Bottom-up market sizing

To determine pricing and sales projections, pricing and demand forecasting of the product are used. This contributes to a market analysis from the bottom-up approach and identifies potential market growth over a specific period, considering factors like changes in market conditions, business growth, increase in brand awareness, economies of scale and regulation changes. The bottom-up approach calculates sales figures based on estimated sales, which is helpful for SOM and emerging markets. For The Lemonade Van, the number of customers, how much they pay for lemonade and how frequently in total will define the market size for a certain time period.

Market analysis is the collection and analysis of market information, including its size, growth potential and competition. Desk research involves analysing sources such as market reports, academic papers, and online databases. It starts with the research question, identifying the relevant data sources to answer the question to be analysed. To make conclusions about the market, this may involve identifying trends, assessing the competitive landscape, and evaluating the potential demand for a product or service.

How to understand the external environment

The market analysis uses frameworks such as SWOT and PESTLE. These models can identify opportunities and threats to provide a comprehensive understanding of the internal capabilities and external environment, which could impact the product's success.

The SWOT analysis assesses the internal strengths and weaknesses of a business or a particular project or product and the external opportunities and threats it faces. The acronym stands for Strengths, Weaknesses, Opportunities and Threats. Questions to analyse these for your business or product or services further are as follows:

— **Strengths:** What advantages does the business have? What do you do better than anyone else? What unique or low-cost resources do you have access to? What do people in your market see as your strengths?
— **Weaknesses:** What could you improve? What should you avoid? What are people in your market likely to see as weaknesses?
— **Opportunities:** What good opportunities can you spot? What interesting trends are you aware of? Is there a need in the market that your business could fill?
— **Threats:** What obstacles do you face? What is your competition doing? Are there emerging trends that threaten your business or your idea?

PESTLE stands for Political, Economic, Social, Technological, Legal and Environmental and is also alternatively known as STEEPLE with the extra E standing for Ethicial. This framework identifies and analyses external factors affecting a business or an idea. The questions to consider include the following:

— **Political:** How do government policies and regulations impact the industry? What is the political stability in the country? What are the current and potential future government interventions?
— **Economic:** What is the state of the economy in the country and globally? How do economic factors like inflation, interest, and exchange rates affect the industry? What is the current economic growth rate?
— **Social:** What are the cultural and demographic trends in the country? What is the population size and age range? What is the level of education and income in the target market?
— **Technological:** What are the latest technological advancements in the industry? How does technology impact the industry? What are the barriers to entry into the industry?
— **Legal:** What is the industry's current and future legal requirements and regulations? Are there any pending legal cases or regulations that may affect the industry?
— **Environmental:** What are the environmental factors that can impact the industry, such as climate change, natural disasters, and resource availability? How is the industry impacting the environment, and are there any regulations to address this?

Together, SWOT and PESTLE provide a robust view of the current position of the business and product to make informed decisions to leverage strengths, address weaknesses, capitalise on opportunities and mitigate threats. By understanding these factors, companies can effectively align their strategies, anticipate changes, and adapt to market conditions.

THE LEMONADE VAN
SWOT & PESTLE ANALYSIS

Sam decides to carry out a SWOT and PESTLE analysis to understand the strengths and weaknesses of The Lemonade Van but also the opportunities and threats to her business coming from outside her business. Sam wants to examine the market opportunity because the initial investment for The Lemonade Van will be substantial for Sam. She wants to understand if this is a financially viable option or if this venture is too risky.

SWOT

STRENGTHS
— This is a mobile and eco-friendly business with low start-up costs.
— The business offers unique and refreshing lemonade.
— Can reach customers in different locations for added convenience.

WEAKNESSES
— Has fewer product options compared to others.
— The market is affected by weather and seasonal changes in demand.
— There is limited storage space for supplies and equipment.

OPPORTUNITIES
— Sam is looking into how we can grow lemons in the UK to help reduce our carbon footprint and we need to understand if this is feasible.
— She is interested in partnering with local businesses or events to expand our product offerings or add-on services, such as snacks or customer orders.
— Sam believes there is potential for growth through social media and word-of-mouth marketing as well.

THREATS
— There are risks to the supply of lemons.
— Competition comes from other food and drink vendors in the local area.
— The changes in consumer trends or preferences that will impact on sales.
— Economic downturns or external factors that affect spending habits of premium drinks or subscriptions.

PESTLE

POLITICAL
— The pricing of wholesale products can be affected by import and export regulations.
— The political situation in the area where the goods are grown may affect the business.
— Running a lemonade van requires obtaining permits and licenses. It is important to adhere to the regulations governing the sale of food and beverages.
— There may be limitations on selling food in public areas that need to be taken into consideration.

ECONOMIC
— The current cost of living crisis is affecting people's spending habits.
— Low sales will make it expensive to buy supplies like lemons, sugar, cups, and running the van.
— It's also important to plan for seasonal fluctuations in demand and keep an eye on competitors in the area that may affect sales.

SOCIAL
— The product is designed for customers who share our ethical values and want to support our brand.
— Keep an eye on social trends and cultural events that could affect sales.
— Assess the demand for mobile food stands to ensure we meet customer needs.

TECHNOLOGICAL
— May only be able to offer lemon-based products when we have lemons in stock.
— To make things easy for customers, we have user-friendly apps that allow them to track their orders and know when to expect them.
— Use portable generators and point-of-sale systems, but in the rare event of a failure, we have a plan in place.
— Recognise that there may be competition from automated vending machines and challenges such as limited internet connectivity for payment systems.

LEGAL
— Consider import regulation and tax on ingredients and packaging.
— Comply with health and safety regulations such as food handling requirements.
— Have legal cover for liabilities such as accidents or injuries.

ENVIRONMENTAL
— Use refillable bottles and environmentally friendly transportation such as Electric Vehicles.
— Reuse the lemon pith and skin for other uses to be more environmentally friendly.
— Waste disposal to be eco-friendly e.g., compostable cups or locally sourced ingredients.
— Energy usage of the van and creating the lemonade.
— Environmental factors that may impact sales such as extreme weather conditions.

THE LEMONADE VAN
MARKET ANALYSIS

Sam wants to understand the commercial risk for The Lemonade Van by analysing the market, particularly if she is to consider expanding into other geographical locations in the future. Below are her findings from the market analysis.

The Lemonade Van will deliver straight to customers, and she will also sell at festivals, farmer's markets, and other events, as well as stocking at local cafes and artisan shops. She is B2C (Business to Customer) and B2B (Business to Business). Each business model will have a different market and approach.

Sam has looked at the market statistics online and found that lemonade is growing. It has a Compound Annual Growth Rate (CAGR) of 6.24% between 2023-2030. The market was worth $8.7bn in 2022.

Drivers in the lemonade market are:
— Organic lemonade is typically better quality, so there is a higher demand for it.
— There is innovation happening in the space as to what types and colours of lemonade there are.
— Lemonade has health benefits. For example, it is high in Vitamin C.
— The most common form of packaging is bottles. However, The Lemonade Van can use glass bottles over plastic bottles as they can be recycled.

Blockers in the lemonade market are:
— Major market players are investing in this space, which means it's very competitive.
— It's highly seasonal, and most sales are made in the summer.

Barriers to entry are low as lemonade is easy to make, made from lemons, water, and sugar/honey.

The **Total Addressable Market** is the total number of potential customers for a mobile lemonade business. In this case, the TAM is the area's entire population where The Lemonade Van would operate, including locals and tourists.

The **Serviceable Available Market** is the segment of the TAM The Lemonade Van could realistically target with its marketing and sales efforts. For example, the SAM might be narrowed down to just the population of the area where The Lemonade Van will be located since it might not be practical to reach out to customers who are too far away.

The **Serviceable Obtainable Market** would be the portion of the SAM that the business could realistically capture as customers. For example, the SOM might be further narrowed down to just the population of the area where The Lemonade Van will be located, who are likely to be thirsty, looking for refreshments, willing to buy lemonade or want it delivered.

Sam's mind map to capture reflections on her market research and analysis.

How to analyse the competition

Entrepreneurs, marketers, product teams and Innovation Leads can all benefit from assessing the competition and have this as a continuous activity as markets change quickly.

Competition analysis is the process of identifying and evaluating the strengths and weaknesses of competitors in a particular industry or market. The aim is to gain a better understanding of what competitors are doing, what their strategies are, and how they may impact your own business. This analysis involves various factors, such as the products or services offered, pricing strategies, distribution channels to reach customers and sell the product, marketing and branding efforts, and overall market position. The goal of competition analysis is to identify market opportunities and threats and develop strategies that enable a business to compete effectively stand out and succeed in its industry.

The Jobs to be Done (JTBD) framework was outlined earlier in the book. The JTBD competitor analysis is a method of analysing competitors through the lens of understanding the jobs that customers are trying to accomplish. This approach focuses on identifying the needs and desires of customers and mapping them to the products and services offered by competitors. By understanding the jobs customers are trying to get done, businesses can identify gaps in the market and create new products or services that better address those needs.

The process of JTBD competitor analysis involves several steps:

— **Identify the jobs customers are trying to accomplish:** Businesses should research to understand their customers' underlying motivations and desires. This can be done through surveys, interviews, and other forms of market research.
— **Map the jobs to existing products and services:** Once the jobs have been identified, businesses should map them to the products and services offered by their competitors. This can help identify areas where the competition is intense and areas where there may be gaps in the market.
— **Evaluate the competition's strengths and weaknesses:** By understanding the jobs that customers are trying to accomplish and how competitors are currently serving them, businesses can identify the strengths and weaknesses of their competitors.
— **Identify opportunities for innovation:** Based on the insights gained from the JTBD competitor analysis, businesses can identify opportunities for innovation. This might involve creating new products or services that better address customers' needs or improving existing products to compete.

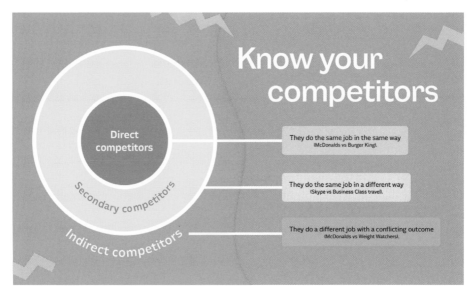

Traynor, D. and Alexiacas, Understanding your competitors, Intercom: https://www.intercom.com/blog/understanding-your-competitors/

Overall, JTBD competitor analysis is a customer-centric approach to analysing the competition that can help businesses better understand the needs and desires of their customers and create products and services that better serve those needs. You can analyse competition using both primary and secondary research methods. Primary research involves consulting experts to identify key players in the market and customer or user interviews to identify what products and services the target audience currently uses.

Desk research can help gather relevant information on competitor products, services, pricing, marketing strategies, market share, distribution channels, how they position their product to customers, indications of customer jobs or needs, successful funding rounds and customer feedback from online reviews.

Also, identify the key players, which can be found in market reports for larger markets. Remember that competition is not always direct, so consider both direct and secondary competition if they are targeting the same audience. Interviews with industry experts would be useful to do alongside desk research.

The conclusions made from assessing the competition can help identify areas where a business can differentiate itself from competitors, develop new products or services to fill gaps in the market or identify opportunities to expand into new markets.

THE LEMONADE VAN
DESK RESEARCH

Sam wants to learn about the market and competition in more detail, so she does desk research to understand the market conditions locally as her first market is the local area. Below is an overview of what Sam found.

Direct competition

The direct competition for The Lemonade Van could be other beverage and snack vendors, such as mobile food trucks, ice cream trucks, coffee carts, or even cafes and restaurants that sell cold drinks. Other potential competition could come from grocery stores or convenience stores that sell pre-made lemonade or other beverages. The weather could also be considered competition, as customers may be less likely to purchase cold drinks during colder or rainy weather.

For B2C, the direct competition may be delivery companies that can provide lemonade on demand through services such as Starship and Deliveroo.

For B2B, the direct competition would be other lemonade suppliers available to the restaurant, café or similar.

Secondary competition

The secondary competition for a lemonade van could be other businesses or vendors that offer similar products or services but are not direct competitors. For example, a coffee shop or ice cream truck may be considered secondary competition for a lemonade van as they offer beverages and treats with different flavours and offerings. Other secondary competitors could include convenience stores, vending machines, and other beverage stands or food trucks. A lemonade van must be aware of its secondary competition as it can impact its pricing, and marketing strategies.

Indirect competition

This is a different job with a conflicting outcome. In this case, the options would be water, hot drinks or similar, as the customer may want a drink for a different reason. Due to the sugar content, a conflicting outcome would be dental or health campaigns encouraging people to drink fewer sugary drinks.

Desk or online research on the competition

Sam looked at the competitors' websites and social media for her local area who would be her key competitors:

Name of the competitor and customer job	Strengths	Weaknesses	Lessons for your business or product idea
Bo's Juice Bar Quenching thirst from high-quality, tasty drink static location when close-by.	Established brand with a loyal customer base – it's nearly ten years old. Consistent product quality and taste (from the reviews). Central location and close to beaches and parks. High quality ingredients, locally sourced.	Limited options provide lemonade and fruit juice options only. High prices as based in the city centre. Customers must go to the bar.	Could offer other juices and smoothies to increase the product range. Strong, memorable brand and great quality service shows that this can grow and retain a customer base.
Lemon Squeezy Require a drink option which is convenient and onsite.	Lemon-themed mobile food truck that specialises in events and has a strong social media presence. Has a memorable brand experience, such as wearing props, elaborate drink presentation and backdrops, so it's a fun experience at events.	Has limited options as is around the variations of lemon flavours such as elderflower or ginger. Limited distribution and small-scale operations.	Change the name from The Lemonade Van to one which doesn't limit the product range. Or could include food that are fruit and veg based to expand product range such as lemon cake, cheesecake, carrot cake. Ideas for creating memorable experiences.
Tutti Fruity Tasty drinks delivered to customers' homes.	A local subscription provider of independent alcoholic and non-alcoholic beverages which changes each month and keeps the client engaged. Nationally sourced beverages – quarterly subscription as monthly may be too often – a premium treat with options to top-up and buy more.	Higher costs of acquisition for subscription clients and costs for delivery and packaging to protect the bottles. Pressure to change the offering every three months.	Shows the higher costs for providing subscriptions and deliveries. Could provide this later once the van is established in the local area at events and ad-hoc visits to residential areas similar to an ice-cream van.

How to understand the attractiveness of a market

Porter's Five Forces can be used to identify the primary sources of competition in a sector or industry. Michael E. Porter (1980), a renowned economist and professor at Harvard Business School, developed the model to analyse the competitive forces within an industry in the book *Competitive Strategy: Techniques for Analysing Industries and Competitors*. It provides a structured approach for assessing an industry's competitive dynamics and evaluating its attractiveness for potential profitability. It can be used as a strategic decision-making tool to identify ways to enhance competitiveness, explore new market segments or develop strategies to mitigate competitive pressures.

This knowledge benefits new entrants if you're developing a new product or service or seeking to identify potential opportunities for existing products and services.

1. **Threat of new entrants**: Assesses the likelihood of new competitors entering the industry. Industries with low barriers to entry, such as low capital requirements or minimal regulatory restrictions, tend to have a higher threat of new entrants, which can increase competition and potentially reduce profitability for existing players.
2. **Bargaining power of suppliers**: Examines the power and influence of suppliers over the industry. Suppliers with strong bargaining power, such as those who provide unique or critical inputs, can demand higher prices or better terms, which can impact the profitability of companies in the industry.
3. **Bargaining power of buyers**: Evaluates the power and influence of buyers or customers in the industry. Buyers with strong bargaining power, such as large customers or those with multiple options, can demand lower prices, better quality, or other favourable terms, which can affect the profitability of firms in the industry.
4. **Threat of substitute products or services**: Considers the availability and attractiveness of substitute products or services that can fulfil the same need or function as the industry's offerings. Industries with many readily available substitutes may face increased competition and pressure on pricing and profitability.
5. **Intensity of competitive rivalry**: Assesses the competition level among existing industry firms. Factors such as the number of competitors, their size, and the level of product differentiation can impact the intensity of competition, which in turn can affect profitability.

You can learn about these broader factors from desk research, particularly from reading thought-leadership articles from market leaders, industry reports, and market analysis reports. If you want to understand these aspects in more depth, you can include these topics when speaking to experts and stakeholders to understand the broader context of the customer and market.

THE LEMONADE VAN
PORTER'S FIVE FORCES

Sam decides to analyse her business using Porter's Five Forces as she hasn't considered the wider context yet, and she may be missing something that may be a risk to her venture.

1. As a new entrant to The Lemonade Van is low, as there are few barriers to entry, such as obtaining necessary permits and licences, securing a suitable location, and acquiring a mobile lemonade van. There may be a moderate threat of new competitors entering the market, which could increase competition and potentially impact profitability.
2. The bargaining power of suppliers is moderate, as The Lemonade Van may require suppliers for ingredients such as lemons, sugar, and cups. If there are limited suppliers or if the Sam relies heavily on a single supplier, the bargaining power of suppliers may be higher, which could impact costs and profitability.
3. The bargaining power of buyers is moderate, as customers typically have other beverage options and can easily switch to a different vendor. However, suppose The Lemonade Van has established a strong brand presence, unique recipes, or a loyal customer base. In that case, it may have more bargaining power with customers, which could impact pricing and customer retention.
4. The threat of substitute products or services is high, as customers have many options for refreshing beverages, such as other beverage stands, convenience stores, or cafes. The Lemonade Van may face competition from other beverage providers, as well as other substitute products or services, such as bottled beverages or homemade lemonade.
5. The intensity of competitive rivalry is high, as other mobile beverage vendors or food trucks in the exact locations may compete for customers. Factors such as pricing, quality, customer service, and marketing efforts may impact the level of competition in the local market.

The Lemonade Van may face moderate-to-high competitive forces in the market, including potential threats from new entrants, suppliers, buyers, substitute products/services, and existing competitors. It's crucial for Sam to carefully consider and address these forces in her business strategy, such as by differentiating offerings through unique recipes, branding, customer service, and marketing efforts and building customer loyalty to mitigate the impact of these competitive forces and achieve business success.

This chapter explored how to analyse the competition and the market. For businesses to be aware of the external environment and how it is changing, it is useful to stay competitive and innovative. The next chapter will focus on customer and user needs specifically through market, user, design research and Open Innovation methods.

How to Plan Project-Based Research

Introduction

Good research takes planning. This chapter focuses on project-based research but can be used in Lean Start-up approaches to plan experiments explained later in this book to assist in the allocation of resources and time. We will explore the different considerations for putting together a plan for a research project and how to define the research questions and aims. An overview of different types of research methods is provided to show you the purpose of the data collection. Where methods overlap such as interviews, the interview guide is different depending on the research type and goals for the research. We finish with ethics in research which is a key consideration for looking after participants and their data.

How to plan project-based research

A research project doesn't have to take months and be expensive. Still, it will be distinctly different for entrepreneurs doing research independently compared to businesses with dedicated project teams. Ultimately, it is an investment whether an entrepreneur, an SME, or a large organisation to get reliable insights into product development.

Now we'll focus on how to scope and plan a research project. Below are the areas you need to consider when planning project-based research. They can also apply to tests and experiments, such as usability tests and MVP lean experiments.

Background to the research	Why you're doing this research, what problem you want to explore in more detail and how you intend to apply the findings.
Research question and aim	What the research question is and what the research aims are to focus the research project purpose and have explicit goals. These may have come from the Assumptions Mapping and Unknown-Knowns exercises to create the hypothesis you'll test.
Research design	What methods you'll use to answer the research question and test the hypotheses.

Sample size	The user groups or customer groups included in the research and how many people per user group are needed.
Data collection methods	How you'll collect the data to answer the research question and aims. This could be interviews and Ethnography for deeper insights or data analysis.
Data analysis	The method used for collecting the data will influence the data analysis method. We'll explore data analysis for the different data collection methods later in this book.
Team and expertise	The number of team members required and their level of knowledge to plan for outsourcing, training, or hiring team members with the skills needed.
Resources and technology	The availability and cost of resources and technology needed for the research, such as software, hardware, and equipment, can impact the budget.
Project plan	Outline what the timeline of the project is likely to be and assign different activities across the team.
Project outputs	Show what will be produced at the end of the research project to disseminate the findings. This could be a report or a presentation.
Communication plan	How will the team and broader business be updated with the progress made in the project.
Budget	How much will this project cost, and what is the budget being spent on.
Risks	Demonstrate potential risks in the project and how these could be mitigated and reduced.
Ethical considerations	Obtaining informed consent, protecting participant confidentiality, ensuring the research is conducted ethically, and considering any sensitive topics and if there needs to be support for participants.

Now that we have these outlined, we'll review some of the items on this list in more detail, in particular the research question, aim, sample, data collection method and ethics.

Research question

A research questions is a specific, focused question guiding research projects or studies. It aims to identify and answer specific information gaps or knowledge deficiencies related to the research topic. The research question should be clear, concise, and answerable through data collection and analysis. It can be used to structure the research design, data collection methods, and analysis strategies. A research question can help focus the research and make it answerable through data collection and the chosen method.

Research aims

Research aims are specific goals or objectives a researcher intends to achieve through their research study. They are typically based on the research question and outline what the researcher wants to achieve or learn from the study. Research aims can vary depending on the type of research being conducted and the specific research question being addressed. The assumptions will be the basis for the research aim. You'll know what to test and why and with whom. The hypothesis are predictions of what may be the outcomes of the research, when testing assumptions.

Example research aims are:
— To identify user perceptions of the product concept.
— To understand the market and ecosystem of the beverage industry.

Sample: Who can take part in the research

Generally speaking, for qualitative research (e.g. focus groups and interviews), the number of people you need to talk to is based on the depth of insights. You know when you've spoken enough people when you're starting to hear the same thing, this is called saturation. In user research, or other types of insights research, the sample size is smaller, but the number of insights is greater (Polaine and Reason, 2013).

The number of people that take part is called a sample size. Quantitative research has a sample size that is usually large, and that is because you'll want to consider statistical significance, which is how reliable the findings are and whether results happen by chance or if there is a genuine relationship or effect.

Nikki Anderson, founder of the User Research Academy, suggests sample sizes for the generative and evaluative research. Generative research involves exploring and uncovering new insights and ideas to inform the early stages of product or service development. Evaluative research assesses and validates existing concepts or prototypes to make informed refinements and improvements.

For generative research, Anderson suggests the following sample sizes:
— **1-2-1 interviews**: 15–25 participants per segment
— **Diary studies**: At least 10 participants per segment (user group)
— **Contextual inquiry**: 10–12 participants per segment
— **Mental model interviews**: 15–20 interviews per segment
— **Participatory design**: 10–12 participants per segment

For evaluative research, Anderson suggests the following sample sizes:
— **Usability testing**
  - Moderated: At least 5 participants per segment
  - Unmoderated: At least 15 participants per segment
— **Concept testing**
  - Moderated: At least 8 participants per segment
  - Unmoderated: At least 15 participants per segment
— **Card sorting**: 20–30 participants per segment
— **Benchmarking**: 25+ per segment as looking at quantitative data

There are different ways to sample in qualitative research, including purposeful sampling, which involves deliberately selecting participants with specific characteristics and experiences relevant to the research objectives. This is the sampling method I use the most for market and user research.

For a purposeful sample, use exclusion and inclusion criteria based on personas to decide whom to include or exclude in research. This will help focus your research and recruit suitable participants. These are based on the personas that stemmed from the assumptions and hypotheses. Each persona will show the segment or user group and are grouped based on shared motivations, needs and behaviours rather than demographics (i.e., age, location).

Specific criteria can be used to screen potential candidates to ensure that your research is focused and that you can find the ideal participants. You can use screening surveys and ask relevant questions to identify the most suitable people who meet the inclusion and exclusion criteria for your user group or market segment. It is also helpful to include availability and contact information to streamline the process of organising interviews, focus groups or observations.

In addition to purposeful sampling, I use snowball sampling. This is when it is challenging to identify and access potential participants directly, so the participants are asked to refer other individuals that may fit the research criteria. As user groups are typically specific, this method can be beneficial.

Other types of sampling include convenience sampling, which is the selection of participants based on their availability and accessibility; homogeneous sampling, to select participants who share specific characteristics or experiences and helps explore a particular experience with a homogeneous group; and finally, expert sampling who are individuals who have specialised knowledge and this is the sampling method used for considering experts and stakeholders to involve in the research.

There are many strategies for recruiting participants; recruitment is the most time-consuming part of a research project. It is essential to keep the momentum going and speak to people soon after starting to recruit participants. Recruitment methods that have worked for me are: Building relationships with gatekeepers of groups to disseminate information about the research to the group, investing in paid advertisements on social media and using a networking approach to invite personal and professional people to tell their colleagues and friends. At the end of the project, it is good to give feedback to the participants in an infographic or short form, the critical insights found and how they were implemented or impacted the product or service.

I also use incentives to encourage people to take part in research. Incentives typically help to motivate people to be involved in your research. However, in some cases, they are not appropriate. You could include the option of having an online shopping voucher or a donation to a charity. If you do, provide vouchers to participants, give them a receipt for the voucher to demonstrate that they were given this.

THE LEMONADE VAN
RESEARCH QUESTION AND AIMS

Sam plans to research independently and wants to focus her time and efforts as much as possible. She's interested in understanding her potential customers for The Lemonade Van at events and the delivery of lemonade in the local area on a subscription model. Here, Sam outlines her research plan.

Research Question:
What are the needs and preferences of potential customers for The Lemonade Van for both value propositions?

Research Aims:
— To identify the target market for the lemonade stand, at events and home delivery.
— To understand the needs and preferences of potential customers in terms of flavours, pricing, and location.
— To identify the factors that influence potential customers' decision to purchase lemonade at events and through a subscription or delivery service.

Timeline and budget
Sam has approximately three months and £2,500 to spend on research. She may get some support from freelance researchers with the data collection or analysis. She may use the budget for incentives.

Target Audience
The two user groups that Sam has prioritised are:

— The parents of young families who attend local family events and visit local venues such as parks and beaches are likely to purchase organic lemonade for parents and children at events and locations.
— Health-conscious adults in the local area who are looking for convenient drink options that could be delivered to their door.

Research method for understanding customer needs

Ethnography and problem/solution interviews will be used to evaluate customer and user needs. Ethnography will be used to understand the event context and what can be learned about buying beverages.

Interviews will be with both user groups to understand approaches toward choosing and buying beverages and if organic lemonade is commonly chosen. What factors influence choices and for them to try flavours to see which is most popular.

Analysis and outputs

The interview data will be analysed using thematic analysis to understand patterns, and the outputs will be presented in a short report which could be used in the business plan.

Types of data collection methods

"Get the hell out of the building." (Steve Blank)

It's easy to say, 'Go and talk to your customers,' but what tools are best to get the information needed? Several factors influence what research methods to use. The specific research goals will determine the type of research method that is most appropriate. If the goal is to gain a deeper understanding of user needs, then interviews or focus groups may be more suitable.

Focus groups help understand how people feel about a topic on a broad level. One research study I did explored how older people felt about predictive analytics used on datasets. The datasets planned to be analysed were for older people, so it was essential to understand their feelings. All the data would be anonymised and aggregated, followed by strict ethical and data handling protocols—the research aimed to understand the perception toward the datasets analysed together from an older person's view.

Primary and secondary research

There are two types of research methods: primary research and secondary research. In primary research, you design and use the tools for a specific purpose. Secondary research is where you use existing research for a different purpose. These two types of research have different uses depending on the context they're used in, such as user, design, or market research.

There are two ways to collect data: qualitative research and quantitative research.

Qualitative research
Qualitative research is a type of research that focuses on exploring and understanding people's beliefs, values, attitudes, experiences, and behaviours in depth. It seeks to obtain rich and detailed data through interviews, focus groups, observation, and case studies.

Qualitative research aims to generate insights, meanings, and understanding about a particular topic, issue, or phenomenon. It explores complex and subjective aspects of human behaviour that cannot be easily quantified or measured.

One of the strengths of qualitative research is its flexibility, allowing researchers to adjust their approach and questions based on emerging insights from the data. However, it has limitations, including the potential for researcher bias and difficulty generalising findings to larger populations. Using a mix of both qualitative and quantitative research can overcome the weaknesses of using one type on its own.

Quantitative research
Quantitative research often involves measuring attitudes, behaviours, preferences, or demographic characteristics. It is often used to gather data on large populations, as the data can be generalised.

Examples of quantitative research include surveys, experiments, and clinical trials. The advantage of quantitative research is that it provides precise and objective data that can be analysed statistically. However, it may not capture the full complexity of human behaviour, and the data collected may be limited by the questions and methods used to collect it. It also requires a large sample size to be statistically meaningful, which can be time-consuming and expensive.

Generative research and evaluative research

Generative research aims to understand the user's day-to-day life and circumstances deeply and is typically qualitative research. Evaluative research considers testing ideas and concepts with users, generally using qualitative and quantitative research.

Different types of generative research
Market research, user/UX research, design research, and Open Innovation are all related to understanding and designing products or services. Behavioural research aims to observe people and their actions, and attitudinal research looks to understand or measure beliefs to understand customer and user needs.

— **Market research:** A systematic process of gathering and analysing data to gain insights into customers, competitors, and marketing trends. It involves various methods such as surveys, interviews, and data analysis to understand consumer preferences, market dynamics and growth opportunities.
— **User research:** User research focuses on understanding users' needs, behaviours, and preferences and how they interact with a product or service. User research aims to create a user-centred design that meets the target audience's needs and provides a positive user experience.
— **UX research:** A subset of user research that focuses specifically on the user experience of a product or service. UX research aims to understand how users interact with a product or service and identify opportunities for improving the user experience.
— **Design research:** Design research is focused on understanding the design process and how design can be used to solve problems and create innovative

solutions. Design research aims to inform the design process and ensure design decisions are based on data and insights.
— **Open Innovation:** A process that involves collaborating with external partners, such as customers, suppliers, and other stakeholders, to generate new ideas and solutions. Open Innovation uses external partners' knowledge and expertise to create innovative solutions and drive growth.

While these research and innovation approaches share similarities, their focus and goals differ. Market research aims to understand the market and customer behaviour. User research and UX research are focused on understanding users' needs, behaviours, and preferences and improving their experience, design research informs the design process, and Open Innovation is focused on collaborating with external partners to generate innovative solutions and obtaining outside perspectives.

Important! Don't ask what people want.
You aim to understand the customer's problems and challenges. Generative research is a tool to get a deep understanding of the person, their thought processes, how they make decisions, what tools they use, and what workarounds they do to solve their problem. It is not to ask for ideas for your product or what they want.

The tools for generative research

There are different types of research and tools to use as each research type has a different purpose for identifying customer and user needs.

User research and design research: Understand user needs for products
User research aims to understand users' behaviour, motivations, and how they achieve their goals. By understanding these, designs can be developed to improve their lives and processes. User research can answer critical questions to validate assumptions about key product/service ideas. Tomer Sharon (2016) wrote *Lean User Research* and suggested that user research can answer the following questions:

— What do people need?
— Who are the users?
— How do people currently solve the problem?
— What is the user's workflow?
— Do people want the product?
— Which design generates better results?
— How do people find stuff?

The answers to these questions can feed into business models, branding, strategy, and growth.

The main aim of **user and design research** is to understand user behaviour, and the methods that are typically used are qualitative and can be generative and evaluative:

— **Ethnography**: You can digitally, or in-person observe people in their natural environment to understand behaviours.
— **Interviews:** If you want to investigate how users perceive challenges and issues thoroughly, you can engage in detailed conversations focused on a specific topic; this could be the problem for the duration of the interview.
— **Problem/Solution Interviews:** Interviews enable you to gain qualitative insights on challenges, perspectives and needs. The solution is provided at the end of the interview for the concept to be tested. This seeks to test business models and ideas.
— **Focus Groups:** To get a broad understanding of a topic, focus groups are a good option and can be done before deep diving through interviews.
— **Contextual Inquiry:** You observe and interview users in the context of their work environment to understand their needs and behaviours.
— **Small-Scale Surveys:** When conducting user research, surveys may not have a large sample size, but they can still help reach a broader range of users and provide insights into findings from qualitative methods like focus groups.
— **Experience Sampling (aka Ecological Momentary Assessment (EMA)):** This is a method where the same questions are asked at different and various times. It helps to understand the factors that influence behaviours.
— **Low-Fidelity Prototype Test:** One way to present a product concept quickly and affordably. You can conduct problem/solution interviews to explore potential solutions and gauge reactions to the proposed solution.
— **Guerrilla Research:** A fast and affordable way to gain insight into experiences, usually research is conducted in public places using convenience sampling to invite participants to be involved as they are available at the time.
— **Diary Studies:** This method enables you to gather information on user behaviours, activities, and experiences over an extended period as participants keep a diary to track a particular activity.
— **Field Studies:** One way to better understand user behaviour, needs, and motivations is by observing and interacting with them in their natural environment. This can be done through contextual inquiry, ethnographic observation, diary studies, shadowing, and in-home interviews.
— **Concept Testing:** A way to present your ideas to your target audience and receive feedback to explore your most important concepts and determine which ones are most likely to resonate. This may be a low-fidelity prototype to visualise the idea or an explanation of the concept.
— **Max Diff and Conjoint Analysis:** To enhance your concept testing, try replicating the real-world decisions that your target audience makes. For instance, compare different products and weigh the trade-offs between various

configurations. This exercise will enable you to determine the most successful combination of features for your product and test pricing models.

The conjoint analysis assesses customer preferences for different product attributes by analysing their choices or trade-offs among various alternatives. Conjoint analysis can help identify the most important product features and inform product design decisions. Outputs include preference scores for each product attribute and the relative importance of each attribute, informing product design decisions based on customer preferences.

— **Co-Creation Workshops:** You could use a participatory design approach that involves stakeholders and end users working together to solve design problems.

In my experience as a researcher, I have discovered that incorporating interactive and participatory methods can significantly enhance the effectiveness and engagement of various research methods.

For example, a client asked us to determine the common travel routes of people arriving and departing from a London tube station. This involved conducting a Participatory Mapping activity, where passers-by placed a dot on a map to indicate their travel destination. We also used this method to understand employees' travel patterns at a company's headquarters during lunch breaks to understand travel behaviour at work. During the Participatory Mapping activity, we interviewed participants to gather information about their travel behaviour using three key questions, as time was limited.

Market research: Understand market needs for the product
Market research aims to evaluate the market and customers' behaviour by investigating customer needs, preferences, and actions and observing market trends and competitors. The common goal of market research is to inform marketing and sales strategies and, in the product development process, to identify if there is a substantial commercial opportunity.

Market research can be used to see if a product or service is feasible, if there is a market for it – especially for emerging technologies and markets – to test if there is a demand for the particular product or service, and to learn from competitors what customer needs are, as well as looking at market trends to find ways to innovate and get ahead of the competition.

Market research is typically quantitative, looking at what people want, will buy, and what people say rather than do, with much larger, statistically significant sample sizes and broader insights. Relying too heavily on data and statistics can mean losing meaning and context. Using qualitative approaches such as interviews can be helpful to understand the 'why' to delve into the observations you're seeing from desk research or surveys in more detail. The typical methods for market research are as follows:

— **Wide-Scale Surveys:** These are useful for understanding perceptions and what customers say about a particular challenge, product, or issue. Large sample sizes participate in wider-scale surveys, and statistical methods are applied to determine the statistical significance.
— **Social Listening:** Social media, reviews, and forums are good places to learn what people say about your competitors. This can give an understanding of how customers use a product or service and what they like and dislike about it.
— **Community Online Research:** Qualitative methods are suitable for understanding specific customers from an existing pool.
— **Expert and Customer Interviews and Focus Groups:** We've seen these in user research, but they can also be used to understand customer needs and how they use competitor products to learn more about their weaknesses and strengths. Interviewing experts and industry influencers can give an in-depth view of the trends and challenges for new entrants to the market. It can be an excellent tool to use alongside desk research. Customer interviews can help understand the ecosystem, processes and systems, challenges with existing products and services provided by competitors and decisions they may make around buying products and services.
— **Customer Discovery:** Conduct interviews with prospective customers to understand their difficulties. Inquire about the challenges and pain points, the reasons behind the difficulties, their previous attempts to solve the problem, and the assistance they wish were accessible.
— **Mystery Shopping:** This involves hiring someone to act as a customer and evaluate the customer experience at a store or with a product. The feedback from the mystery shopper can provide insights into the customer experience and areas for improvement.
— **Biometrics:** Biometrics methods include eye-tracking, galvanic skin response (GSR), heart rate variability (HRV), and facial coding can be used to identify how someone is interacting with something or how they react to something. Other research disciplines that use biometric research methods include psychology, neuroscience, and human-computer interaction research. These methods are increasingly used in user experience research and usability testing.

Validating the market can be done using various experiment or testing methods, so you don't build a product no one wants. These include cold calling, collecting pre-orders, crowdfunding, offering a sample, running test adverts, analysing trends and keywords and spoof landing pages.

Without a clear understanding of the market, a business may guess what its customers want, which can be costly. Guessing may lead to misguided investments in product development, marketing, or sales strategies that do not resonate with the target audience.

Market and user research can be used together to 'power up' and build a complete picture of what users want from your design, broader industry trends, and what the business can feasibly do. The User Experience, marketing and product teams ideally work together to get to know the customer, the market, and the product design. Leah Buley in her book, *The User Experience Team of One* explains that CX and UX – Customer Experience and User Experience, can't work together as they are based in different areas of an organisation—however, their work overlaps in strategy, customer understanding and governance, which can create tension.

Jobs-To-Be-Done interview
A type of interview that can be helpful is the Job Map Interview, a component of the Jobs-To-Be-Done approach. A job map usually consists of 10-20 steps listed to accomplish the job in the most efficient manner possible. Each step should be written as a verb, followed by an object and a contextual clarifier for example, drink (verb), fresh lemonade (an object) at a local event (a contextual clarifier). Questions can be used to confirm the steps and find areas where innovation is needed.

Service design research: Understand user needs for services
Service design methods refer to the techniques and approaches used to understand the users and their needs, the context in which the service operates, and the touchpoints where it is delivered. Some of the commonly used methods for Service Design discovery, alongside user research and contextual inquiry, are:

— **Journey Mapping:** Journey mapping is a visualisation technique that maps the user's journey from start to finish to identify pain points and areas of opportunity. The method involves creating a visual representation of the user's experience through each touchpoint in the service
— **Co-Creation Workshops**: Co-creation workshops bring together the service providers and users to collaborate in ideating, prototyping, and testing solutions. The method promotes the generation of new ideas and the co-creation of solutions that meet user needs.

— **Service Safaris**: Service safaris are field trips that involve service providers and users exploring other services to gain insights and inspiration. The method involves visiting and observing different services to identify good and bad practices and understand what makes a service successful.
— **Rapid Prototyping**: Rapid prototyping involves creating a simple, low-fidelity version of a service or product to test with users. The method helps to quickly test assumptions and ideas before investing significant time and resources.

Open Innovation research
Open Innovation has its methods that differ significantly from user research and market research, and these include:

— **Co-Creation:** Co-creation is working with the product's end users to extract knowledge to deliver a positive user experience. It is *"an active, creative and social process, based on collaboration between producers and users initiated by the firm to generate value for customers"* (Prahalad and Ramaswamy, 2000).
— **Crowdsourcing:** An organisation can outsource projects to the public to gather a broader range of knowledge and insights by seeking input from a diverse and unspecified group of individuals. The public is given the opportunity to offer feedback and opinions.
— **Webscouting**: Webscouting is gathering information and conducting research through online sources, platforms, and digital channels. It involves two types: Netnography, which are online observations and interactions and is a variation of Ethnography. It helps in reflecting cultural interaction in a particular context. The other type is social media solution scouting, which involves searching for customer-generated content online to understand solutions to a company's problems. This process is comparable to the 'social listening' concept used in market research.
— **Hackathons:** A collaborative event where software developers, designers, and other participants work together to create new solutions or solve a particular problem.
— **Open Innovation Platforms:** Online platforms allow organisations to share their problems and challenges with a broad community of innovators and experts who can contribute ideas and solutions.
— **Innovation Contests:** Competitions that encourage participants to develop innovative solutions to specific problems, with prizes for the best ideas.
— **Lead User Analysis:** A method for identifying trends and innovations by studying users who face similar challenges or have similar needs to those of the target audience.

- **Participatory Design:** A collaborative design approach that involves end users and other stakeholders in the design process to ensure that the resulting product or service meets their needs and expectations.
- **Open-Source Development:** A collaborative approach to software development in which the source code is made available to the public, allowing anyone to contribute to its improvement and development.

These methods can help organisations by adopting Open Innovation approaches to access new sources of knowledge and expertise and to develop more innovative and compelling products and services.

Research picker

From the lists above, which cover different types of research, you'll find that there are various approaches that you can use to collect data. Below is a table based on the most common goals that I've seen and the methods I've used. The pros and cons of each technique are outlined to help you decide if it is a suitable method for you.

Goal	Method	Pros	Cons
"I have no idea what my users want, and I want to learn about their challenges".	User Research: Focus Groups	Get broad views quickly. Good starting point for a new topic.	Difficult to organise. Participants may not feel they can be open.
	User research: Interviews	Get deeper understanding. Participants more likely to be open.	Time-consuming as need to speak to people individually. Self-reported behaviours which may not be accurate.
"I want to know how people might use my product or service."	User research/ Observation User research: Conceptual Inquiry (Observation plus interview)	Find out how people approach their challenges. Can identify real-life behaviour rather than self-reported.	Can be difficult to recruit people to let you observe them. They may not behave the same with someone observing.
"I have an early idea of my solution; I want to know if people will pay for it"	User research/ Market research: Concept testing	Can get quick feedback on early ideas. Can identify if the concept may be close to a problem-solution fit.	Can't find out from an abstract idea if people will pay for it
	User research: Max Diff and Conjoint Analysis	Understand how people use competitor or similar products. Understand decision making between choices.	Limited options. Could get decision fatigue.

Goal	Method	Pros	Cons
"I'm struggling with ideas after collecting data"	Open Innovation: Co-creation	Generate ideas with users. Likely to be relevant solutions.	Facilitation to manage user input if have lots or not many ideas. Ambiguity as to who owns the Intellectual Property.
	Open Innovation: Hackathon	Can generate ideas and solutions to specific problems. Outside input can spur creative solutions.	Carefully managed and organised. May be expensive to run.
"I want to understand potential customer and user needs online without talking to people"	Open Innovation: Webscouting, social listening	Relatively easy to access the information. Could uncover insights that may not be found by talking to people directly.	Time-consuming as may need to search for relevant information. Will need to have training as to what to identify for Webscouting if not experienced.

Research methods for the public sector and charity

The research methods we've covered that can be used for product development and innovation can also be applied to products and services for community, charity, and social issues. There are specific research methods for community and social research: participatory research methods and Social Innovation.

Community and social research: Participatory research methods
Participatory research methods involve active collaboration and engagement between researchers and the community being studied. This approach recognises that the community members are experts in their own experiences and knowledge and should be involved in the research process as equal partners.

One standard participatory research method is Community-Based Participatory Research (CBPR). This method involves the community being studied in all aspects of the research process, including research design, data collection, and analysis. CBPR aims to create a collaborative and empowering process rooted in the community's values and needs and seeks to address community-identified problems and concerns.

Other participatory research methods include Participatory Action Research (PAR) and co-research. PAR are working with a community to identify a problem or issue and then collaboratively developing and implementing an action plan to address the issue. Co-research aims for an equal partnership between researchers and community members, with both parties contributing equally to the research process and decision-making.

Participatory research methods have been used in various settings, including healthcare, education, and community development. They have been shown to promote community engagement, empowerment, and ownership of research outcomes. They can help ensure that research is more relevant and valuable to the studied communities.

Public sector and charity: Social Innovation
Social Innovation is developing and implementing new ideas, products, services, and models to meet social needs and improve quality of life. It can involve collaboration among various stakeholders, including government agencies, businesses, non-profit organisations, and individuals. It may include using new technologies or business models to address social issues such as poverty, inequality, health, education, and environmental sustainability. Social Innovation

aims to create positive social change and can be driven by profit and non-profit motives. It often takes a multidisciplinary approach, drawing on insights from fields such as Design Thinking, human-centred design, and systems thinking. Systems thinking is an approach to analyse the parts and interactions between them within a whole system.

Healthcare: Randomised Control Trials and Quasi-Experimental Designs
Randomised Control Trials (RCTs) randomly assign individuals or groups to receive an intervention (treatment group) or not (control group) and then compare outcomes between these groups. This method helps to establish causality between the intervention and the observed changes.

When randomisation is not feasible, quasi-experimental designs can be used. These designs compare outcomes between groups that have been exposed to the intervention and those that have not, without random assignment. Common design approaches include difference-in-differences, propensity score matching, and regression discontinuity designs.

Both RCT and quasi-experimental design methods are commonly used in healthcare and testing the effectiveness of medicines but these can be applied to impact evaluation and understanding the effect that a product or service has had on a particular group.

Ethics in research

As a researcher, it is good practice to consider the ethics of your research. It is essential to obtain a consent before recording or using any data in adherence to GDPR and Data Protection policies. This can be documented using a consent form.

For qualitative research, have a Participant Information Sheet to cover the main areas of the research's purpose, what they need to do for the research, what the findings are used for, and their rights as participants. Ideally, send this to the participants at least 24 hours before the interview so they can read through and understand the research. I've found that the consent form and participant information sheet can both be done using a survey tool.

For interviews, consider the Interviewer-Interviewee power relationship, particularly your role as the interviewer. Ensure the interviewee knows they don't need to answer all the questions. Also be aware of how much people may be biased in their responses, perhaps influenced by the phrasing of your questions and if they are aware that you are a founder.

Commonly followed protocols for the ethical Code of Conduct include the Market Research Society Code of Conduct and the Social Research Association Research Ethics Guide. It is critical to comply with GDPR to use and collect personal data when doing research. In the UK, it is necessary if handling data to register with Information Commissioning Office.

To ensure ethical discussions are approached from various perspectives, consider forming an Ethics Committee that includes board members and individuals with diverse views and experiences. Implement a clear process for submitting and receiving feedback on ethical decisions, relating to research such as the design of an experiment. Ethics is part of the duty of care.

THE LEMONADE VAN
PARTICIPANT INFORMATION FORM

Sam will conduct research with potential local customers as outlined in her research plan. Sam provides a Participant Information Form and Consent Form ahead of the interviews to ensure that the participants of her research understand their rights and have a good understanding of the research.

Introduction
I appreciate your interest in our research. The purpose of this form is to provide you with information about the research. If you have any questions, please do not hesitate to contact the researcher.

Study Purpose
This research aims to understand how you make beverage choices, what factors you consider when buying drinks at local events and what your views are toward beverage delivery services.

Why you've been invited to participate
You've been invited to participate in the research because you live locally and are likely to attend local events.

What the research entails
If you agree to participate, you will be asked to participate in an interview that will last approximately one hour. During the interview, you will be asked questions related to beverage choices. The discussion will be audio-recorded to ensure accuracy and may be transcribed for analysis.

Confidentiality
Your participation is entirely voluntary, and you may withdraw at any time. All information collected will be kept confidential. Your name and other identifying information will not be associated with published results. Data will be stored securely and only accessed by the research team in a password-protected folder.

Risks and benefits
There are no known risks associated with participating in this study. The benefits include contributing toward a better understanding of beverage choices to help develop drink choices and customer experiences.

Contact information
If you have any questions or concerns about the research, please feel free to contact the researcher: Sam Chan, at sam@chan.me.co or 012345 678 910

CONSENT FORM

I have read and understood the information provided in the Participant Information Form for the research 'Beverage choices at events and for home delivery'. I have had the opportunity to ask questions, and any questions I had have been answered satisfactorily. I agree to participate in the research.

I understand that my participation is confidential, and my name and other identifying information will not be associated with published results. I understand that I may withdraw from the research at any time.

— I give consent to the research being recorded.
— I do not give my consent to the research being recorded

I confirm that I consent to participate in this study by signing below.

Participant's Name

Date

Researcher's Name

Date

Incentive Voucher Receipt
I can confirm that I have received the [voucher].

Participant's Name

Date

Limitations and challenges in research

Research is not without its limitations. Sometimes compromises need to be made for the research to be completed within tight deadlines and budgets. It is always good practice to be transparent with the limitations and challenges experienced in a research project. When the research report is produced later, the reader can have this in their mind as they read through to understand why conclusions may be drawn as they have been or why further research may need to be done on a topic. The table to the right gives examples and explanations to different challenges that can arise when doing research or evaluating the plans for research.

In this chapter, we've explored different ways of doing generative research, which is critical to understanding user needs before building a product, particularly if you need more insights into the market, customer, or user needs. Next, we'll move from planning research to doing research.

Type of limitation	What this limitation can mean for your research
Bias	Researchers may have biases, beliefs, and assumptions that could influence the research outcomes.
Limited access to participants	It can be challenging to find and recruit participants representative of the target audience. This can be due to time constraints, geographical constraints, and privacy concerns.
Sample size	The sample size for a research project can affect the accuracy and generalisability of the results. A small sample size may not represent the target audience, while a large sample size may be costly and time-consuming to recruit and analyse.
Limited resources	Research can be costly in terms of time, money, and other resources. There may have limited resources to conduct comprehensive studies or may need to make trade-offs in terms of the scope and depth of the research.
Changing customer needs	Customer needs and preferences can change rapidly, and research results may become outdated quickly. Researchers may need to update their research regularly to stay current with changing trends and needs.
Difficulty in measuring emotions and motivations	Measuring emotions and motivations can be challenging as they are subjective experiences that are difficult to quantify. Researchers may need alternative methods like observation and interviews to gather data on these factors.
Difficulty in interpreting results	Interpreting research results can be challenging, especially if the data is complex or contradictory. Researchers may need multiple methods and approaches to analyse and interpret the data to arrive at meaningful conclusions.
Opportunity cost	Researching a new product idea may be at the expense of doing another activity, such as business development and can cause distraction or stress and may impact the research.
Lack of expertise	Conducting effective research requires a certain level of knowledge, mainly when designing surveys or experiments, analysing data, and interpreting results. Entrepreneurs may not have the necessary skills or experience to research independently. However, research can be outsourced to consultants.
Changing market conditions	The market and customer needs can change rapidly, making it difficult to keep up with the latest trends and adjust their products accordingly. This can make research findings obsolete or irrelevant.

How to Collect Data to Understand User and Customer Needs

Introduction

This chapter will guide you on how to manage and conduct project-based research. We will provide an example interview guide for customers, users, experts, and stakeholders and a sample data analysis. We will also cover other qualitative methods, such as observations and Contextual Inquiry, to understand the problem better. We'll review how to use surveys to understand user and customer needs and finally, delve into secondary analysis to analyse any existing datasets you may have.

Kicking off a research project

Once the project begins, the project team can benefit from having a Problem Statement from the outset to summarise the key points of the research project. This provides an overview of the problem space and the project goals for the entire team. The Problem Statement can be used for both large projects and smaller experiments to keep track of the projects and align the team.

— **Motivation:** What is the motivation behind the project? What do you hope to achieve?
— **Users:** Who are the targeted user groups for the project?
— **Outcome:** What specific outcomes are you expecting from the project?
— **Problem to solve:** What problem are you attempting to address in the project?
— **Success:** What does success look like to you for this project? How will you measure it?

The second activity that project teams can benefit from is the exercise Hopes and Fears. Simply put, there are two columns: 'Hopes', which outlines the goals you hope to achieve, and 'Fears' (IBM) which identifies any potential concerns about not meeting project goals. These are grouped and reflected on and help to manage expectations.

It is helpful to know these to understand concerns regarding the project goals and potential risks to its success.

THE LEMONADE VAN
HOPES AND FEARS

Although Sam is doing the research herself, she wants to consider what she may be concerned or excited about and have these in mind when collecting data. She completes the Hopes and Fears exercise.

Sam's Hopes:
— Gain a better understanding of our customer's preferences and needs.
— Discover new opportunities to attract more customers.
— Find ways to differentiate ourselves from competitors based on customer preferences.

Sam's Fears:
— Customers may not be interested in participating in the research.
— Results may show that assumptions about customers are incorrect.
— Target market is smaller than we initially thought, limiting our potential customer base.
— Research may uncover intense competition in the market, making it difficult to differentiate ourselves based on customer preferences.
— Research may require significant time and resources, taking away from other important business activities.

How to be an effective qualitative researcher

To become a successful researcher, there are several skills that one must possess. The goal is to explore the context and challenges thoroughly. Here are some tips on how to conduct effective interviews:

— Build rapport with the participant.
— Ask questions that encourage a conversational tone.
— Use neutral language and avoid judgement or defensiveness; there are no right or wrong answers.
— Take notes while actively engaging with the participant.
— Pay attention to non-verbal communication.
— Create a safe and honest environment.
— Practice deep listening by being fully present in the moment.
— Be adaptable and think on your feet if unexpected answers arise or if you need further clarification.
— Allow the participant to speak more than you; aim to talk no more than 20% of the time.
— Practice note-taking and engaging in conversation while reading the interview guide.
— Respect the participant's time and effort in participating in your research
— Be organised and diligent in processing data.
— Be analytical and able to identify patterns without giving too much emphasis to small outliers.

Be aware of your bias

Erika Hall (2013) outlines that pure research is the creation of new knowledge based on experiments and observations, and applied research is using ideas and techniques from pure research to serve a real-world goal. The research covered in this book is primarily applied research, where we use concepts, techniques, and tools from pure research, such as hypotheses, testing and experimentation, to gather evidence.

When conducting research, it's essential to be aware of bias as it can affect the questions asked, how they are asked, how open-ended they are, how responses are listened to and how data is analysed. Hall (2013) outlines several types of bias.

The first type is **Design Bias**, which occurs when the research is designed based on the researcher's biases. It's important to question these biases and remain aware of them when planning and designing your research. The second type is **Sampling Bias**, which influences the selection of participants for the research.

Third is **Interview Bias**, which can be challenging to avoid, but researchers must remain impartial to prevent results from being skewed. Fourth is **Sponsor Bias**, where results may be affected by the organisation funding the research. Fifth is **Social Desirability Bias**, where participants may say what they think the researcher wants to hear, especially in group situations like focus groups. Using multiple methods such as observations, interviews, and quantitative data, called triangulation, can help reduce the impact of this bias. Finally, there is **The Hawthorne Effect**, where behaviour may change when observed or when the researcher is present in the environment being studied.

Asking the right questions is the key for effective interviews

The most common research methods to understand users and customers are interviews and Ethnography (observation). Steve Jobs said that you should avoid using focus groups for design:

> "*It's really hard to design products by focus groups. Often, people don't know what they want until you show it to them.*"

However, use focus groups if you're looking at getting a breadth of views, but they will be at the surface level, and people are less inclined to open and share in a group environment. They can be an excellent tool to get a broad understanding of a problem and discuss shared experiences.

Now, we're going to explore how to plan an interview guide and what to consider when doing interviews. In the interview, your aim is to understand user needs, behaviours, motivations, goals, and existing processes and systems they work within.

— **Interview question funnel:** Start with open questions about the participants and become more specific over the interview, encouraging them to give you examples through stories.
— **Ask open questions:** An example of an open question is 'Tell me about a time when...' rather than closed questions with fixed responses such as 'Do you use Google to search for local lemonade products?'
— **Use prompts:** Throughout the interview, you can use prompts to understand something further, such as 'Why?' and 'Tell me more about that...' Or, if you want examples of tools, you can add to the question, 'What tools do you use? (e.g., X, Y, Z)' if you're discussing tools.

- **Use vignettes:** Vignettes are scenarios and stories that someone may relate to, and you can use this to base questions on.
- **Have a conversation-type feel:** The interview should feel like a discussion on the topic rather than a formal interview.
- **Be adaptable:** If a response intrigues you, stay curious and ask questions to explore it further but stay on track to ensure the whole interview is completed.
- **Stick to core questions:** Consider your main aim for the session and your fundamental core questions. Sometimes if interviews run behind schedule and you can't get through all your questions, you can cover the core ones.

When choosing interviews for user research, I typically use problem/solution interviews where the first half of the session is understanding the person and their current challenges. The second half focuses on the solution and their thoughts about a proposed idea. This is a mix of the problem interview and the solution interview. However, if this is entirely exploratory, I use the time to understand the problem for the whole interview purely to gain empathy.

An interview guide for a problem/solution interview or focus group generally has this structure.

- **Warm-up questions:** Ask about a general aspect of the topic, such as their job role if doing B2B research, for example.
- **Behaviours and processes around the topic area:** What are their thought processes and approaches to solving their problem? Ask for examples of when they did something that your research is related to.
- **Challenges and pain points:** What are their challenges? What do they wish they had available to make their life easier? You may ask them how they currently use tools to solve their problem, which you can ask them to walk you through.
- **Introduction to the prototype or product/solution idea:** Give a high-level overview of the solution; what are their initial impressions?
- **Demonstration:** Show a demonstration, slides, or diagrams of the solution if you have it in a basic format. Or talk through a higher fidelity prototype. Then ask them again about their thoughts. What's missing? Is this something they would use? You could look at the prototype screen by screen and discuss further with the participant. This section depends on how far along the prototype is.
- **Wrap-Up:** Do they have any further comments? Would they like to take part in other research? If you need more participants, you could ask if they'd recommend anyone to participate in the research.

THE LEMONADE VAN
PROBLEM/SOLUTION INTERVIEW GUIDE: USERS AND CUSTOMERS

Sam is now ready to start doing her research. She's chosen interviews with potential customers and will use a problem/solution Interview approach as she has an idea for a solution she wants to explore. However, she will begin with the problem in the interview to not skew participants' answers toward the solution she has in mind as a product and service for the local area to provide lemonade at events in a mobile food truck and to deliver organic, fresh lemonade locally. She is focusing on the delivery and subscription value proposition.

Recruitment
Sam wanted to interview potential customers in her local area to test The Lemonade Van's idea of Electric Vehicles delivering lemonade and an app to order and track deliveries. She went to the shopping centre to a department store that sold organic drinks to recruit participants who lived within a 2-3 mile vicinity of her home where she makes the lemonade. The interviews were conducted in person in a local hotel lobby that was quiet and where she could record interviews and give them a sample of the lemonade to taste. Consider the location of your interviews as you wouldn't use a hotel lobby as a place to discuss sensitive topics.

Interview guide
Hello. Thank you for taking the time to speak with me today. My name is Sam, and I am researching a new business idea for a lemonade van. This interview aims to understand your thoughts and opinions on drinks and buying beverages.

1. Can you tell me a bit about yourself and your favourite drink?
2. I'd like to understand more about how you purchase drinks at home and when you're not at home.
    - If you're at home, what drinks do you typically consume? Where do you usually buy drinks?
    - If you're outside the home, what drinks do you typically consume?
    - What are your biggest challenges or frustrations with buying drinks outside the house?
    - Tell me about the last time you encountered this problem.
3. Do you currently have any subscriptions where items are regularly delivered to your home?
    - (If yes) Tell me more about these.
    - Would you have subscriptions for food or drink?
    - (If no) Why do you not have subscriptions?

4. What factors are most important to you when choosing a drink? (Prompts: taste, quality of ingredients, price, convenience, environmental impact)
5. How important is it to you that your drinks are made with organic ingredients? Would you be willing to pay a premium price for organic drinks? Why? Which other factors do you consider when purchasing organic drinks?
6. How significantly does the environment impact on your decisions about food and drink you buy?
7. Would you consider having a subscription to drinks delivered regularly to your home?
   - (If yes) Why? What types of drinks would you order? How frequently would you expect drinks to be delivered? How likely is it that you would order fresh lemonade regularly?
   - (If no) Why not?
8. At The Lemonade Van, we are considering developing an app to manage deliveries of drinks ordered on a subscription. What features would you expect to see on this app?
   - Do you use an app for your subscriptions? What features do you like? What features do you think are missing?
9. Would you be willing to try samples of the fresh lemonade?
   - (If yes) what are your initial thoughts? Would you put in an order to buy this today? Why?

Thank you for taking the time to speak with me today.

Expert Interviews: Exploring the systems, processes and industry

Until now, we've focused on customer and user interviews and focus groups to understand needs and what reactions are to concepts for solutions. You could do expert and stakeholder interviews parallel to customer and user interviews to understand the context and market. An expert has specialist knowledge, and a stakeholder has a vested interest or influence in a project, organisation, or decision-making process.

Organisational stakeholders are *"groups without whose support the organisation would cease to exist"* (Hall, 2013). If you work in an SME or large organisation, it may be helpful for you to interview organisational stakeholders to understand business priorities, get buy-in, understand how the project/product affects the organisation, and understand workflow and potential requirements.

First, as you did with the users and customers, brainstorm the potential experts and stakeholders you wish to speak to fill the knowledge gaps you have about the market. You may be able to find these experts at conferences who are keynote speakers, influencers on LinkedIn, or similar.

Interviews that I've done with industry experts have focused on how the industry works, upcoming market trends, what new entrants may need to consider, and what processes and systems there are to operate in the market or with a particular potential customer if it is a large organisation. Interviews with highly experienced individuals within the systems of a particular industry have focused on the decision-making process, how procurement processes work, and what needs to be considered as a new entrant delivering a particular solution. When designing the interview guide, consider the interview's goal and the key questions you want to discuss. Suggestions for the interview guide for experts are as follows:

— Tell me about your experience of working in [name of the industry]
— What approach would you recommend a business looking to enter this industry take?
— What are the critical challenges in this industry for businesses?
— Who are the key competitors or key players in this industry?
— What changes do you see in the future for this industry?

Knowledge gaps may have arisen after desk research for market and competition analysis. This may show the type of expert that you'd like to learn from. Experts can be recruited from your network, trade shows and conferences to identify the key speakers and from social media by looking through relevant profiles and what they may have written or spoken about. Experts can expect to be reimbursed for their time, which may be a consideration for incentivising an hour's interview or a shorter discussion if they are time poor.

THE LEMONADE VAN
BEVERAGE INDUSTRY EXPERT INTERVIEW

Sam wanted to learn from an expert about the drinks industry broadly as well as lemonade specifically in addition to her desk research. She decided to speak to a beverage expert. After an online search, an expert was recruited from LinkedIn after analysis to identify the industry's key players and thought leaders.

Introduction
Thank you for your time today. I want to learn more about the beverage industry, specifically the organic lemonade market.

Background information
— Can you tell me about your experience in the beverage industry?
  • Tell me more about the fresh lemonade market specifically *(these secondary bullet points here are called prompts. Prompts remind you to cover a topic in more detail in case the participant doesn't cover it in their answer)*
— What has been the most significant change in the beverage market in recent years?
  • What changes have you seen in the fresh lemonade market?
— What excites you about the fresh lemonade market?

Market demand and trends
— Where do you see any demand for fresh lemonade?
  • At events? Home delivery?
— How do you see this demand changing in the future?
— What are the key factors influencing the demand?
  • What may be driving demand?
— Are there any emerging trends, such as flavours, that we should be aware of?
  • What do you think is driving these trends? What do you think could happen to these trends? What could inhibit or block these trends in the future?

Customer preferences and behaviour
— How would you describe the typical customer who buys fresh lemonade?
  • At events? Uses a home delivery service?
— What factors do customers typically consider when buying beverages?
  • Taste? Ingredients? Location? Convenience? Packaging? Price? Experience? Brand?
— Are there any specific pain points or unmet needs among fresh lemonade consumers? Why?

Technology and innovation
— How has technology influenced the beverage industry? The fresh lemonade industry?
  • Are there any notable examples of technology-driven innovations in the market?
— In what ways do you think technology could further disrupt or improve the beverage industry in the future?
— Are there any emerging technologies or innovations that could impact the beverage industry in production, distribution, or consumption?

Challenges and Opportunities
— What are the main challenges facing the beverage industry?
  • Product development? Market growth?
— Are there any untapped opportunities or niches within the fresh lemonade market that have not been fully explored yet?
— What advice would you give to a new business entering the fresh lemonade market?
  • How can the business be different? What challenges might the business experience?

Close
Thank you again for your time. Do you have any final comments you'd like to share?

Who else would you recommend I speak to?

Your feedback has been very valuable. Thank you.

Sam will also be talking to experienced food and drink business owners in the area, particularly those that have mobile trucks to understand what the opportunities and pitfalls are and what it's like to be a business owner in this industry.

Checklist for your interview

Take notes during the interview, and where you have permission, record interviews that can be transcribed for analysis. Consider your GDPR and data policies on storage and usage of data.

Before your interview, write a checklist to ensure you have what you need on the day. For me, my list is usually:

— Consent form (signed or on an online form which they've digitally signed)
— Participant information form (previously sent)
— Incentive voucher receipts
— Incentives
— Interview guide
— Pen and paper for notes
— Voice recorder and camera if in person
— Laptop with camera and microphone if remote

Making observations to learn customer and user needs

I find making observations enjoyable as it's like people-watching. Once, I worked with a brand consultancy interested in learning more about how their client could rebrand their business. By conducting interviews with the employees, observing the employee's different branch offices, and asking them a questionnaire, we learned a great deal about the business's challenges and how a rebrand could be done. The brand company was able to evidence how the client could build on its USP and strengthen its position in the market.

Ethnography is a qualitative research method that involves observing and studying people in their natural environment to understand their behaviours, experiences, and beliefs. This can be done in person and online.

Make observations with permission and set-up similarly as interviews in that there is a Participant Information Sheet and Consent Form.

Ethnography aims to understand how people do things and behaviours in a natural environment to see how people solve problems and their approaches. Here, you may take notes and make recordings such as photos and videos. When doing Contextual Inquiry, a mix of interviews and ethnography, this is a great method for unpicking thought processes and a deep understanding of the context of the observed behaviours as you're being talked through it.

These questions can be used to understand a particular culture or social group.

— **What?**: What refers to the physical and material aspects of the culture or social group, such as their artefacts, tools, and environment. Ethnographers may observe and document the physical surroundings of the people they study and the objects they use and interact with.
— **How?**: How refers to the actions, behaviours, and practices of the culture or social group. Ethnographers may observe and document how people carry out their daily routines, how they interact with each other, and how they use objects and tool.
— **Why?**: Why refers to the underlying beliefs, values, and motivations that guide the actions and behaviours of the culture or social group. Ethnographers may seek to understand why people do certain things, what motivates them, and what values they hold. By understanding the more profound cultural meanings behind behaviours and practices, ethnographers can gain insights into the worldview of the people they are studying.

Erika Hall (2013) adds the 4 Ds of Ethnography:

— **Deep Dive:** Understand a small but sufficient number of representative users well.
— **Daily Life:** Learn how people behave where they live and work.
— **Data Analysis:** Systematic analysis is the difference between actual Ethnography and meeting interesting people.
— **Drama!** Lively stories help to engage team members and act on the same interpretation of user behaviour.

Ethnography can be a digital form of observation called Digital Ethnography. Digital Ethnography is a research method that applies ethnographic techniques to study digital or online communities, social networks, and virtual worlds. It involves using digital tools and platforms to collect and analyse data on online behaviours, interactions, and experiences of people in their natural settings. Digital Ethnography allows researchers to observe and record online communities' social practices, cultural norms, and values and gain insights into how people use digital technologies to create meaning and social connections. The method may involve various data collection techniques, such as online surveys, online interviews, digital diaries, and content analysis of online conversations, images, and videos. Digital Ethnography is helpful for businesses, marketers, and researchers to understand consumer behaviour, preferences, and attitudes in the digital age.

Contextual Inquiry: Observation and an interview

Contextual Inquiry is a user-centred research method that aims to understand individuals' needs, behaviours, and motivations within their natural environment. It involves observing and interacting with users as they engage in regular activities, whether using a product, completing a task, or solving a problem. The primary objective of Contextual Inquiry is to gather rich, qualitative data by immersing oneself in the users' context. This enables researchers to gain deep insights and uncover valuable information that might be missed through traditional surveys or interviews alone. By observing users in their real-world settings, researchers can better understand their challenges, the context in which they operate, and the underlying reasons behind their actions. This method helps designers, developers, and product teams to create genuinely user-centred solutions, addressing real needs and delivering optimal user experiences.

Examples of Contextual Inquiry questions are:

1. How do you typically approach [specific task or activity] in your daily routine?
2. Can you walk me through your steps to complete [specific task]?
3. What challenges or difficulties have you encountered while performing [specific task]?
4. Why do you make certain choices or decisions when engaging in [specific activity]?
5. How does [specific task or activity] fit into the broader context of your work/ lifestyle/goals?

Next, we have an example of Ethnography in practice with Oral-B and how it can be used as a research tool.

The analysis of qualitative data collected from focus groups, interviews and observations has a dedicated chapter (Chapter 8). If you want to understand more about analysing qualitative data, skip to the next chapter. We'll be explaining more about quantitative data for the remainder of the chapter, particularly surveys and secondary analysis of existing data for new insights.

Case Study: Braun/Oral-B Electric Toothbrush for Children – Using Observation

In 1996, parents complained about their children refusing to clean their teeth. Oral-B saw this as a market opportunity. Oral-B worked with IDEO to design new toothbrushes. IDEO observed Oral-B customers and how children brushed their teeth.

Using observation, they found that children hold the toothbrush differently from adults as they have less dexterity than adults, and so hold the toothbrush in their fists rather than fingers. It was harder for children to hold narrow toothbrushes.

The problem was defined, which led to the design of the solution to fit comfortably in a child's fist. Their solution was a 'squish gripper', and they designed it initially as a prototype to test in the same households, and it was a shape that worked well in children's hands. Bright colours and graphics were added to be more engaging for children.

Understanding customer and user needs using surveys

Quantitative research can be used to understand customer perspectives through questionnaires. It is a method of empirical investigation that aims to gather numerical data that can be analysed statistically to identify patterns and relationships. Quantitative research typically involves collecting data from a large sample of participants using structured surveys, questionnaires, or experiments and analysing the data using statistical methods to identify significant differences or correlations.

There are vital aspects to consider for quantitative research: question design, defining the sample, the sample size, how to encourage respondents to complete the survey, and how to analyse the findings.

Later in the book, we'll explore other quantitative data sources for existing products or products launched in the market.

Planning your survey

Surveys can be used for market and user research purposes. It is typically used in market research to understand customer needs and behaviours. For your survey, you'll need to consider who you want to include using the inclusion and exclusion criteria for the user and/or customer groups you want to focus on. Then consider where you'll find this group of people to answer your survey and how you can incentivise responding to the survey as responses are usually low. Depending on the number of people that need to answer the survey to be reliable, it can take a long time and be labour-intensive to engage a high number of respondents. You could consider speaking to gatekeepers of communities and networks who could post a link to the survey in an online group or contact relevant organisations that could access the target audience. User research typically uses surveys for evaluative research for continuous feedback and learning across a small, focused group of users and customers.

Sample sizes, the number of people you need to answer the survey from a particular group, are generally calculated to consider several factors:

— **Population size**: The larger the population size, the larger the sample size needed to achieve a representative sample.
— **Level of precision**: The level of precision or margin of error you are willing to tolerate. A smaller margin of error requires a larger sample size.
— **Confidence level**: The confidence level you want to achieve. A higher confidence level requires a larger sample size.
— **Variability**: The level of variability or dispersion within the population. A high variability requires a larger sample size.
— **Analysis method**: The statistical analysis method you plan to use. Some methods require larger sample sizes than others.

Once you have determined these factors, you can use statistical formulas or online sample size calculators to calculate the appropriate sample size for your study. These calculators usually require you to input the population size, margin of error, confidence level, and variability. The output will be the size of the sample needed for your study.

It is important to note that determining the appropriate sample size for quantitative research is crucial for obtaining reliable and accurate results. A sample that is too small can lead to unreliable results, while a sample that is too large can be unnecessary. Therefore, it is essential to carefully consider the factors mentioned above and select an appropriate sample size for your study.

Small sample sizes can be used for indications of user and customer needs in some scenarios, it depends on whether the results need to have the reliability and validity that the large sample size brings. Large-scale surveys can be helpful for market research and understanding perceptions and purchasing decisions.

Question design

Using tools such as Google Forms, SurveyMonkey, or TypeForm can make the survey engaging, but having the right questions and the correct number of questions will help you get the data you need.

If you're doing evaluative research and using questionnaires to understand a behaviour change or identify the impact of using the product or service, you'll need to use a pre-post-test design. This method involves measuring outcomes before and after the implementation of the product or service used by selected groups. While it does not account for external factors that may influence the results, it can still provide insights into changes during the usage period.

When designing a questionnaire, knowing how you will analyse the results can influence the question design. You'll need to choose the appropriate question type, such as multiple choice, Likert scale, ranking or open-ended, to get the data you need for the desired analysis method. Consider the following when designing your survey.

— Have a clear research aim.
— Don't include too many questions, as this can put people off responding properly. Consider the critical purpose of the questionnaire and each question to ask as few questions as possible.
— Avoid leading questions which could skew answers, such as 'Do you like lemonade?'
— Ask one question at a time, using clear, simple language.
— Have a mixture of closed and open questions. A closed question has a yes or no answer or multiple-choice response, and an open question can let the respondent provide their answer using short or long text boxes.
— Consider using response structures such as a Likert scale, a structure used to rate on a scale of 1–10 where one is highly unlikely, and ten is highly likely, rate the likelihood of repurchasing this product in the future.
— Have 'logics' in your questionnaire; logic is a way to set up the survey to give the respondent the relevant questions and give them a personalised route through the survey based on their responses. This means that the respondent does not see all the questions for the whole survey.

- Plan for missing data and design the survey to minimise the impact of having insufficient data to analyse.
- Pilot test the survey before you distribute it to your target audience.
- Consider ethics and consent and how this will be explained to respondents, in particular the purpose of the survey, how the data will be used and any risks or benefits to participating.

You can use questionnaire banks to help you design surveys. SurveyMonkey has a question bank you can refer to. There are online repositories and databases for validated questionnaires. A validated questionnaire means it's been tested and measures what it intends to measure. Databases include FAIRsharing, HealthMeasures and the EQUATOR Network. Validated questionnaires usually show the data analysis technique.

Quantitative data analysis

The research aims, and objectives will determine the choice of research design and data analysis approach.

When we do data analysis for quantitative data, we need to understand what variables and the different types of data are. A variable is a characteristic or attribute that can vary or take on different values within a sample (group of people). Variables can be classified into different types, such as **nominal** or **ordinal**, which show discrete levels, or quantitative (**interval** or **ratio**), which represent numerical quantities. Variables measure and describe characteristics of interest in an experiment and are the basis for statistical calculations and analysis to uncover patterns, relationships, and insights. If you want to use more complex statistics, in the planning stage, you'll need to consider variables you may want to test and possible and null hypotheses. A null hypothesis suggests there is no significant difference or relationship between variables being studied, and any observed differences are due to random chance or sampling error.

Interval data is numerical data with no true zero point where the difference between any two values is meaningful. The intervals between values are consistent and can be compared, for example, calendar years or temperature in Celsius or Fahrenheit. **Ratio data** has a true zero point, meaning there is a complete absence of the variable being measured, and this allows for meaningful comparisons that can be made of both differences and ratios between values, for example, height, age, and distance. **Nominal data** consists of categorical variables that can be sorted into distinct groups or categories without any inherent order, such as colors or types of fruits. On the other hand, **ordinal data** also represents categories, but they possess a meaningful order or ranking among them, like education levels or customer satisfaction ratings. Consider confounding variables that may impact the relationship between variables. Design questions that could control for or measure this. A confounding variable can influence the estimated relationship between the dependent variable and independent variable. The independent variable represents the cause and the dependent variable represents the effect.

There are three main ways to analyse data: Descriptive Statistics, Inferential Statistics and Statistical Analysis. We will look at the various types of analysis and tests in turn below.

Descriptive statistics

Descriptive statistics summarise the mean, median, mode, range, and standard deviation data. It provides an overview of the data distribution and can help identify trends, patterns, or outliers. Descriptive statistics can be used in market research to identify a population's key features to help market segmentation. A survey may show outliers or extreme values across a user or customer group to identify where to focus qualitative research efforts.

Frequency distribution is where the data is organised into categories or intervals to show how often each category occurs. This shows patterns and identifies popular features or preferences among customers. Examples of the visualisation of frequency distribution include a table, chart, or histogram showing the frequency of each category or interval, enabling the visualisation of data distribution patterns.

Cross-tabulation analyses the relationship between two or more variables by creating a contingency table. Cross-tabulation can help identify associations or dependencies between variables, such as the relationship between customer demographics and product preferences. A contingency table may be used for displaying the frequency distribution of two or more variables, allowing the identification of relationships or associations between them.

Inferential statistics

Inferential statistics is commonly used in market research to make inferences about a population based on a sample and helps to draw conclusions beyond observations. Techniques such as t-tests, ANOVA (analysis of variance), chi-square tests or correlation analysis are commonly used in inferential statistics for market research.

Analysis of Variance (ANOVA) analyses the differences between the means of three or more groups. ANOVA can help determine if there is a significant difference in the performance of various product features or designs. Consist of F-statistic, p-value, and the decision to accept or reject the null hypothesis, enabling the comparison of means across multiple groups. The F-statistic in ANOVA is a ratio of the variance between group means to the variance within groups, and the p-value represents the probability of obtaining such an F-statistic by chance alone, indicating whether there is a significant difference among the group means ANOVA may be applied in different ways in market research and product development.

In market research, ANOVA can be used to analyse data from market research surveys or experiments to identify significant differences in customer preferences, behaviours, or attitudes among the different market segments to determine if there are distinct groups within the market based on variables of interest. ANOVA can also be used to assess the impact of different product variations on customer perceptions or preferences to compare the means of multiple groups (e.g., packaging designs or pricing levels) to understand which options customers prefer. It can also be used in UX/user research to assess the impact of different design variations, interface layouts or user interactions on usability, satisfaction, or performance measures. It helps identify a significant difference in user experience outputs across different experimental conditions or user groups.

A chi-square test assesses the association between two categorical variables. It determines whether there is a significant relationship or dependency between the variables based on observed and expected frequencies. The test compares the observed frequencies in different categories with the frequencies that would be expected if there were no associations between the variables. The chi-square test calculates a test statistic and compares it to a critical value from the chi-square distribution. If the test statistic exceeds the critical value, it indicates a significant association between the variables. Chi-square tests are commonly used in social sciences, market research, and other fields where categorical data is analysed to understand relationships and dependencies.

A chi-square test could be used for market segmentation as the chi-square test can help assess the relationship between demographic variables and consumer preferences, behaviours or purchasing patterns. The chi-square test can examine the association between customer satisfaction levels (e.g., satisfied, neutral or dissatisfied) and various factors, such as service quality, pricing, or delivery speed. It helps identify if there are significant differences in satisfaction across different customer segments or experiences. Also, when analysing user feedback or reviews, the chi-square test can be applied to explore associations between sentiment (e.g., positive, neutral, or negative) and product features or customer attributes. It identifies if certain features or customer characteristics are significantly associated with sentiments.

Correlation analysis measures the strength and direction of the relationship between two variables. Correlation analysis can help determine if there is a linear association between variables, such as the impact of a product feature on customer satisfaction. The outputs include the correlation coefficient (r) and p-value, indicating the strength, direction, and significance of the relationship between the two variables. Correlation analysis can examine relationships between variables in market research survey data. For example, it can measure the correlation between customer satisfaction ratings and factors such as product quality and customer service. Correlation analysis can also uncover relationships between customer behaviours and various metrics, such as measuring the correlation between purchase frequency and customer loyalty or between website engagement metrics and purchase conversion rates.

Statistical analysis

Statistical analysis involves collecting, organising, and interpreting numerical data to uncover patterns, relationships and insights and draw valid conclusions. It uses various statistical techniques and methods to analyse data, identify trends, test hypotheses, and make inferences about populations based on sample data.

Regression analysis or time series analysis can be used to develop predictive models to forecast market trends, customer demand or sales projections to anticipate future market conditions. **Regression analysis** models the relationship between a dependent variable and one or more independent variables. Regression analysis can help identify the factors that influence a particular outcome, such as sales, and predict future performance based on these variables.

Time series analysis is used to identify trends, patterns, and seasonal variations. Time series analysis can help forecast future demand, sales, or other key performance indicators, enabling data-driven decision-making in product development. Outputs include trend, seasonal, and residual components, and forecasts for future data points, allowing for better planning and decision-making based on historical patterns.

Market segmentation may also be done by using cluster analysis or factor analysis to segment the market and target specific customer segments with tailored market strategies. **Cluster analysis** groups data points with similar characteristics into clusters. Cluster analysis can help identify customer segments with distinct preferences or needs, enabling targeted product development and marketing strategies.

Factor analysis is a statistical method used to identify underlying latent factors that explain the correlation patterns among observed variables, helping simplify complex data and reveal meaningful relationships.

Statistical analysis helps understand the characteristics of market data, such as trends or purchasing behaviour, through understanding variabilities and data distribution. In product development, it can be useful for hypothesis testing to assess the significance of relationships, compare groups or variables or determine if observed patterns are statistically significant or happened by chance.

Hypothesis testing tests the validity of a claim or assumption about the data by comparing it to a null hypothesis. Hypothesis testing can help determine if there is a significant difference between groups, such as the effectiveness of different product designs or marketing strategies. Hypothesis testing here is different to the assumptions and hypothesis exercises we've previously explored as this test compares groups.

The tools for analysing quantitative data vary as it depends on the type you are doing. A spreadsheet is enough for some types of analysis, such as descriptive statistics. However, you may need software such as SPSS, STATA, and SAS. SPSS is typically used for social sciences, marketing, and business research. It can be used for most analytic techniques, such as cross-tabulation, regression, ANOVA, cluster, and time series analysis. R is an open-source programming language and environment for statistical computing and graphics, and it has data analysis tools for descriptive statistics through ANOVA. SAS is a statistical software suite used in healthcare, finances and marketing and offers analytical tools for regression, hypothesis testing, to time series analysis. STATA is usually used in economics, sociology and public health research and supports data analysis, including time series analysis. You can use data visualisation tools such as Tableau when sharing your results.

THE LEMONADE VAN
SURVEY

Sam wants to use a survey and interviews to evaluate her potential customers' needs. In this survey, her focus is on understanding customer preferences and potential interest in The Lemonade Van.

Introduction

My name is Sam, and I'm interested in learning about your drink preferences and where you purchase drinks. This survey will help me understand more about a business I'm interested in setting up locally to provide organic lemonade at events and to deliver to local communities.

Thank you for your interest and time in completing this survey. All the data you provide will be anonymous, and you can provide your email at the end if you're interested in a follow-up discussion. Data will be stored according to Data Protection and Data Privacy policies and regulations. You can withdraw from the survey anytime, and your responses will be removed.

What postcode do you live in? *(This is to screen responses and could be a list but will be open in this example, and if they don't meet the criteria will be led to a screen that thanks them for their time)*

About you

1. What is your age group?
- [ ] Under 18
- [ ] 18-24
- [ ] 25-34
- [ ] 35-44
- [ ] 45-54
- [ ] 55-64
- [ ] Over 65

2. What is your gender?
- [ ] Female
- [ ] Male
- [ ] Non-binary
- [ ] Prefer not to say

Lemonade Delivery Services

3. How often do you order home-delivered beverages (e.g., soft drinks, coffee?)

- [ ] Never
- [ ] Rarely
- [ ] Monthly
- [ ] Weekly
- [ ] Daily

4. If a lemonade delivery service was available in your area, how likely would you be to use it?

- [ ] Very unlikely
- [ ] Unlikely
- [ ] Neutral
- [ ] Likely
- [ ] Very Likely

5. What factors would you consider in using a lemonade delivery service? (Select all that apply)

- [ ] Price
- [ ] Convenience
- [ ] Quality/taste of the lemonade
- [ ] Variety of flavours/options
- [ ] Eco-friendly packaging
- [ ] Organic ingredients
- [ ] Special promotions or discounts

6. Which of the following options would you prefer for a lemonade delivery service? (Select one)

- [ ] On-demand (1-2 hours)
- [ ] Scheduled (choose a specific date and time)
- [ ] Subscription-based (regular deliveries on a set schedule)

Lemonade Stand at Local Events

7. How often do you attend local events (e.g., outdoor concerts, sports events)?

- [ ] Never
- [ ] Rarely
- [ ] Monthly
- [ ] Weekly
- [ ] Daily

8. What types of events do you attend most regularly?

9. If a lemonade stand was available at events, how likely would you be to purchase from it?
- [ ] Very unlikely
- [ ] Unlikely
- [ ] Neutral
- [ ] Likely
- [ ] Very Likely

10. What factors would you consider purchasing lemonade from a mobile lemonade van at a local event? (Select all that apply)
- [ ] Price
- [ ] Convenience
- [ ] Quality/taste of the lemonade
- [ ] Variety of flavours/options
- [ ] Eco-friendly packaging
- [ ] Organic ingredients
- [ ] Special promotions or discounts

Closing

11. What are your suggestions for a lemonade delivery service or van at local events?

12. Please provide your email if you'd like to be invited to a research interview.

Thank you for completing the survey. Your feedback is valuable.

Survey Analysis

Descriptive statistics will be used to analyse the findings to understand the popular responses and displayed visually using bar graphs and pie charts.

Analysing existing data for new insights

Secondary analysis is the evaluation of existing information but for a different purpose. Analytics tools can glean valuable user engagement and feedback information to understand pain points, and customer needs better.

The following data is captured with a clear purpose, however once it can be analysed again, seperately or together where the analyst asks a new question. Ethics may be considered here and if any permissions are needed.

- **Usage Data:** The information about how users have interacted with a product or service, such as number of visits, session duration, pages visited and user engagement patterns.
- **Conversion Data:** Measures the success of specific goals such as completing a purchase or signing up for a newsletter. This data can help uncover the user experience's effectiveness and design.
- **Customer Demographics:** This data that may be housed in internal databases could be used to segment users and identify target audiences, which may help to provide some evidence for the proto-personas to start to build this on actual data and evidence rather than assumptions.
- **Performance Data:** Metrics such as page load times, service response times and error rates to identify bottlenecks, diagnose technical issues and optimise the product or service's performance.
- **Customer Feedback:** Quantitative feedback through surveys we've looked at, ratings and reviews provided on platforms to get insights into customer satisfaction, preferences, and pain points. This data can be used to prioritise improvements, gauge customer sentiment, and measure the impact of any changes made.
- **Sales and CRM Data:** Sales data includes information about revenue, transactions, and customer lifetime value to track financial performance and identify trends.
- **Social Media Metrics:** On social media platforms, the number of followers, likes, and interactions (such as shares and comments) are monitored. This data is used to gauge online presence, evaluate the success of social media tactics, and determine the type of content most appeals to the audience.
- **Big Data:** Identifying big datasets available where multiple datasets could be analysed together may uncover insights if new questions are asked of the data.

To carry out secondary analysis, you must have a clear research objective, e.g. 'To evaluate existing customer needs and gaps in addressing needs'. Identify the relevant data points that can answer your research objective, gather, and organise the data from internal systems such as Customer Relationship Management

(CRM) systems and analytics tools and organise the data in a spreadsheet or database for analysis. There may be different types of data to analyse, such as structured and unstructured. Unstructured is usually comments and qualitative notes. You may need to clean or pre-process the data to ensure it is accurate, consistent, and complete. Analyse the data using quantitative analysis techniques to understand patterns, trends and relationships understand relationships between variables. Interpret the results and report the findings to the product team. It may also be helpful to interview product, research, and sales/marketing colleagues to learn more about the context of wider company data.

When I worked on one database analysis study, we took existing NHS Health Check data and analysed these data. We wanted to know what invitation method was most successful for various groups of people and how communication methods could influence the uptake. The recommendations from this analysis were to improve the service design to increase engagement. There may be data within your business that you could use to ask it different questions from its initial purpose for collecting it.

In the past few chapters, we have learned various ways to identify user and customer problems, such as interviews, focus groups, observations, and surveys. In the upcoming chapter, we will delve into how to synthesise and analyse the qualitative data collected.

How to Analyse Qualitative Data to Define Customer and User Needs

Introduction

In this chapter, we will explore how to analyse the data from the qualitative research to make sense of the data and turn data into insights to define the problem and identify user needs. To ensure research projects are not forgotten about, using a ResearchOps framework can help to capture, store, and manage research findings so they are accessible not only to the project team but the organisation.

When to stop collecting qualitative data

Data can be analysed throughout the data collection to determine when you're not learning anything new. This is called saturation.

When collecting the data, taking notes, and reflecting on what you've learned as you go along is beneficial. This can help you determine if you've reached a saturation point and if your initial assumptions and hypotheses have been validated or modified. There may be some 'Surprise-to-Insights Leaps' in these reflections and debrief discussions with the team. This leap is when key insights are found, typically through empathising with the user. One way of structuring this reflection that could be a leap may be, 'I wonder if this means that the user _____.'

If you have project team members or organisational stakeholders included in running interviews, having a debrief to discuss the interviews and noting reflections can be helpful as you go along. These insights can be used later in the data analysis. These reflection notes are called memos. Once you feel that you have gathered enough data for your research, it is time to conduct a thorough data analysis. This typically happens at the end of the data collection period when you have reached saturation.

Preparing the data for analysis and synthesis sessions

An analysis and synthesis session comprises a group of key stakeholders coming together to generate insights. Ahead of the session, you may feel it's relevant to analyse and synthesise the data yourself, mainly because you'll likely have many data in the form of notes, photos, interview recordings, interview transcripts and reflections from qualitative project-based research. You may also have some data from the quantitative research; however, this section will focus on the qualitative data. The quantitative data and results could be referred to in the synthesis sessions as they could reinforce some insights.

Ahead of the analysis and synthesis session, you could consider the following:

— **Organise the data:** Organise the data in a way that makes sense. This could be on a spreadsheet or a platform such as Notion. Make it easy for you to access. The data should be clean, meaning data that isn't included in the analysis should be removed.
— **Anonymise the data:** When you organise the data, you may need to aggregate or anonymise the data. If you use pseudonyms, ensure the individual is not discoverable to protect their identity.
— **Comply with data protection regulation:** It's essential to ensure that all data follows GDPR and privacy regulations. To keep the data secure, encryption or password protection should be used when storing, accessing, and sharing it.
— **Cleaning data for analysis:** You will need to clean the data by tidying up transcripts and notes before you review and analyse the data.
— **Tagging data points:** You may begin to tag, highlight, and identify data points within the qualitative data. When analysed, these data points and their frequency will identify common themes from what is repeated frequently and outliers or sub-themes from what is mentioned less commonly.

You could tag transcripts to process the data. Tags can be defined, and as you analyse more transcripts, you may group tags if you see overlap. Data analysis can carry bias. Having a colleague check random samples of tagging to see if they'd tag and possibly start to group things, in the same way, can help to provide some rigour in the data analysis. You may wish to use software to tag findings such as NVivo.

Analysis and synthesis sessions with stakeholders

You can share clean, anonymised data sets, such as individual transcripts, for other stakeholders to analyse before the analysis and synthesis session. The stakeholders could analyse 1–3 interview transcripts by answering the questions below for each participant:

— What problem can they find the users having?
— What are the solutions available to users?
— What surprised them?
— What did they learn?

Each stakeholder can advocate for the research participants whose interview transcripts they have analysed. Sharing analysis in this way means that data analysis is not all reliant on one person. Typically, the researcher does the complete analysis, but the collaborative, stakeholder and individual analysis approaches can be done together, particularly for complex problems and research topics.

THE LEMONADE VAN
EXAMPLE INTERVIEW TEXT AND NOTES ORGANISED AND READY FOR ANALYSIS

Sam has had her interviews transcribed. In this section, I will show areas of the interview guide, highlight passages that I believe show a piece of data, and, in black, show my reflections and thoughts as I go. This is an example of one excerpt of the interview guide, but Sam will continue with the rest of the transcripts, reflect on what she is reading, and then look at patterns to identify themes and sub-themes.

Interview Text

Chris: My name is Chris, and I'm a 32-year-old graphic designer living in the city. I love spending my free time exploring new restaurants, going to concerts, and playing sports. My favourite drink is probably iced coffee, especially during the summer months. I find it very refreshing and a great way to start my day.

My reflections: From this highlighted section, I'm interested to see where Chris goes and the possible locations to sell lemonade locally. These were venues that hadn't been considered before.

Sam: I'd like to understand more about how you purchase drinks at home and when you're not at home.

Chris: I usually drink water, coffee, and occasionally some fruit juice at home. I typically buy my drinks from the local grocery store or sometimes order them online if there's a good deal. When I'm outside, I mostly go for coffee, tea, or soft drinks, depending on my mood and the time of day. One of my biggest challenges when buying drinks outside is finding a balance between taste, quality, and price. The last time I encountered this problem was when I wanted to grab a coffee, but the only nearby option was a pricey, high-end coffee shop. I didn't want to spend that much on a coffee, so I had to walk a few blocks to find a more affordable option.

My reflections Here, I've learned the types of drinks Chris likes and that lemonade may fit into one of those categories. This could have been followed up with a question to clarify. I'd keep this in mind to modify the guide for the following interview. I see here that price is essential when buying drinks and is something Sam needs to consider.

Sam: What factors are most important to you when choosing a drink?

Chris: *When choosing a drink, taste and ingredient quality are my top priorities. I also consider the price, but I'm willing to pay a bit more for a drink that tastes great and has high-quality ingredients. Convenience and environmental impact are also important to me, especially regarding reducing plastic waste.*

My reflections: *Here, I've learned more about what buyers are looking for and what the customers' needs are for drinks: taste, quality of ingredients, price, convenience and environmental impact of the product and packaging.*

Sam: How important is it to you that your drinks are made with organic ingredients?

Chris: *I think organic ingredients are necessary, but it's not always my top priority. If there's an option for an organic drink that tastes good and is reasonably priced, I'd be willing to pay a premium for it. However, if the price difference is too significant, I might choose a non-organic option. When purchasing organic drinks, I also look for fair trade certification and environmentally friendly packaging to ensure I make a responsible choice.*

My reflections: *Chris likes to make 'responsible choices'; interestingly, organic is not essential. It's interesting to see how organic and non-organic ingredients can influence price differences, and if it is too high, this could put people off buying the lemonade. Using Fairtrade ingredients and using environmentally friendly packaging is essential.*

THE LEMONADE VAN
OBSERVING CUSTOMERS AT EVENTS

Sam's Approach: Sam makes observations by attending local events where there are several food stands to identify what types of stands would typically be present and their price points. Her research aims to understand customer behaviour regarding food and drink purchases at events in her local area.

Observation: Sam will observe her environment and take note of the types of people who attend, the time of day and any other relevant factors that may impact sales. She'll pay attention to the behaviour of people walking by, such as whether they stop at food and drink vendors, how long they linger, and what they're looking for when making decisions.

Observe other vendors: Sam will observe food and drink vendors at the event and consider what she thinks makes a successful stand and how they've attracted customers. She will pay attention to the event attendees and what kind of food and drink items are selling well.

Reflection: Sam will reflect on her observations, and consider the changes she could make for her event based on observations. She may set up a follow-up experiment, such as doing a dummy lemonade stand and testing different pricing strategies or display options, offering free samples to see how people react to the product, or changing flavours to see which is most popular.

Notes from Sam's observations

Below are Sam's notes from the event. She walked around the event to make observations about the environment. Below are her notes, and Sam analyses these to show the key themes derived from the interview data analysis.

What I'm observing:
— People attended the local festival in groups, often with friends or family.
— Many attendees are seeking refreshments, especially on this hot day.
— Some event goers are explicitly looking for cold, non-alcoholic beverages.
— There are a few existing food and drink vendors at the event, offering a variety of options.
— Attendees prefer quick and convenient service with minimal waiting time.

How I'm making observations:

— I've positioned myself in a central location at the event, allowing me to observe people's interactions with the existing vendors and each other.
— I'm paying close attention to customer choices, expressions, and conversations with vendors.
— I take notes on customer behaviours and preferences, ensuring not to interfere with or influence their actions.

Why I'm making observations:

— I want to understand the motivations behind attendees' preferences for certain refreshments and their expectations for convenience and service.
— I'm looking for potential gaps in the market or unmet needs that a mobile lemonade van could address.

Reflections:

— On hot days like today, people are more likely to choose cold and refreshing drinks, like lemonade, to quench their thirst and cool down, as most drinks have ice. The Lemonade Van at events could cater to this demand.
— Attendees appreciate quick and efficient service, as they want to spend more time enjoying the event rather than waiting in line. The Lemonade Van should prioritise minimising waiting times and streamlining the ordering process.
— Since many people attend group events, offering group-sized portions or multi-serving containers could encourage group purchases and increase overall sales.
— People have different tastes and preferences; offering customisable options such as flavoured lemonades or different sweetness levels could make The Lemonade Van more appealing. Each vendor had a range of at least ten cold drinks, some were cans of fizzy drinks, and few were homemade.
— It wasn't easy to understand why customers made the choices that they did from making observations.

Sam's notes for analysis

From my interviews, I've found that local customers are looking for a drink to cool down on a hot day at events, and this was found here too. When at an event, getting a drink quickly is essential, meaning I need to consider reducing queue times. I could make it easier to make group purchases and have containers to hold many drinks at the same times for group orders as people attend events with family and friends. I found that vendors offer a range of drink options. However, these were pre-bought ahead of the event. I will need to consider how I can pre-make lemonade before attending events and what packaging will make it easy to sell pre-made drinks.

Finding themes in interview data to get insights

For product teams and researchers, the primary purpose of the analysis is linked to the research objectives. The focus is typically on behaviours, decisions and thought processes to find customer and user needs.

As a researcher, you have various options for analysing qualitative interview data. You can use Concept Analysis to identify how often words, phrases, or concepts come up. Narrative Analysis helps you understand the structure, content, and context of narratives to grasp the meaning and importance of experiences. Discourse Analysis lets you examine the use of words, phrases, and linguistic features to comprehend the social dynamics, power relations, and implications conveyed through language. Finally, Thematic Analysis is a popular technique that involves identifying patterns in the data and grouping them into themes. This method is frequently used to analyse qualitative data from user, UX, design, and market research.

Finding patterns and themes in the data

Take the data points or tags and start to group them and find patterns. Patterns can show themes. Group the patterns into themes and look at what the strong , main themes are and the weaker themes. Thematic analysis is typically used by an individual where the person starts to map out all the findings and then groups them by theme. You may choose to do this as you're going along to see where you hit the saturation point, meaning you're not learning anything new, or you could wait until the end.

When analysing data on your own, it's recommended to have a team member act as a 'spot checker.' This person can attempt to reproduce the analysis using a small sample, which helps to ensure thoroughness and decrease any potential bias in qualitative research.

When you find patterns in your data points, you may find some strong key themes and others that relate to the main theme, called sub-themes. For example, a key theme for Sam may be a positive view toward a healthy alternative to soft drinks, but the sub-themes may be that there is a preference for having this available conveniently.

Although some patterns may be weaker due to fewer data points, they can still provide valuable insights that challenge common views. These insights are referred to as 'outliers', and it is essential to showcase them in the analysis to highlight what was common and what was not. This is known as weighting analysis, a reliable approach to data analysis since it acknowledges that not all themes are equally significant, but influenced by frequency of the data points occurring in the qualitative data.

During the analysis stage, it is useful to identify and highlight quotes that accurately reflect what was said to capture critical themes and sub-themes effectively. These quotes will help bring your analysis to life and make it more engaging when you write it up later or present findings.

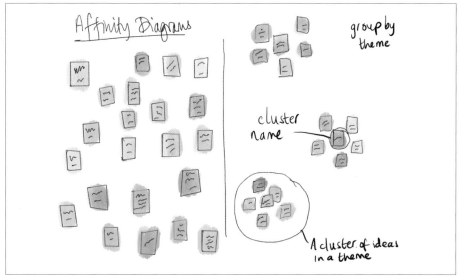

Affinity Diagram Sketch, Sharp, C. (2023)

Using Affinity Diagrams in a group analysis

Affinity diagrams is an analysis technique that allows groups to collaborate and quickly distil insights into clusters and themes and vote on the highest priority. You may wish to do this as a workshop. The steps for affinity diagrams are as follows:

1. Determine the objective or problem you want to address, as this will determine the type of information you'll gather and how it'll be organised
2. To start, gather input from team members or stakeholders. Each person should analyse a transcript or two and share their findings on a Post-it note. These notes can be placed on an online whiteboard like FigJam, Miro, or Mural, or a physical whiteboard or wall. At this point, all ideas and inputs should be gathered and placed randomly without grouping them.
3. Group related ideas or inputs on the Post-it notes to form clusters. Avoid discussing or debating ideas at this point. The focus is on identifying patterns and relationships.

4. Create header cards summarising the common theme or relationship across the Post-it notes in that cluster or group.
5. Review and refine the grouped ideas and header cards to ensure the relationships and themes are accurately represented and adjust where necessary.
6. Analyse the groups and post-it notes to discuss the findings and insights.
7. There is the option to vote on a cluster to prioritise it based on the objective of the analysis.

In one research project, we conducted expert interviews for a food sector client looking to analyse customer habits to understand the ecosystem. We also interviewed customers to find out what their needs were. The client helped analyse the interview transcripts and found that the idea and problem they thought they were solving, they weren't. User needs were more straightforward than anticipated, and the market conditions differed from what they'd assumed. The outcome of the affinity mapping exercise was that they changed their value proposition to meet user and customer needs closely, as these needs clustered together showed precise requirements.

Defining the problem and customer/user needs from analysis

"If I were given one hour to save the planet, I would spend 59 minutes defining the problem and one minute resolving it." (Albert Einstein)

Entrepreneurs, product teams and researchers could take a Challenge-Oriented Innovation (COI) perspective, where innovation focuses on addressing specific problems, needs or challenges faced by individuals, organisations, or society. Within this approach, innovators identify pressing issues or difficulties and then develop new ideas, products, or services to tackle them. Defining the problem, you're looking to solve and why this is important will keep a clear goal and vision for product development (Spradlin, 2012). We can apply this to the analysis to ensure we have a clearly defined problem by understanding user needs and empathising with the user. The defined problem can be built on in the following Ideation Session based on clear customer and user needs.

Types of user needs from the problem

A customer need is a driver for a customer to buy a product or service. Understanding and anticipating needs will help a product or service cater to customers before they request it. If companies can fulfill needs before they aren't fulfilled, this leads to innovation. There are three most common types of user needs, according to Stobierski (2020), which are functional, social, and emotional. **Functional** needs are where customers evaluate solutions based on whether they will help them achieve a particular task or function. **Social** needs are how a person wants to be perceived by others when using a product or service. They can be challenging to identify and usually arise by finding patterns across user needs. **Emotional** needs are how a customer or user wants to feel.

Maslow's (1942) hierarchy of needs can help to understand motivations for human behaviour. Based on this, Bradley (2010) developed a framework for understanding and defining user needs called *"Hierarchy of User Needs"*. The framework outlines five levels of user needs that must be met for a product or service to be successful.

1. **Functionality:** The product or service must perform its intended function or task effectively and efficiently.
2. **Reliability:** The product or service must be dependable and consistently perform its function over time.
3. **Usability:** The product or service must be easy to use and understand, with a minimal learning curve.
4. **Proficiency:** The product or service must enable the user to achieve mastery or proficiency, allowing them to use it more efficiently and effectively over time.
5. **Creativity:** The product or service should inspire and enable the user to be creative and achieve their goals innovatively.

Using these categories can help businesses understand the most important needs and prioritise them in product development. Steve Jobs said "*You've got to start with customer experience and work backwards to technology. You cannot start with the technology and try to figure out where you are going to sell it.*" Ultimately, the customer and user needs demonstrate products and services need to be functional, fulfill the job they need it to do, be easy and delightful to use, reliable and efficient.

Needs Statements (Customer/User Problem Statements) can be used to identify what customers and users need and define the problem. These statements are brief descriptions of a particular problem or deficiency in a product, service, or solution that needs to be addressed. By utilising these statements, the development process can be directed towards the needs and pain points of the target audience. A well-crafted needs statement is crucial for aligning stakeholders, establishing priorities, and measuring the effectiveness of a solution.

A Needs Statement should include the target audience and what problem they are facing, with this problem being clearly defined. Describe the primary problem, challenge, or unmet need that the target audience is experiencing. Provide context about the problem, including the environment in which it happens. This can help you to understand the contributing factors and potential barriers to addressing the issue. Then, explain the impact by identifying the consequences or implications of not addressing the need, such as lost opportunities or adverse outcomes for the target audience. Finally, outline the ideal outcome that would be achieved by successfully managing the problem to provide a clear goal to aim toward. The Needs Statement should be clear, concise, specific, actionable, and measurable.

A concise version of a customer Need Statement is made up of the user, problem, and solution in the following structure: I am... (user/customer) I'm trying to... (outlines solution they want) But... (what the problem is) Because... (the reason for the problem) Which makes me feel... (shows the emotion because of the problem) This is demonstrated below:

'**I am** a customer buying lemonade at a local festival. **I'm trying to** buy a healthy drink from a drinks stand at the event. **But** I don't know which lemonade varieties are available. **Because** the information isn't communicated, and the descriptions on The Lemonade Van menu are too small from a distance. **Which makes me feel** frustrated because I would like to know what I want to buy before queuing.'
At this point, you can return to the proto-personas and assumptions to validate needs and develop personas based on evidence.

The broader context of the problem: Culture and systems

As entrepreneurs, product teams, and researchers, we study user needs and behaviours. However, it's useful to be aware that broader social or cultural factors may influence these behaviours and needs. To gain a deeper understanding, social psychology and cultural analysis can help us assess why certain things, like colours, shapes, used in products and service design and social environments, hold meanings to people and how they interpret them.

Consider the broader cultural and social environment of user behaviour observed as people make decisions and act in a complex environment. Social factors include reference groups such as peers and friends and role and status. Cultural aspects include social class and rituals. Combined, there are social-cultural factors such as values and beliefs, moral standards, shared views among groups and traditions. These can all impact user and buyer behaviour. The systems, processes and infrastructure of organisations, environments and ecosystems can impact how people behave.

Systems thinking identifies how different processes and ways of working are interrelated and interconnected and impact one another, and can provide some context of the user or customer problem. The systems thinking approach breaks down systems and stories into smaller parts.

The systems thinking framework is the third principle of humanity-centred design, a discipline that links to Design Thinking. The Interaction Design Foundation (2016) describes systems thinking as being people-centred, solving the right problem, considering everything as a system and then proceeding toward a viable solution using incrementalism – testing small and iterating. It reframes problems to expose underlying causes that may be addressable. Systems thinking is usually used to understand problems in large, complex systems such as healthcare or issues facing complex organisations, meaning that simple solutions won't be suitable. (When considering involving experts and stakeholders in understanding a problem and how a system works, the problem being explored may be part of a system and understanding its context may be critical to understanding needs.)

Presenting insights visually using experience maps

After analysing and synthesising data to uncover user and customer needs, a report may outline the findings and include visual representations of some insights or analysis. These reports serve as a record of the process and findings and usually have a specific structure that tells the story of the research. This structure includes providing background and context, identifying the research problem and objectives, outlining the scope and limitations, presenting relevant concepts and areas for further investigation, explaining the research methods used, detailing the participants and how they were recruited, describing how the data was collected and analysed, the overall themes through describing the findings, and concluding with recommendations and reflections on improvements.

There are many ways to present the insights from analysis and synthesis. To visually present needs, experience mapping is a method to quickly demonstrate user and customer needs. Nielsen Norman Group suggest that before any mapping takes place, three decisions need to be made:

— **Current (as-is) vs future (to-be):** Is the map showing the everyday or desired world?
— **Hypothesis vs research:** What is the input used to build the map? Is it hypotheses or research?
— **Low-fidelity vs. high-fidelity:** Will the map be polished or unrefined?

Morales (2020) outlines the different types of experience mapping. Experience mapping is a tool that UX designers use to build empathy with users. A user experience map visualises the end-to-end user experience. It allows teams to visualise the basic understanding of the experience before considering a particular product or service. There are four types of mapping:

— Empathy mapping
— Experience mapping
— Customer journey mapping
— Service design (blueprint) mapping

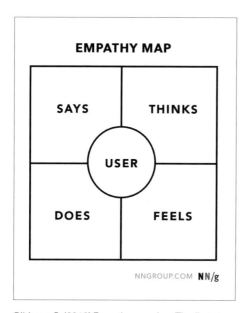

Empathy Maps: A visualisation of a user to show what we think we know about how they think, feel, say, do and hear. Empathy mapping helps understand a user's mindset in the matrix below.

Customer Journey Mapping: A Customer Journey Map displays the interactions and relationships between customers and organisations over time. It visually represents the process that someone undergoes to achieve a goal, from start to finish. The map also highlights touchpoints with the business and can provide insight into the customer's sentiment.

Gibbons, S. (2018) Empathy mapping: The first step in design thinking, NNGroup: https://www.nngroup. com/articles/empathy-mapping/

Service Blueprint: A Service Map is a visual representation of a service process to make it easier to design or improve a new process. It uses a Customer Journey Map to show when the customer interacts with the service and how the combination of the customer's experience with all employee actions and support processes may not be visible to the customer.

Experience Mapping: Experience mapping is a way to understand a customer's processes, needs, and perceptions as they work towards their goals. It involves observing and mapping out the customer's touchpoints and interactions in a larger context. This technique can be used before designing a product and helps companies understand how users approach and solve problems without the proposed solution.

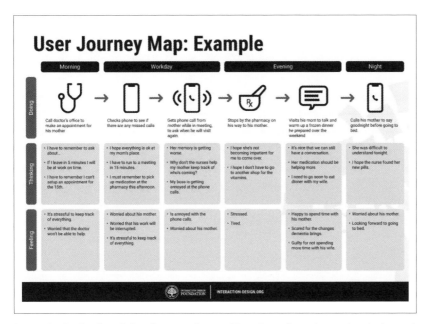

Interaction Design Foundation, Customer Journey Maps: https://www.interaction-design.org/literature/topics/customer-journey-map

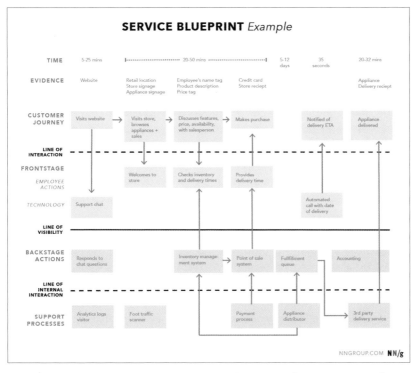

Gibbons, S. (2017) Service Blueprints: Definition, NNGroup: https://www.nngroup.com/articles/service-blueprints-definition/

EXPERIENCE MAP *Example (Pregnancy)*

TRIMESTER	1ST	2ND	3RD
ANXIETY LEVELS + COMMON TESTS	Positive Pregnancy Tests Urine analysis – – – – – – → Maternal Serum Chorionic Villus Sampling	Fetal Development and Gender Detemination – – – – – – – – – – – – – – → Fetal Heartbeat Monitoring – – – – – – – – – – – – – – – → Alpha-fetoprotein screening, hCG, estirol, inhibin Glucose Tolerance Tests – – – – – – – – – – – – – →	3D Ultrasound Fetal Non-Stress Tests
SHARING	Partner Close Friends/Family	Other Friends/Work	Obvious in Public
PLANNING	Name Generation	Maternity Leave Plans Nursery and Supplies Prep	Birthing Classes Baby Shower + Hospital Bag
PHYSICAL EXPERIENCE Energy · · · · · Weight —— Discomfort – – –			

NNGROUP.COM **NN/g**

Gibbons, S. (2018) Empathy mapping: The first step in design thinking, NNGroup: https://www.nngroup.com/articles/empathy-mapping/https://www.nngroup.com/articles/ux-mapping-cheat-sheet/

Alongside these types of maps are other specific maps used in UX to better understand processes and the context, for example:

— **Ecosystem maps:** *"A UX ecosystem is a set of interdependent relationships that emerge between components within an information environment."* (Dave Jones)
— **Scenario maps:** A user scenario describes the story of a user's goal. A scenario map is a group exercise that enables the design team to think about how the persona segments may approach a task or activity through the product or service.

Experience maps can be used with products and services that are already in existence and don't always need to be applied to new products being developed. It can be a helpful way to visualise the customer journey and how internal processes impact customers. It can also identify customer sentiment from end-to-end, where complaints, drop-offs or friction may occur, and highlight where improvements or innovations can be made. Suppose little is known about existing customers and users. In that case, this can be a useful starting point, and it may highlight gaps in knowledge and where further research could be valuable to understand customers.

Managing research findings through ResearchOps: Building a repository

Now you have the analysis done, needs identified and maps completed, it's time to think about how you manage knowledge from research internally. Sharon (2017) argues that there are problems with research and insight management:

— **Bad research memory:** Not having a clear view of who has been involved in research previously and details of past research projects.
— **Research silos:** Research being carried out across the organisation in a siloed manner rather than collaborative and cohesive.
— **Reports:** Long reports to show insights that may not be read and don't portray insights properly.
— **Research dictatorship:** Where certain people or groups are 'allowed' to do research.

ResearchOps is the term used to describe the people, mechanisms, and strategies involved in user research. The ResearchOps Community defines it as providing the necessary roles, tools, and processes to support researchers in maximising the impact of their work across an organisation. Establishing research activities and managing the resulting insights is crucial to allow for easy searching, sharing, and collaboration as the research repository expands. This repository should be continuously updated throughout the entire product development process.

ResearchOps enables user research and other types of research to be scaled and for the impact of research to span wider across the organisation. To implement it, one needs to take the following steps:

— Create a research framework.
— Have key stakeholders involved.
— Build a habitual practice.
— Make research easy to access in the future through repository tools.
— Carry out research with care and quality.

In this chapter, we have explored data analysis, user needs and how to present these needs through experience maps. These will act as a foundation for the next phase, generating ideas for potential solutions.

How to Ideate
to Generate Solutions

Introduction

The previous chapter covered defining the problem by analysing user and customer interview data. Having a well-defined problem from the user's perspective is a strong foundation for generating ideas. There are several options for ideation methods that will lead to effective outcomes for the workshop. A starting point for ideation is outlining the 'How might we...?' question and having a Point of View, which comes from the Needs Statement we looked at in the previous chapter. This could be shared with the attendees before the ideation workshop to help them prepare.

In this chapter, the facilitation of an ideation workshop will be outlined. Once ideas have been generated for potential solutions, selecting the ones to take forward as the possible solution is a crucial step, as this sets the grounds for the subsequent phases of prototyping and building the MVP and then the product.

Some business practices, such as brainstorming, can lead to internal opinions being the primary source of feedback. Tom Chi (2015) calls conjecture and views in these types of meetings 'guess-a-thons', where people have feedback about something they've not experienced. Also, there is the idea of 'bike-shedding', where the more trivial the detail, the more time and energy is wasted and too little time discussing important, highly technical matters. This means that where people have opinions on something like colours or fonts, there are many points of view, but for the complex problem, where people are not experts on the matter, they are more likely to guess. The types of ideation sessions we discuss in this chapter are collaborative and based on evidence, meaning there isn't a reliance on internal opinions and 'guess-a-thons'.

Define the design challenge: Point of View and How might we...?

"It's very, very rare to find cases where somebody on their own, working on their own, in a moment of sudden clarity has a breakthrough that changes the world." (Steve Johnson)

For entrepreneurs, UX researchers and product teams facilitating the product development process and looking to generate ideas based on insights, starting with the Point of View (POV) and How might we...? (HMW) approaches is a strong foundation as it begins with the user and the problem rather than the solution.

The POV is an actionable problem statement that you can use as a basis for generating ideas for solutions. You need to define the user, choose their fundamental needs and the insight to show the evidence for that need. You can refer to the Needs Statements outlined in the previous chapter, which were generated from the analysis.

The POV brings together all the work done to define the design challenge. A POV is structured as follows:

> (*User*) needs to (*user's need*) because (*insight*).

A POV can be used as a basis for a Why-How laddering exercise to understand that POV or user need in a more meaningful and actionable way. Why-How Laddering is a technique to uncover the underlying motivations and values that drive behaviour. It involves probing questions exploring the reasons behind choices and actions, delving deeper into the 'why' behind their behaviours; by repeatedly asking 'why' and linking the responses to subsequent 'how' questions, we can reveal the hierarchical structure of customer or user motivations, providing insights for marketing strategies and product development. It can be used to go into further detail about user needs and find what's meaningful and actionable. Asking *Why?* to understand the meaning and *How?* to identify the action.

A *How might we...?* question helps define pain points and consider how a problem might be solved. If your POV is:

"Domesticated cats need fresh water to drink in the home to keep hydrated and healthy."

HMW questions may be:

— How might we make water appealing to cats inside the home?
— How might we educate cat owners about the importance of fresh water available for cats?

Ideation methods picker

This is Service Design Doing (2018) is a book by editors Stickdorn et al that explains methods for Service Design and outlines several pre-ideation and ideation techniques. In this table are some ideas from *This is Service Design Doing* to demonstrate how many ways exist to generate potential solutions. The table brings together a selection of methods with the types of outcomes that can be expected to help you decide which ideation method would best suit your workshop.

Pre-Ideation:
Slicing the Elephant – Make a Big Challenge into Smaller Challenges

Method Name	How it works	Outcome
Attribute Listing	Take the different attributes of a problem and look at them individually and create ideas around each one.	For a broad overview of a problem ahead of an ideation session.
Six Thinking Hats	Invented by Edward de Bono, participants adopt different viewpoints by changing hats and ideate from these. The hats are blue for managing the big picture, white for information and facts, red for emotions, black for discernment and logic, yellow for optimistic response, and green for creativity.	To enable people to come out of their usual ways of thinking and look at ideas in different ways.
5 Ws and H	Participants ask themselves six questions (who, what, when, where, why and how) to look at the variations of the answers.	To focus on one problem and discuss from a variety of perspectives to explore it in more depth.
5 Whys	Toyota used this method to look at a problem, asking 'Why?' five times or more.	To explore fewer problems in more detail to generate focused ideas.

Generate Lots of Ideas

Crazy 8s	8 minutes for 8 quick ideas for 1 minute sketches.	To generate ideas quickly which visually represent ideas.
Doodling Ideas	Doodling and sketching ideas of the solution.	To give people time to consider what they think solutions could look like and how they could work before discussed.
Brainstorming	Generating many ideas simultaneously, using phrases such as 'Yes and...!' to build on each other's ideas.	To create lots of ideas and build on each other's ideas and thoughts.
Worst Possible Idea	Seek the worst possible solutions, designed to boost creative thinking.	To consider not only the positive but the worst ideas to start ideas from a different perspective.
Scenario Mapping	Using the personas generated and place the persona into different scenarios.	To consider different users and solutions from different perspectives.

Add Depth and Diversity to Ideas

Bodystorming	A physical exploration to generate ideas such as role-play.	To act as if the solution exists, to consider it closer to reality.
Octopus Clustering	Standing in front of a wall of sticky notes, people are arranged in rows. The front row sort notes, while the row behind offer support. The rows alternate to analyse the sticky notes, only a few rotations occur.	To filter ideas into clusters without discussion. The sticky notes will need to have a clear message.

Facilitating an ideation session

When planning your workshop, identify the ideation methods you'll use and the key stakeholders involved, including internal and external parties, key customers, and the product team. This will help ensure a clear output or outcome for the workshop.

You may benefit from having an external or experienced internal facilitator run the ideation sessions. You can run these ideation sessions remotely using interactive whiteboards such as Miro, FigJam, and Mural, or in person.

For ideation, David Burkus (2019), author of *Leading from Anywhere* argued there are four rules. First, there are no bad ideas, second the facilitator should ensure to capture everything, third use hybrid brainstorming, which is an approach to blend idea generation and problem-solving, such as silent idea generation followed by group discussion and sharing of ideas and aim to generate lots of ideas and prioritise quantity over quality.

Stevens (2019), from UX Planet suggests the following for facilitating a practical ideation session with stakeholders:

— Invite the right people (these may be critical decision-makers, key customers, or employees such as engineers).
— Designate a facilitator to ask the right questions and keep it problem-centred
— Choose a suitable location.
— Prepare a list of 'How Might We...' questions.
— Break the ice.
— Select your ideation techniques.
— Gather ideas and outline the next steps.

Preparing a clear brief before the workshop is recommended to achieve better results and make the most of your time. This should include background reading, the workshop's purpose, an overview of critical insights, and the purpose of the ideation session.

Having a precise aim for the session's outcome, carefully chosen methods for ideation, and a well-facilitated session will help generate many ideas to address the design challenge.

Keep to time by having a clear and timed agenda. Use a stopwatch to time different elements of the session. In ideation sessions, ideally, we have a setting where we can openly share ideas and build on these; we don't want 'idea killers'. You can build on ideas by saying 'Yes and...' and even have a bell that is rung when an idea is being criticised. We want lots of ideas in this session.

If you're not getting enough ideas, you could crowdsource ideas. This is a method used in Open Innovation approaches, but also as a method for getting external assistance with ideation. Versions of crowdsourcing ideas are hackathons, design competitions or using dedicated platforms such as Ideaken (collaborative crowdsourcing) and 99designs (design crowdsourcing).

Lightning Decision Jam

AJ&Smart, a German design agency, developed the Lightning Decision Jam, a quick and timed way to identify and define the problem, ideate, find the best solution based on effort and impact and arrive at clear action steps.

— Write down problems (7 mins)
— Present problems (4 mins)
— Select problems (6 mins)
— Reframe the problem as challenges (6 mins)
— Produce solutions (7 mins)
— Vote on solutions (10 mins)
— Prioritise solutions (30 secs)
— Decide what to act on (10 mins)
— Turn solutions into actionable tasks to test them (5 mins)

The Lightning Decision Jam may effectively reach decisions quickly about potential solutions. It could be used as a follow-on to an ideation session if no decisions were reached or for Product Discovery research where later-stage product development calls for experiments and learning fast and quick decision-making.

Selecting ideas to take forward

There are multiple tools available to help decide which ideas are worth prototyping. The table explains different techniques for screening and selecting ideas to progress.

Method Name	How it works	Outcome
2x2 matrix	Structures information about users and design to understand the relationship between them, to identify feasibility/effort vs impact of ideas.	To identify the 'big bet' type ideas that would need a lot of investment, and 'quick wins' to identify what could be done quickly.
Business benchmarking	A table comparing the different ideas against key criteria such as uniqueness (how does it compare to other offerings?) and profitability (does it have the potential to be profitable?).	To strategically align ideas against criteria to identify what fits business needs as well as user needs.
£100 distribution test	If each person had £100, how would they distribute their money across the different ideas?	To get an understanding of gut reaction or a way of voting on ideas.
Dot voting	Selecting ideas with dots to vote for ideas to see which ones are most popular.	To quickly vote on ideas to identify popular potential solutions.
Identify a variable	Rather than prototyping a complete version of a solution, you could focus on one variable, and you can test multiple prototypes.	To identify the core value that could be offered to users as a basic solution as a starting point.
Decision Matrix	Using criteria, which is weighted, can help the group decide which option to address first.	To use criteria to make decisions on ideas.
Four Categories Method	Categorise ideas according to abstractness from the most rational choice to the 'long shot'. The four categories are: the rational choice, the most likely to delight, the darling, and the long shot.	This is like the 2x2 matrix with different categories and positions and divides ideas.
Bingo Selection	To categorize ideas according to form such as physical, digital or experience prototype.	To identify how the idea could be prototyped for the next phase.
Now-Wow-How Matrix	This evaluates ideas on a scale of: **Now:** Ideas lack novelty but can be implemented immediately. **Wow:** Ideas can be implemented and are innovative. **How:** Ideas that could be implemented in the future.	To rank and evaluate ideas to reduce the number of ideas.

Screening ideas is crucial when developing products and services as businesses identify the most promising concepts. Having a list of criteria for business needs and customer needs will help to whittle down to prioritised ideas.

It's important not to be too quick to dismiss ideas, as there may be factors you haven't considered yet. Consider keeping a record of these ideas in an 'Ideas Parking Lot' for future evaluation.

For the prioritised and selected ideas, go through the list of questions to evaluate the ideas further. As a researcher or product team member, it's critical to involve the key decision makers in assessing the ideas. For entrepreneurs, you may consider these questions with your team.

— Which ideas align with business goals?
— What are the key customer needs we're looking to address?
— What will the benefits of the product idea be to the customer?
— Will the product idea help to grow the customer base?
— Will it be easy or complex to make or develop the product?
— Will it be expensive to make?
— Could it be profitable?
— Are there many similar products or services on the market?
— Will it make the business more competitive?
— What is your gut reaction?
— What other information will you need to help you decide if this is a good idea?
— Ask questions from the three lenses of innovation, plus Cagan's two questions: Is it feasible? Is it viable? Is it desirable? Is it ethical? Is it useful? I would add two questions here: Is it sustainable?
— What are the possible unintended consequences or worst-case scenarios if this product or scenario were
a reality?

The next chapter will provide an overview of prototyping, a way to test visual or physical representations of the idea with users and customers to get their feedback. This can be a helpful method, as it puts something tangible in front of people.

How to Test and Experiment Using Prototypes

Introduction

The focus of this chapter is prototyping. We discuss prototyping, the four categories for prototyping, and what evaluative research is required to iterate and learn needs through prototypes rapidly. There are different levels of prototyping, from low-fidelity which could be made from cardboard and paper and a basic representation of the solution, through to high-fidelity, which could be designs of the solution produced by a UX Designer. At the different levels of fidelity, the ways of testing the prototypes to identify needs vary, and we'll be exploring these experiments and tests in more detail in this chapter. The analysis of the methods used differs and depends on the test being done.

What is prototyping?

"Prototyping is an experimental process where design teams implement ideas into tangible forms from paper to digital. Teams build prototypes of varying degrees of fidelity to capture design concepts and test them on users. With prototypes, you can refine and validate your designs so your brand can release the right products." (Interaction Design Foundation)

Through prototyping, you have a tangible representation of an idea that you can quickly iterate and develop. Having an early prototype means changes aren't expensive and time-consuming as prototypes can be highly adaptable. Receiving early user feedback on basic prototypes enables you to experiment to get closer to solving user needs and problems and Product-Market Fit.

Four categories of prototypes

The Handbook of Human-Computer Interaction (1997) by Apple designers Stephanie Houde and Charles Hill describes four types of prototypes, demonstrating different design dimensions. The four types are:

— **Role Prototypes:** What can it do for the user? What functionality might the user benefit from?
— **Look and Feel Prototypes:** What are the options for its experience? What does it look and feel like to interact with it?
— **Implementation/Feasibility Prototypes:** How does this work technically? What specifications are needed for it to be achieved? What are the technical risks?
— **Integration Prototypes:** How can it all work together?

According to Franks (Austin Centre for Design), there are three types of fidelity:

— **Low-fidelity prototyping:** Early-stage prototyping could be as simple as a sketch or video demonstrating the idea. It allows for rapid iteration and easy customisation.
— **Mid-fidelity prototyping:** A realistic model or functional prototype to enable interactive experiences without any technical development that can be costly.
— **High-fidelity prototyping:** A realistic and functional prototype that can be continuously improved.

Andy Polaine, a design leadership coach, consultant, argues that there are five levels of service prototyping. Prototyping services differ from prototyping products because services are experiences, and products can be tangible. The different levels of service prototyping are as follows:

— Discussion for exploration to identify issues and challenges.
— Participation through co-creation to improve how the touchpoints will work together in a real-world setting.
— Simulation through improvements to refine the experience and explore unknowns.
— Live prototype to validate and iterate the service in natural conditions.
— Pilot through feasibility or sustainability projects to learn what is needed to run a long-term service.

You may see similarities in these five levels to what we've seen with Design Thinking. We start with discussions to understand user needs. However, instead of analysing and ideating internally with key stakeholders, in service design, you may wish to use co-creation, whereby you work closely with users and customers collaboratively to develop the service into a user-led solution. The service can then be designed by the organisation to test through simulation and live prototypes before being piloted in a real-life setting.

Prototyping is crucial as it brings something intangible or conceptual into being tangible and concrete that can be used for direct feedback. Prototyping is a key stage for Design Thinking. Evaluative research is a method of assessing a product or concept by gathering data to refine and enhance it. We will explain each prototype level, the types of prototypes at each stage, and how to test them.

Testing the usability of prototypes

When designing a product, it's essential to consider its usability. The product should be easy to learn, efficient, and memorable, allow users to control and overcome errors, and provide an enjoyable experience. Specifically, **information architecture**, which is the organisation, structure and labelling of information to facilitate intuitive navigation, findability and understanding for users within digital interfaces or physical spaces, it guides how the product functions and includes pages, content, folders, interactions, and behaviours. **Visual design** considers how design elements work together, incorporating principles like balance and scale. Finally, **interaction design** focuses on designing the user's interaction with the product.

When testing prototypes, decide on the touchpoints you want to test and the method that fits the purpose of testing, design your interview questions with the aim of the testing in mind and test with participants. Having a UX expert at this point to guide designs will contribute toward effective prototypes. Ideally, UX/ UI (User Experience and User Interface) designers would have been involved in the previous explorative research phase as the empathy with the user through research would give them a good context for designing prototypes.

When testing prototypes, it's crucial to choose participants carefully. You could focus on one user group and value proposition that will give you a deeper understanding of how the prototype can meet users needs. You can have a mix of past or new participants and conduct brief interviews to test the prototypes depending on the phase and purpose. Additionally, you can use Contextual Inquiry to gain insights into their actions and motivations when undertaking any usability tests.

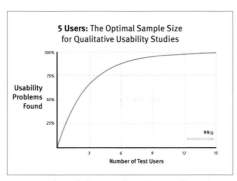

Nielsen, J. (2000) Why You Only Need to Test with 5 Users, NNGroup, nngroup.com

During the prototyping phase, you can use fewer users per group for testing designs and prototypes compared to the discovery period. NNGroup suggests that only five users per group are necessary, as shown in the diagram. Feedback loops will be more frequent but faster than in early-stage research.

Low-Fidelity Prototype

A Low-Fidelity Prototype is low-cost, scrappy, and rough for products and services. Examples include:

— **Paper:** Paper and cardboard versions of digital interfaces.
— **Storyboarding:** A collection of pictures explaining the journey, guiding users through the complete process's experience or scenario.
— **Lego Prototyping:** IDEO, the international design firm, widely uses Lego prototyping, as it sparks creativity and allows rough prototypes to be made.
— **Concept prototyping:** To test the concept of the product as a solution:
  • **Explainer video:** A video visually demonstrates the product or service.
  • **Sketches**: Drawings of the product and how it works.
— **Online Advertisements:** To test demand by running a low-cost ad campaign targeting potential users and customers.

Creating Low-Fidelity Prototypes is a cost-effective and simple way to test assumptions and concepts in the early stages of product development. These prototypes can be used in Problem/Solution Interviews to validate the feasibility of early-stage concepts.

Interviews and Tests for Low-Fidelity Prototypes

Five-Act Interview (Kowitz et al, 2016): is a customer interview to test prototypes. It has five parts to it: 1) A friendly welcome, 2) Context questions similar to the 'problem' part of the Problem/Solution Interview, 3) Introduction to the prototype, 4) Tasks and 5) Quick debrief and close.

Mental Model Interviews: Mental models shape how people use things.
"A mental model represents a person's thought process for how something works (i.e., a person's understanding of the surrounding world). Mental models are based on incomplete facts, past experiences, and intuitive perceptions. They help shape actions and behaviour, influence what people pay attention to in complicated situations, and define how people approach and solve problems." (Susan Carey)

Mental model interviews help to uncover why people do what they do. Mental models show how people think something should function based on their experiences with similar tasks or activities. Some questions you may ask in a mental model interview are:

— What tasks are they completing (or trying to finish)?
— What are the overarching goals people try to achieve with these tasks?
— What is the current end-to-end 'routine' or journey people are going through?
— Where are they encountering problems or frustrations during this routine or journey?
— Once you've understood the journey, what features or products would support these tasks?

Usability Testing: The user aims to complete specific tasks and may interact with a low-fidelity prototype, such as a paper prototype, to help identify fundamental issues.

Concept Testing: This test gives the product team feedback on the overall value proposition, features, and functionality to identify if the solution will address user pain points early on.

Paper Prototype Testing: This test identifies inconsistencies, navigation issues and bottlenecks in the user flow using a paper-based representation of the product that simulates user flows and navigation,

Feedback Capture Matrix: When the researcher captures feedback on the Low-Fidelity Prototype, a feature capture matrix may help to capture real-time feedback. This is a 2x2 matrix, and each of the quadrants are: Plus sign (+) (likes and positive feedback), delta sign (Δ) (constructive criticism), question mark (?) (questions raised), and light bulb sign (Ǫ) (ideas spurred).

Card Sorting: The user sorts labelled cards into logical groups and categorises elements or features of the product, which helps understand user mental models and expectations. It can be used to design the information architecture (structure and order of information to achieve tasks).

Design Critique: A UX Designer reviews the Low-Fidelity Prototype to identify potential issues, provide feedback and suggest improvements.

Cognitive Walkthrough: A researcher or UX expert follows the user flow and simulates the user's thought process and actions to identify usability issues and areas of confusion.

User Flow Testing: The user flow is the process where someone completes a task from end to end, and the navigation paths they take are evaluated. The test shows how the user completed the task.

THE LEMONADE VAN

Sam put together sketches and a storyboard from the findings, which she will test with her target audience. The aim is to understand who would be interested in a lemonade delivery app.

Sam has in mind the competitor analysis, user interview findings and personas. She will work with a UX designer on these early-stage sketches and user flow diagrams to ensure these are useful documents to be tested by users.

Storyboard for lemonade delivery app
The storyboard shows the steps that someone will take to order lemonade and provide feedback on the delivered product.

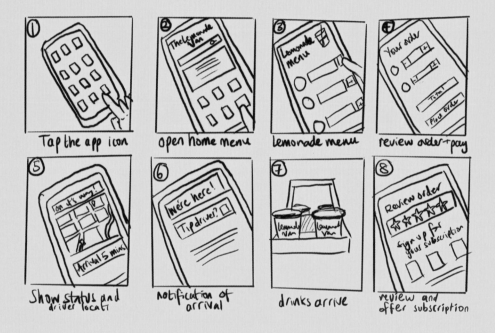

Sketches for the user flow
The user flow shows how Sam expects people to use the app to order lemonade that will be delivered.

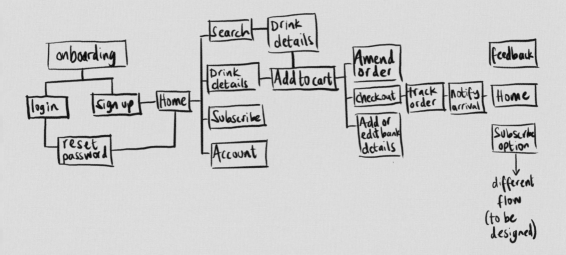

Examples of Prototyping Products and Services

Alexa, the AI assistant, was initially tested as a small device prototype in a controlled environment. Contract workers were hired to walk through rooms and ask scripted questions, for six months, six days a week. This process was used to gather data to train the AI assistant. The data collection was expanded to different cities, which provided a diverse range of acoustic environments, regional phrases, and access.

Dropbox used an Explainer Video MVP to determine if their product could solve people's problems. The video tested the value proposition and assumptions that people were experiencing difficulties with file syncing and whether the concept of Dropbox solved the problem.

The founders of Airbnb faced two challenges: finding a hotel room in cities hosting frequent conferences was difficult, and they needed help paying rent. To test their assumptions, they offered air mattresses in their living room, free Wi-Fi, complimentary breakfast, and the opportunity to network with like-minded individuals. Initially, their website was not very comprehensive, and they only targeted tech conference attendees at sold-out events instead of every potential user. However, they continued to iterate and learn, eventually leading to the development of Airbnb.

Mid-Fidelity Prototyping

A Mid-Fidelity Prototype is a visual representation or mock-up of a product or interface that falls between a Low-Fidelity Prototype and a High-Fidelity Prototype in terms of detail and functionality. Mid-Fidelity Prototypes are often used to test and gather feedback on design concepts, user interactions and overall user experience before investing resources into the High-Fidelity Prototype.

Types of Mid-Fidelity Product Prototypes
Mid-Fidelity Prototypes can help people better understand what the solution, or part of the solution, will look like. They are suitable for refining the solution, with room for changing direction and test options.

— **Clickable Wireframe Prototype:** Several tools can produce mock-ups (non-functional screenshot images) and click-through wireframes (joined up, clickable product pictures), such as Sketch, Invision, Proto.io and POP-app by Marvel.

- **User-Driven Prototyping:** The development of the prototype is closely shaped and designed with the users; the prototype is used as a tool to learn more about the user early on and throughout the prototyping stages to ensure it meets their needs.
- **Live-Data Prototyping**: This refers to creating prototypes that use real or near-real data instead of simulated or placeholder data. The prototype is connected to live data sources or systems, allowing users to interact with and experience the prototype using authentic data. It represents how the final product or system will function and behave in real-world scenarios. Issues, limitations, and opportunities related to data integration, processing or usability can be addressed early.
- **Landing Page:** A web page to outline the product and, sometimes, pricing with a call to action, which may be to register interest or sign up for a waiting list. Landing pages can be great to understand if there is a demand for a product before too much time and effort is put into it. If there is a call-to-action button, it can link to a sign-up page to create a waiting list. This makes it easier later to get testers for Beta or high-fidelity prototyping.

I conducted usability tests on a Live-Data Prototype to determine its practicality in real-life situations. The product was an app designed to assist rail passengers in making decisions about their journey. During the test, I evaluated whether I could use the essential features, receive a mobile phone signal, and if the route options provided were feasible and suitable for my needs. After resolving some technical difficulties, I further tested the product with potential users to see how they used the prototype on various mobile phone networks and devices in a rail environment, both at the station and on the train.

Types of Mid-Fidelity Service Prototyping
To prototype services, as a service designer or product manager designing a technology product that delivers a service, there are different forms of showing users and customers how their customer journey may operate. Users and customers can test service prototypes in the following ways:

- **Desktop Walkthrough:** Mapped out touchpoints through a small version of the service.
- **Touchpoint Prototyping**: To test each touchpoint of the service, a touchpoint is the interaction between the user and the service.
- **Roleplay and Acting:** Acting out the service with users to role-play the service and how it would work in reality.
- **Generative Prototyping:** Prototyping new ideas with stakeholders or experts.
- **Video Prototyping:** A video to demonstrate the service.

Testing Mid-Fidelity Prototypes for Products and Services

When product teams test Mid-Fidelity Prototypes, there are several ways to run experiments to get user feedback. Below is a list of tests that can be run on Mid-Fidelity Prototypes:

— **Happy Path Testing:** To understand the critical user flow throughout the product and ask the users questions about their perspectives of the design and how the flow is structured.
— **Usability Testing:** To identify issues and areas for improvement on the usability and user flow based on functions and features that are maybe there, in theory.
— **Concept Testing:** To test the overall concept of the product to ensure it resonates with the users and their needs. This helps to understand feedback on the value proposition, features, and overall appeal.
— **Card-Sorting:** Group and categorise different elements of features of the product to understand their mental models and expectations to inform the design of the information architecture and navigation.
— **Clickable Prototype Testing:** Based on basic interaction, users can click through the interface and navigate between screens to validate the user flow, loops, confusing paths, and loops and ensure the users can complete key tasks.
— **Heuristic Evaluation:** UX experts can review the prototype against usability principles to identify potential issues or areas for improvement.

High-Fidelity Prototyping

The High-Fidelity Prototype aims to represent what the solution will look like accurately. It may include the expected functionality and could consist of all the functional parts required, although these will be less than ideal in its execution. The aim is to provide *"the closest representation of the idea possible* without *the time and cost required of a final production"* (Interaction Design Foundation). High-Fidelity Prototypes are mock-ups produced in a high level of detail and closely represent the end product. It allows for testing what the end product will look like and can be used to approach the potential market for providing feedback.

Experiments for High-Fidelity Prototypes

High-Fidelity Prototypes are tested in various ways to evaluate the Problem-Solution Fit and Product-Market Fit. The experiments are highly focused on refining the solution as the problem has been validated by this point, and the Problem-Solution Fit is close but may need some refinement. The experiments can start identifying Product-Market Fit by testing a functional product with potential users and customers to refine the core value proposition. This core value is being provided to prioritise features and user requirements for developing the Minimal Viable Product.

— **A/B Testing:** A comparison of two versions of a product or features to find out which one performs the best. It works best with a large set of users for small iterations.
— **Usability Testing:** Usability testing is having users interact with the product. The design, such as how people interact with the prototype, can be tested, and the content and its order, known as information architecture and specific User Interface elements, can be tested.
— **User Acceptance Testing:** Testing the prototype with real users to ensure it meets their needs and expectations. Crucial for validating product features and functionalities that align with the users' requirements and preferences.
— **First Click Testing:** Evaluates the users' initial interactions with the prototype to see how intuitive the interface is for first-time users. Participants are given specific tasks, and researchers observe which UI elements they click first to complete tasks.
— **Cognitive Walkthrough:** The researchers take steps through the prototype, simulating a user's thought process and actions as they complete tasks to identify potential usability issues and areas of confusion.
— **Heuristic Evaluation:** UX experts review the prototype against a set of usability heuristics or principles to identify potential issues or areas of improvement. This method can help uncover usability problems.
— **Task Analysis:** Breaking down user tasks into smaller steps and understanding how well the prototype supports each step. It can help identify gaps in the user flow, leading to a more streamlined process.
— **Accessibility Testing:** This evaluates the prototype's compliance with accessibility guidelines and standards.

THE LEMONADE VAN
INTERVIEW GUIDE FOR HIGH-FIDELITY PROTOTYPE

Sam has decided to develop the app prototype further as a High-Fidelity Prototype and wants to test its usability by setting user tasks.

Introduction
Thank you for your time in testing this prototype. There are no correct answers, as the prototype is being put to the test and not your abilities. Please think aloud and tell me what you're thinking and how you feel during the session. Please let me know if you have any questions or need any clarification.

Task
Sam is watching out for the length of time it takes to complete each task, how many mistakes they make and where they get lost to measure its usability.

I will give you a task individually, and I'd like you to complete them as we go through them.

1. Register and create an account
2. Add a lemonade order to the cart
3. Customise the order
4. Choose a delivery date and time
5. Enter the delivery and payment information
6. Review and confirm the order
7. Track the delivery status
8. Pay the subscription fee
9. Locate and use a support feature

Interview Questions: General Usability and Interaction Design
— How would you describe your overall experience using the software?
— Did you find the interface easy to navigate? Were there any parts that were confusing or difficult to understand?
— How would you rate the ease of use on a scale of 1 to 10, with one being very difficult and ten being very easy? Why did you choose that number?
— Were there any tasks or steps you found challenging or frustrating?
— Were there any features or functionalities you especially liked or found helpful?
— Was there anything you thought was missing you wished was there?

Close
Is there anything you'd like to add?

Thank you for your time today. If you have any further thoughts, please don't hesitate to email them to me.

(Provide incentive and voucher)

Accessibility testing

Accessibility testing ensures that digital products and services are user-friendly for people with varying abilities, including those with disabilities. By incorporating accessibility testing, you can create an inclusive experience and fulfil legal requirements. It's beneficial to consider accessibility during the prototype stage and understand how people with different digital and accessibility needs can use the product or service you're developing. It is useful for accessibility to be considered at the early stages of product development to enable a wide range of people to use products and services.

UK Government Digital Inclusion Scale informs categorising digital skills (Annex 2 of the strategy). Through their user research, they found that people face four key challenges when going online:

— **Access:** The ability to go online and connect to the internet.
— **Skills:** The ability to use the internet.
— **Motivation:** Knowing the reasons why the use of the internet is a good thing.
— **Trust:** A fear of crime or not knowing where to go online.

To carry out accessibility testing on High-Fidelity Prototypes, later, the Minimal Product and product or service to be released, consider the following:

1. **Review the guidelines:** The Web Content Accessibility Guidelines (WCAG) provide recommendations for making web content more accessible. There are four principles: perceivable, operable, understandable, and robust.
2. **Automated testing tools:** Testing tools such as Axe, WAVE or Lighthouse to scan the website or app can help to identify accessibility issues such as missing alternative text, incorrect heading structures and insufficient colour contrast.
3. **Manual testing:** In addition to automated testing tools, manual tools can help identify accessibility issues that may have been missed. Manual testing involves assessing keyboard navigation, the correct use of ARIA (Accessible Rich Internet Applications), and the logical flow of content.
4. **Screen reader testing:** You can use screen readers for testing prototypes and products such as JAWS, NVDA or VoiceOver. This can ensure that visually impaired users can access and understand your content. While testing, pay attention to how the screen reader says content, headings, links, and form elements.
5. **Conduct usability testing with users with disabilities:** Involve users with disabilities in the usability testing process, including participants with a diverse range of abilities, such as visual, auditory, cognitive, and motor impairments.

6. **Test across devices and browsers:** To ensure optimal performance and consistent user experience, it's recommended that you test your product on various devices, including desktops, mobile phones, and tablets, as well as different web browsers.
7. **Accessibility audit:** An accessibility expert can conduct a thorough audit, identify complex issues, and provide recommendations.
8. **Train the team:** Educate the team on the importance of accessibility and provide training on accessibility best practices. Having a culture of accessibility can ensure that everyone is aware of their responsibilities in creating accessible products.
9. **Integrate accessibility into the development process:** Accessibility can be a core part of the development process rather than an afterthought. Include accessibility requirements in the project planning, design, and development stages.
10. **Regularly monitor and update:** Accessibility testing is not a one-time event but part of an ongoing process to monitor for accessibility issues to make updates where content and functionality change.

Some consultancies offer accessibility testing as it is a specialist skill. For user research and testing for products and services that include sensitive topics, underserved groups or vulnerable people, there are special considerations experienced researchers will have expertise in and may be able to carry out on your behalf. Several resources are available, such as Microsoft's Inclusive Design Manual and Google has libraries dedicated to inclusive design.

Design Sprint: Testing challenges, ideas, and prototypes quickly

A Design Sprint is a process during which businesses can validate their ideas and overcome any key obstacles through design, prototyping, and user testing in five days. The process is described in the book *Sprint* by Kowitz, Knapp and Zeratsky (2016).

> *"Design Sprints have built-in exercises for talking to experts, identifying challenges, mapping out the problem, and testing your ideas with users. This fairly rigid format has a wonderful side-benefit of fostering curiosity and a discovery mindset even in the most confident or locked-in client."* (Eran Dror)

I ran a Design Sprint for a marketplace product in its early stages for a small team. There were some ideas as to how the marketplace could work and what the challenges may be. As the team had limited availability, it being a start-up, I ran the Design Sprint across three days. I combined Days Two and Three of the four-day Sprint into one day to speed up the process further. Ahead of the Design Sprint, we all had prepared our ideas about the challenges, what the marketplace could address, and its limitations. We recruited users ahead of the Design Sprint starting. We conducted short user interviews and concept testing in the Design Sprint. It was a great experience, but it felt rushed compared to project-based research, and we didn't get into as much depth. However, it was great for testing ideas quickly and getting users involved by giving them insights into their challenges and how this marketplace could work for them.

The Design Sprint and the Design Sprint 2.0
There are currently two versions of the Design Sprint: A five-day Design Sprint and a four-day Design Sprint (Design Sprint 2.0). For the five-day Design Sprint, there are set tasks per day that you and your team will complete, from defining key questions and long-term goals on a Monday to sketching product or service ideas on a Tuesday, deciding which of these is the best on a Wednesday, building a prototype on a Thursday and, finally on Friday, testing prototypes.

Design Sprint 2.0 is employed to achieve the same end goal as a standard Design Sprint but is condensed into four days. It is structured so that the entire Sprint team is required for less time, thus making it easier to facilitate and even cheaper to run.

Before the Design Sprint 2.0, there is the preparation that needs to be done:

— **Define your big challenge:** What challenge(s) do you hope your Design Sprint will help you overcome? Is it that you want to have designed an entirely new product? Are you trying to develop a specific new feature? Get clear on this, or you could waste four days on something you don't need.
— **Get a Decider:** This person makes all final decisions.
— **Recruit a Sprint team:** These people will participate in the Sprint, representing your company and its relevant faculties.
— **Schedule experts:** Book in to have the relevant experts on the suitable days and times for your Design Sprint.
— **Pick a Facilitator:** You will need someone to help you through this process to stay on track.
— **Block five full days in the calendar:** Perhaps the hardest of these steps!
— **Book a room with two whiteboards:** You will need these throughout the Sprint process.
— **Interview key stakeholders:** Don't go into your Design Sprint blind. Talk to key stakeholders for their thoughts and opinions on what you're creating during the four days.

A typical four-day design Sprint has set tasks on different days:

Day 1: Define the Challenge and Produce Solutions
Day 2: Vote on Solutions and Create a Storyboard
Day 3: Prototyping
Day 4: User Testing

In preparation for the Design Sprint, I completed several tasks beforehand. This included conducting user research outlined in the first phase and scheduling timeslots to speak with users on the fourth day. Additionally, I conducted a competition analysis and background work on the problem area.

What comes after the Design Sprint is essential. The activities following a Design Sprint could include distributing next steps decided at the end of the four-day Sprint, what needs to happen to continue developing the product, creating a business plan or case, and using systems such as ResearchOps to distribute, store and communicate the Design Sprint activities and conclusions.

I've saved the Design Sprint until now because this shows the quicker process version. The early-stage research outlined to this point is for slow, in-depth research and testing. However, Design Sprints can be more suitable for understanding problems and creating prototypes to test. Typically, Design Sprints are run when the concept is relatively mature and there is a high willingness to invest in the idea and its execution.

This chapter explored prototyping from low-fidelity to high-fidelity prototyping and suitable experiments and tests that can be run to get a Problem-Solution Fit before building a Minimal Viable Product based on the prioritised features and functionality of the product.

11

How to Prioritise Needs and Features for The MVP

"Customers don't know what they want, and they can't give you ideas."
(Rob Fitzpatrick)

Introduction

Throughout the prototyping phase, whilst tests and experiments run, the product team will evaluate and refine Problem-Solution Fit to identify the critical value the product delivers to the customer based on the prioritised user needs. This chapter explores the prioritisation of user needs throughout the prototyping phase to get to the core features and functionality the product or service will need when the Minimal Viable Product is built to experiment in the market to identify Product-Market Fit. A range of prioritisation methods can be used, and the most common types are outlined in this chapter.

Kano Model and Kano Diagram

The Kano Model and the Kano Diagram by the Japanese researcher Noriaki Kano help identify and prioritise customer needs and preferences. There are three categories:

— **Basic needs** are a product's most fundamental requirements to be considered usable. The customer expects these needs to be met and may not notice when they are.
— **Performance needs** are things that customers explicitly state that they want and relate to the features and functions of a product. These needs vary in importance and can be used to differentiate products.
— **Excitement needs** determine the emotional needs of customers who positively respond to a product. This can lead to higher levels of customer loyalty and satisfaction.

The Kano diagram is a visual representation of these types of needs and helps identify the features of functions of a product that fall into each category. The diagram plots customer satisfaction against the level of fulfilment of each need. The three categories of needs are represented as curves in the diagram.

Basic needs are a flat line, showing that the increased fulfilment of basic needs doesn't increase customer satisfaction as customers expect this need to be met. The performance needs curve is upward-sloping, indicating that customer satisfaction increases as more needs are fulfilled. The excitement needs curve is a downward-sloping curve, meaning that too much fulfilment of excitement needs can lead to decreased customer satisfaction. Satisfaction decreases because there is a diminishing impact of certain product features or attributes on customer delight or excitement over time.

In the Kano Diagram, the customer needs can be identified and prioritised:

— **Must-Be:** Basic requirements a product must meet to be considered acceptable by customers. If these needs are unmet, customers will be dissatisfied and may even reject the product entirely.
— **Attractive requirements (Latent needs):** These latent or unspoken needs go beyond customer expectations and can increase customer loyalty and satisfaction. Delighters are unexpected and can differentiate a product in the market.
— **One-dimensional requirements:** Needs that increase customer satisfaction as they are fulfilled and decrease satisfaction as they are not. These needs are typically explicitly stated by customers and are related to the features and functions of a product.
— **Neutrals:** Needs that have no impact on customer satisfaction or dissatisfaction. They are features or functions that customers do not care about.

The best way to start is to identify customer needs, and you can refer to the primary and desk research discussed in the book's earlier sections. Then, categorise customer needs into the following groups: Basic (Must-have), Performance (One-dimensional), Excitement (Attractive), Indifferent, and Reverse to identify which features are primary and which are secondary. The Basic category are features necessary for a product to be considered functional and acceptable to the market. The Performance category includes features explicitly stated by customers and is often used to compare competing products in the market. Excitement categorises features that provide a competitive advantage and can lead to customer loyalty and differentiation. Indifferent category encapsulates the 'nice-to-have' but is not critical in influencing customer perceptions or decision-making. Reverse characterises a category where the absence of a feature leads to customer satisfaction, as its presence does not significantly impact satisfaction or may result in dissatisfaction.

Once you've categorised customer needs, develop the Kano questionnaire to understand customer preferences better, each need has a paired question. A paired question is a functional question (how the customer would feel if the feature were present) and a dysfunctional question (how the customer would feel if it was absent). You need to measure the responses on a scale of 1-5. This questionnaire collects data across the target audience and analyses the data by determining the level of satisfaction and dissatisfaction for each need. Calculate the average score for each pair of questions.

Using the scores, plot the Kano diagram to create a scatter plot with the x-axis representing satisfaction (functional questions) and the y-axis representing dissatisfaction (dysfunctional questions). Place each need on the plot based on its average scores. Basic (Must-have) needs are in the lower-right quadrant, where satisfaction is low when absent, but dissatisfaction is high when absent. Performance (One-dimensional) needs are in the upper-right quadrant, where both satisfaction and dissatisfaction increase with the presence/absence of the feature. Excitement (Attractive) needs are in the upper-left quadrant, where satisfaction is high when present, but dissatisfaction is low when absent. Indifferent needs are near the centre, where neither satisfaction nor dissatisfaction is significantly affected by the presence/absence of the feature. Reverse needs are in the lower-left quadrant, where satisfaction is low when present and dissatisfaction is low when absent.

Finally, interpret the results to prioritise features. You can inform the product strategy in particular basic needs, differentiators through performance needs and delight customers through excitement needs.

Prioritising needs: MoSCoW

Developed by Dai Clegg, a software development expert, in the 1990s, MoSCoW helps to prioritise requirements: Must-have, should-have, could have, and won't have or will not have right now. It is commonly used in software development, project management and business analysis to prioritise requirements, features, and functions.

— **Must-have:** Essential features or requirements that are critical for the product or project's success.
— **Should-have:** Essential features or requirements that are not necessary but should be included if possible.
— **Could-have:** Desirable features or requirements that can be included if resources and time permit but are not crucial to the success of the product or project.
— **Won't-have:** Features or requirements that are not planned for the current project or release but could be considered in the future.

This can be used for identifying and prioritising requirements, product backlog, determining which features or requirements are for each release, and, as the product develops, prioritising new features that may emerge during reviews or retrospectives to adjust.

The MoSCoW approach is sometimes criticised for being biased and subjective. However, by adopting a collaborative approach, this issue can be addressed. To prioritise features using the MoSCoW method, I present a screenshot for each screen and provide feedback in a colour-coded format based on the groups mentioned above. This allows me to discuss and prioritise the features with design and development teams.

RICE scoring for prioritisation

RICE scoring is a prioritisation framework used to evaluate and rank ideas, projects or initiatives based on their potential impact, effort required, confidence level and reach. It provides a structured approach to prioritise and allocate resources effectively. RICE has four components: Reach, Impact, Confidence and Effort.

Reach refers to the number of people or customers who will be affected or benefit from the idea or project. It quantifies the potential audience or market size impacted and a higher reach indicates a broader impact. **Impact** measures the idea or project's potential positive or negative effect on the target audience or business goals. It assesses the significance or magnitude of the expected outcome. A high impact implies a greater positive influence. **Confidence** reflects the level of certainty or confidence in the estimates of reach and impact. It considers the availability of data, research or evidence supporting the projected outcomes. A high confidence indicates more reliable and validated assumptions. **Effort** represents the resources, time and level of work required to implement the idea or project successfully. It considers factors such as workforce, technical complexity, financial investment, and timeline. A high effort implies more resources are needed. RICE scoring involves assigning a numerical value or score to each component on a predefined scale, typically from 1 to 10. The scores are multiplied (Reach x Impact x Confidence) and divided by Effort to calculate the overall score. The higher the RICE score, the higher the priority of the idea or project.

Action Priority/Impact Effort Matrix

Developed by Anderson et al, the Impact Effort Matrix helps to decide what to implement and why. To map out your prioritised features/ideas, if you have several, you can use the Action Priority Matrix, similar to Lean Prioritisation, which has 'value' on the y-axis instead of impact. This is a visual representation to help the product team and critical stakeholders decide which tasks to focus on and the order in which to focus them on. The graph has two axes and four boxes. The y-axis has impact, and the x-axis has effort. You can plot initiatives on the matrix. This matrix can be used to prioritse ideas and projects.

These distil into:
— **High impact and low effort**: Quick wins
— **High impact and high effort**: Major projects
— **Low impact and low effort**: Fill-ins
— **Low impact and high effort**: Thankless tasks

The matrix helps teams prioritise which features to work on by assessing their potential value to customers. This is done by evaluating each feature's impact, considering factors such as revenue generation, customer satisfaction, market share, or process improvement. Additionally, the matrix can help to determine the amount of work and resources required to complete a feature by considering budget, resources, or development time. It can also identify potential risks that could impact the successful implementation of a feature, such as technical complexity, competition, regulation, or stakeholder dependencies.

Prioritised user/design requirements for the product

Once the customer and/or user needs and product and service features are prioritised, you can now consider the user and design requirements for the product. The requirements for the product will fall into different categories as listed below:

— **Functional Requirements:** These describe the product's features, capabilities, and functionalities to meet its intended purposes. These usually come from customer needs, user and market research collected in the discovery phase.
— **Non-Functional Requirements:** These define the product's characteristics that it must have to ensure usability, performance, reliability, and other quality factors. They are usually identified in the prototyping phase and may include performance, scalability, security, accessibility, maintainability, and usability.
— **User Interface Requirements:** The prototyping process is likely to have highlighted user interface requirements to ensure the product is visually attractive, user-friendly, and consistent with the brand image UI could include layout, colour palette and typography.
— **User Experience Requirements:** During prototyping and user testing, UX requirements are identified to ensure the product delivers an intuitive and delightful user experience. UX requirements are usually navigation, interaction patterns, information structure, and overall flow.
— **Data Requirements:** Requirements that define the type, format, and structure of data the product will use, store or process. Data requirements are often identified during discovery when understanding customer needs and the product's context. They may include input and output data, data storage and processing specifications.
— **Integration Requirements:** Integrating with other services or APIs may be necessary. This requires defining the protocols, formats, and methods of communication and data exchange necessary for the interface. These integration requirements are discovered during primary research while analysing the product's ecosystem and dependencies.
— **Compliance and Regulatory Requirements:** Depending on the industry and target market, the product may need to adhere to regulations, laws, or standards. These requirements are identified during discovery, too and can include aspects such as privacy, security, and industry-specific standards.

You must log the user requirements that were not prioritised, as these may be addressed or evaluated later. A product roadmap determines the direction of the product and outlines the vision and priorities. We will discuss product roadmaps in Chapter 15 when we look at product management.

Design and user requirements for the Minimal Viable Product

There are different ways to express user needs and prioritised features for the Minimal Viable Product, a basic product version, to the design and development teams to turn insights into an MVP.

— **Use Cases:** To understand the requirements and functionality from a user's perspective, a use case describes how users interact with a system, product, or service to achieve a specific goal or complete a task.

— **User Flow:** A user flow diagram shows the expected tasks, in what order the tasks are likely to take, and who the actors are. These could be shown on a process flow diagram.

— **User Stories:** These are concise, user-centred descriptions of specific features or functionalities written from the user's perspective to capture requirements and guide software development.

— **Acceptance Criteria:** This list of criteria shows what users will accept and can be used as the basis for design and User Acceptance Testing (UAT).

In this chapter, we've outlined how to prioritise user and customer needs to create the requirements for the product and ways to communicate this to the design and development team. In the next chapter, we're moving from user research to find Product-Solution Fit to Minimal Viable Products and testing in the market.

12

How to Use Lean Start-Up and Test MVPs

Introduction

This chapter will explore the approach of *Lean Start-up*, a hugely influential book by Eric Ries that has inspired the Lean Canvas and Lean Experimentation methods. The main principles are learning fast, continuous learning, and quick iterations to improve based on feedback. This section will provide an overview of Minimal Viable Products, which has several versions. The Minimal Viable Product can be used to conduct experiments in the market with larger user groups and test the product in the market to get feedback.

Lean Start-up and Steve Blank: Starting with learning

Ries wrote the book *Lean Start-up* in 2011. It is popular among start-ups and has significantly influenced building products, particularly in the technology, software, and digital sectors. There are five principles to Lean Start-up, which are as follows:

1. **Entrepreneurs are everywhere:** Many opportunities exist to build a successful business.
2. **Entrepreneurship is management:** To be flexible and adopt continuous learning.
3. **Validated learning:** Lean start-ups serve customers needing their products. They adapt to the market's needs by understanding what customers want through experimentation.
4. **Innovation accounting:** Keep detailed records of tests and analyses to understand what works best and gauge progress to learn about innovation. This crosses over with the ResearchOps and research repository idea to carefully log feedback, analysis and decisions based on evidence.
5. **Build-measure-learn:** Lean start-ups start by building the simplest product, the Minimal Viable Product, which then goes through rigorous tests and user feedback to understand how users accept the product and then iterate to improve.

Steve Blank is widely recognised as a key thought leader and pioneer in the Lean Start-up movement. He is credited with developing the 'Customer Development' methodology, a fundamental component of the Lean Start-up approach. His work has heavily influenced the principles and practices in Eric Ries's book and significantly shaped the concepts and frameworks associated with Lean Start-up methodology.

Blank wrote the *Four Steps to Epiphany* in 2005, outlining the four stages. The first stage is **Customer Discovery**, where one needs to 'get out of the building' to engage with potential customers, identify their needs and validate assumptions about the problem being solved and the target market. It emphasises the importance of continuous customer feedback and iteration.

The second stage is **Customer Validation** where the goal is to validate the Product-Market Fit by building and testing Minimal Viable Products (MVPs) with early adopters. The emphasis is gathering data, refining the value proposition, and ensuring a viable market for the product or solution. A value proposition is a unique combination of benefits, values, and advantages that a product, service or company offers to its customers. It is a concise statement that communicates the value that a customer will receive by choosing a particular product or service over alternatives in the market. A strong value proposition articulates the key reasons why a customer chooses a specific offering and how it addresses their needs, pain points or desires. It should resonate with the target audience and convey value, benefits, and outcomes that customers can expect to achieve.

The third stage is **Customer Creation**, at this point, once the Product-Market Fit is validated, the focus shifts to customer acquisition and scaling the business. This step involves developing and executing strategies to attract customers while continually iterating and refining the business model. The fourth and final stage is **Customer Building** which involves transitioning from a start-up to a scalable and sustainable company. It includes establishing processes, building the organisation, and refining the business model to support growth and profitability. Blank's book emphasises the importance of customer-centricity, iterative learning, and market validation through the start-up journey. It provides a framework for testing hypotheses, and adapting the product to market feedback to increase a business's chance of success.

In her book *Lean Customer Development: Build Products Your Customers Need*, Cindy Alverez (2014), director of User Experience at Yammer (acquired by Microsoft). She challenges how Lean Start-up-based approaches are applied today. Alverez proposes a different Customer Development approach compared to Blank's called Lean Customer Development, which has five steps:

1. Form a hypothesis based on what you know about your customer
2. Go out and find real potential customers and talk to them
3. Ask them questions to validate or disprove your hypothesis
4. Analyse their responses and identify needs
5. Work out what to build and test so you can keep learning

There are similarities to what we've examined using the Design Thinking model. Lean Customer Development demonstrates that starting with learning before building can inform the formation of the solution, so your insights are more focused when talking to people about the product.

Product-Market Fit in Lean Start-Up

Dan Olsen created the Product-Market Fit period pyramid in his book The Lean Product Playbook in 2015. He explained to achieve Product-Market Fit we need a model. His lean approach guides process teams and entrepreneurs through testing key hypotheses.

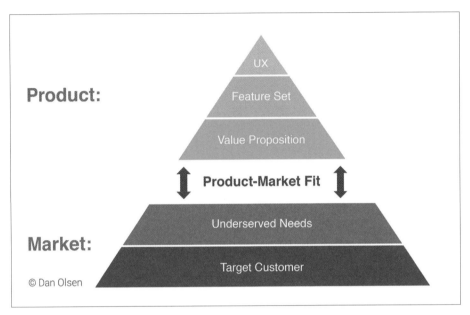

© Olsen, D. (2015) The Lean Product Playbook, Wiley: https://dan-olsen.com

Product-Market Fit is a goal where the product value and market need connect. Usually found in the overlap of unmet needs and the relevant solution to meet the needs.

Sean Ellis, the co-author of *Hacking Growth* with Morgan Brown (2017), developed the 40% rule as the decisive indicator of product-market fit. He benchmarked around 100 start-ups and found that, in those cases where the product user would be very disappointed if the product disappeared, the company would grow faster compared to those with a low score below 40%.

The Four Quadrants of Product-Market Fit by Adam Fisher (2019) from Bessemer Venture Partners explain the true indicators of Product-Market Fit and caution against misleading indicators. He plotted Product-Market Fit across four quadrants with axes: depth of customer engagement and vision for your company. A high-level of both leads to PMF. Sometimes, companies may simply be capitalising on a trendy idea or telling a compelling story. Ultimately, customer and user validation must come from the market itself.

Lean Canvas

The Lean Canvas, created by Ash Maurya, is a strategic tool entrepreneurs, start-ups, and established businesses use to develop, refine, and communicate their business models. It is based on the Business Model Canvas (this is featured later in the book) but focuses on the lean start-up methodology. It also can be helpful as a tool to focus on exploring the product idea in more detail.

Maurya, A. Lean Canvas/Lean Stack. Licenced under the Creative Commons Attribution-Share Alike 3.0 Un-ported Licence: https://thetractionstage.com/wp-content/uploads/2021/09/The-Lean-Canvas.pdf

The Lean Canvas has nine building blocks to describe, design and evaluate a business model.

1. **Problem:** The problem that the business aims to solve or the need that it seeks to fulfil for its customers.
2. **Solution:** The solution that the business offers to address the problem or need to be identified.
3. **Key Metrics:** The measurable data that the business will use to evaluate its success and progress.
4. **Unique Value Proposition:** The unique value that the business offers to its customers that differentiates it from competitors.

5. **Unfair Advantage:** The unique strengths, assets, or capabilities that the business has that give it a competitive advantage.
6. **Channels:** The methods through which a business delivers its value proposition to its customers.
7. **Customer Segments:** The groups of people or organisations that a business aims to serve.
8. **Cost Structure:** The costs that a business incurs to create and deliver its value proposition.
9. **Revenue Streams:** The sources of revenue that a business generates from its customers.

The steps for using Lean Canvas are as follows:

— **Identify the problem**: The first step is to identify the problem that your business aims to solve or the need that it aims to fulfil.
— **Define the solution**: Determine the solution that your business offers to address the identified problem or need.
— **Determine key metrics**: Identify the measurable data that your business will use to evaluate its success and progress.
— **Develop a unique value proposition**: Determine the unique value that your business offers its customers that differentiates it from competitors.
— **Identify unfair advantage**: Determine the unique strengths, assets, or capabilities that your business has that give it a competitive advantage.
— **Design channels**: Identify the methods through which your business will deliver its value proposition to customers.
— **Define customer segments**: Determine the groups of people or organisations that your business aims to serve.
— **Determine cost structure**: Identify the costs that your business will incur to create and deliver its value proposition.
— **Identify revenue streams**: Determine the sources of revenue that your business will generate from its customers.

Previously, we discussed the Riskiest Assumption Test (RAT). The Lean Canvas and RAT are interconnected. The Lean Canvas captures and organises key assumptions within the business model, and RAT helps identify the most critical assumptions to focus on for testing and validation. By using the Lean Canvas, RAT can be identified by start-ups and from this, can design targeted Lean Experiments to gather insights and validate or pivot their business model accordingly. The RAT informs the refinement and iteration of the Lean Canvas, ensuring a more robust and validated business model.

THE LEMONADE VAN
LEAN CANVAS TO EVALUATE ASSUMPTIONS

Sam has lots of insights from the research on her early idea from interviews, and testing the High-Fidelity Prototype. Sam uses the Lean Canvas to understand her assumptions and identify the riskiest assumptions to create lean experiments for. Here, she focuses on the value proposition of delivery and subscription service.

— **Problem**: Difficulty in finding consistent, high-quality lemonade delivery services.
— **Customer Segments**: Families and individuals who enjoy lemonade and are health-conscious and would prefer regular deliveries, and local businesses looking for a refreshing beverage option for their customers or employees.
— **Unique Value Proposition**: A lemonade van offering fresh, high-quality lemonade through a subscription-based delivery model. Convenient and consistent access to delicious lemonade without the hassle of making it at home or searching for quality alternatives.
— **Solution**: A subscription service that delivers lemonade to customers ensuring a constant supply of high-quality lemonade, delivered by The Lemonade Van.
— **Channels**: Social media and online advertising, local business partnerships for delivery. Promotions and word-of-mouth campaigns to encourage customers to spread the word.
— **Revenue Streams**: Subscription fees, partnerships, or sponsorships.
— **Cost Structure**: Initial investment in the van and equipment app development, inventory costs such as ingredients, packaging materials and supplies, operating expenses such as fuel, maintenance and insurance, marketing and promotional costs and labour costs for operating the van and managing deliveries.
— **Key Metrics**: Number of subscription customers and retention rate, revenue growth and profitability and customer satisfaction and feedback.
— **Unfair Advantage**: Unique brand identity and experience, exclusive recipes and high-quality ingredients and strong relationships with local businesses.

Sam can identify the critical components of the business model and test and validate assumptions to develop the strategy to create a successful business. She has identified that Channels and Cost Structure are potentially her riskiest assumptions as she has validated the problem and demand, and now she needs to refine her business model.

Assumptions and Lean Experiments

Return to Chapter 4 to revisit the overview of the assumptions. To test the assumptions in Lean Start-up through evaluative research or Lean Experimentation, which involves swiftly testing assumptions and hypotheses through low-cost and fast experiments to obtain information and insights into customer behaviour, preferences, and requirements.

The basic steps of Lean Experimentation are:

— **Identify the problem**: Define the problem you are trying to solve and your assumptions about your customers and their needs.
— **Develop a hypothesis**: Based on your assumptions, develop a hypothesis about how your product or business idea can solve the problem.
— **Design an experiment**: Create a small-scale experiment that tests your hypothesis and can be completed quickly and with a low budget. This can involve creating a prototype of your product, testing different marketing messages, or pricing strategies, or conducting user interviews.
— **Run the experiment**: Run the experiment and gather data on customer behaviour and feedback.
— **Analyse the data**: Review the data collected during the experiment to see if it supports or disproves your hypothesis.
— **Make a decision**: Based on the data and insights gathered, decide whether to pivot, persevere, or abandon the idea.
— **Iterate**: If you continue with the idea, use the data and feedback gathered to improve and iterate the product or business idea.

Experiment Pairing is a term coined by David Bland (2018), meaning to use pairs of Lean Experiment methods depending on the prototype's fidelity level. An example of Experiment Pairing could be to run an online ad (one experiment) plus have a Landing Page (second experiment), so the results of these experiments will demonstrate interest and follow-on engagement to simulate a real-world marketing campaign and buying behaviour.

Using Lean Experiments gives entrepreneurs and product teams the facility to learn fast. Tom Chi (2015), a Silicon Valley Entrepreneur, advocates for reducing the time between guessing and observing the actual data through usage and testing to reduce 'loop length'. One way Chi did this was through quick prototypes to share ideas and prototypes early and rapidly iterate these with his teams.

© Strategyzer AG, The Test Card, Strategyzer: https://www.strategyzer.com/resources/canvas-tools-guides

© Strategyzer AG, The Learning Card, Strategyzer: https://www.strategyzer.com/resources/canvas-tools-guides

Planning Lean Experiments

Strategyzer's Test Card is designed to guide and document the testing process for a specific assumption or hypothesis. It helps to structure the testing approach, track results, and capture key learnings.

Here are the steps to using the Test Card:

— Start by identifying the assumption or hypothesis you want to test. It could be related to a new product, feature, or service.
— Write down the assumption or hypothesis in the "What we want to test" section of the Test Card.
— In the 'Why we think it's true' section, list the evidence or reasons that led you to believe the hypothesis or assumption is true.
— In the 'What we'll measure' section, define the metrics or key performance indicators (KPIs) you will use to measure the success or failure of the hypothesis or assumption.
— In the 'What success looks like' section, describe success if the hypothesis or assumption is validated.
— Finally, in the 'What we'll do' section, outline the steps you will take to test the hypothesis or assumption, including the experiments or tests you will conduct, the data you will collect, and the analysis you will perform.

Paired with the Test Card is the Learning Card. Strategyzer's Learning Card helps capture and summarise the key learnings and insights derived from the testing process. It is a tool for synthesising information and identifying the implications of the test results.

Strategyzer's Test Card and Learning Card can be used to structure prototype testing efforts, gather relevant data, and analyse the results. These tools support a systematic approach to learning and iterating, refine the value proposition, validate assumptions, and enhance the product or service being developed.

Design of Experiments for Lean Start-up

Design of Experiments (DoE) is a statistical and systematic approach used to plan, conduct, and analyse experiments in order to optimise processes, improve product quality, and gain insights into the relationship between variables. It allows researchers and engineers to efficiently identify significant variables dependent and independent, that affect the outcome of an experiment and determine the optimal conditions for achieving desired results.

It is an approach that can be used in product development and Lean Start-up. First, optimise design and performance by exploring various design options and combinations of features, materials, or components to determine their impact on product performance, reliability, and user experience. This helps teams identify the best design solution and optimise the product. Second, it can reduce development time and cost as DoE allows for simultaneous evaluation for multiple factors, which can reduce the number of experiments needed for a more efficient product development process. Third, it could minimise risks and uncertainties by systematically testing different variables and their interactions. DoE can identify potential risks, failure points or performance issues early on and enable teams to address these issues. Finally, DoE provides a structured approach to collecting and analysing data, which can inform evidence-based decisions during product development.

Statistical models are used to analyse the findings such as ANOVA, which you can learn more about in Chapter 7. It can be used to analyse innovation and design thinking on a deeper level using statistical modelling to see relationships between variables.

Minimal Viable Product (MVP)

The Minimal Viable Product (MVP) is core to the Lean Start-up approach. An MVP is a functional product with minimal features tested in the market. It differs from a High-Fidelity Prototype, and it's essential that these are both not confused as they have different purposes and functionality. A High-Fidelity Prototype is a representation of the final product's design and user experience to gather feedback on the visual and interactive aspects of the product, it may have limited functionality, but its main aim is to emphasise the visual design, user interface and interaction details to replicate the look, feel and experience of the final product. The MVP has enough functionality to deliver the core value proposition and allow users to accomplish key tasks or solve a specific problem.

The primary purpose of the MVP is to test the product's core value proposition and assess its market viability. It is a fully functioning product that real customers can use with a limited feature set to learn more about customer needs, preferences, and willingness to pay or use the product. It allows developers to iterate and improve the product based on real-world usage and customer feedback.

Marty Cagan stated, *"the MVP is the smallest possible experiment to test a specific hypothesis."* (2011) to get to to Product Market-Fit. In Product Discovery, the core questions are similar: Is the solution valuable? Is it usable? Would customers buy it? Could they use it? Can we build it? Can our stakeholders support it? Is it ethical? Should we build it? An MVP can go through many iterations daily from tests and insights using qualitative and quantitative approaches.

Aaron Humphrey (2023), founder of Intrface argues that there is a rush to build the MVP, and it takes many months, and features can be created that users don't need. According to the Start-up Genome, an innovation foundation, this rush may explain why 74% of start-ups fail due to premature scaling. MVPs are for testing and learning and not software ready to ship. It's a test to measure its viability and use it to talk to target customers, understand problems, define a clear value proposition, to iterate and improve.

Different types of MVPs can be used to gather feedback for future development.

— **Concierge MVP**: Manually performing a service for customers rather than building an automated product to focus on understanding customer needs and validating the value proposition.
— **Wizard of Oz MVP (Smoke test or fake door)**: An apparently (to users) functional product, but the functionality is carried out manually by the team, used to gauge interest and demand.
— **Piecemeal MVP**: Leveraging existing tools, services, or platforms to create an MVP rather than building from scratch. The solution is assembled using existing components to validate the idea with minimal investment.
— **Single-Feature MVP**: Build and launch a product with one core feature that addresses the primary customer need to test the value proposition and gather feedback before expanding the feature set.

- **Functional MVP**: Building a simple, functional product version with limited features set to launch quickly, father user feedback and iterating based on real-world usage.
- **Pre-Order MVP**: Offering the product for pre-order or crowdfunding before it is built. The goal is to gauge demand and generate revenue to fund product development.
- **Explainer MVP**: Using a video or presentation to showcase the product concept and benefits without building the product to generate interest and gather feedback.

Lean Experimentation to iterate the MVP

In the Lean Start-up approach, the MVP has a crucial role in validating hypotheses, learning about customers, and iterating on the product based on user feedback. The MVP is a simplified version of a product with enough features to be functional and valuable to early users to test core assumptions about Product-Market Fit and gather real-world data to inform further development.

David Bland, an author and founder of from Precoil reflects on MVPs for the Lean Start-up approach and has found that when creating a Minimal Viable Product (MVP), it's important to remember that it's designed for learning rather than scaling. The Build-Measure-Learn loop should start with understanding what you need to know about the customer, market, and problem. The business or start-up determines the minimum requirements, but it's ultimately up to the customer to decide if it's viable. The main objective of the MVP is not to generate revenue or scale but rather to learn more about the market and identify if there is a scaleable business model.

MVPs can be used to validate the value proposition, assess market viability, and gather customer feedback. The MVP needs to have a clear goal of what is being tested, what needs to be validated, and what success looks like to build the product.

Lean Experimentation allows businesses to test ideas and gather data to inform decision-making quickly and cost-effectively. By testing assumptions early and often, companies can avoid investing time and resources in ideas that are unlikely to succeed and can focus on building products and services that meet real customer needs.

Return to the prototyping section to identify suitable experiments to test the MVP. Some of the experiments will be similar, such as usability testing, A/B Testing, customer interviews and surveys and social media and online engagement through monitoring social media. Instead of testing the prototype for Problem-Solution Fit with a small set of users, the MVP is a minimally functioning product seeking to evaluate Product-Market Fit with a larger group of users.

The MVP is a stepping stone towards the first release to ensure the final product is valuable and usable for the target audience. To summarise the Lean Experiments that can be run on MVPs, the table below outlines the types of tests and critical goals for each MVP approach. Overall, MVPs and Lean Experiments aim to test and validate feasibility, desirability, and viability.

Type of MVP	Relevant Lean Experiments	Goals
Concierge MVP	· **Customer Interviews**: Gather insights into behaviours, interactions, and expectations. · **Shadowing**: Observe users interacting with the MVP and evaluate behaviours and expectations. · **Landing Page Testing**: Test needs and willingness to pay for manual or concierge-type service. · **Manual Service Delivery**: Validate responses to manual interactions and level of customer engagement. · **Pre-Orders or Waiting List**: Gauge demand for the concierge service, validate pricing and assess willingness to commit to the service. · **A/B Testing**: Test variations of the service experience and test approaches, pricing, and features with different customer groups. · **Pilot Programme**: Run a pilot with a select group of customers to refine the service, collect feedback and validate assumptions before scaling.	To test the response and willingness to pay for manual services to customers before building a fully automated service.
Wizard of Oz MVP	· **User Interviews:** Validate assumptions about the problem customer behaviour and desired features. · **Prototype Demos:** Visually appealing prototype that appears to be an automated system but is manually operated. Demonstrate to potential users and gather feedback on reactions, expectations, and usability. · **Shadowing:** Observe users interact with the MVP and gather insights into behaviour and interactions. · **Wizard Role-Playing:** Act as the 'wizard' to manually operate the system, engage with users and provide intended experience and gather feedback on perceptions, interactions, preferences, and satisfaction. · **Usability Testing:** Capture feedback on functionality, clarity of instructions and any frustrations or confusion encountered. · **Feature Prioritisation Survey:** Interview or survey users to prioritise desired features and functionality of the system to validate assumptions about most important aspects	To evaluate user feedback on features, usability, preferences, and functionality before committing to building the system.

Type of MVP	Relevant Lean Experiments	Goals
Piecemeal MVP	• **Feature Prioritisation Survey:** Survey importance and desirability of different features or components to prioritise based on user preference and develop most desired first. • **Feature Testing:** Develop and test individual features separately to gauge interest and usability for incremental validation and improvements. Test user satisfaction, engagement, and usability issues. • **A/B Testing:** Test variations of the product with different features to determine with version performs better based on engagement conversion rates or other metrics. • **User Feedback Sessions:** Interviews, surveys, or usability test to understand preferences, pain points and satisfaction levels. • **Minimal Marketable Feature (MMF):** Identify the most valuable feature that can stand alone as a marketable product. Develop and launch the feature separately to test acceptance, engagement, and demand. • **Iterative Prototyping:** Create mock-ups of individual components and gather feedback on design, functionality, and user experience before integrating into final product.	To test individual components and features of a product independently with user feedback.
Single-feature MVP	• **Problem-Solution Interviews:** Understand the problem, need, and pain points related to the specific feature being developed • **Usability Testing:** Test the single features with users to evaluate its usability, ease of use and effectiveness. • **Pre-Launch Landing Page:** Create a landing page that shows the single feature and its value proposition. Collect email address or expression of interest from users to gauge demand and validate the appeal of the feature. • **Wizard of Oz Testing:** Simulate the functionality of the feature to validate assumptions and refine the feature. • **A/B Testing:** Create variations of the feature or user interface and split user base into different groups and show each group a different version of the feature to measure engagement and conversion rates. • **Usage Analytics:** Implement analytics tools to track user interactions and behaviour with the single features and analyse data such as click-through rate, usage patterns or time spent. • **Cohort Analysis:** Analyse user feedback and usage data to identify patters and trends among different user groups or segments. Find whether different subsets of users interact with the feature or if it resonates with certain user profiles.	To evaluate and refine the product feature by feature and determine which is the key feature to develop first.

Type of MVP	Relevant Lean Experiments	Goals
Functional MVP	• **User Testing:** Observe interactions by users and assess ease of user, intuitiveness and overall user experience and usability. • **Metrics Tracking:** Implement analytics tools to track user behaviour and engagement to measure acquisition, retention, conversion rates or time spent on certain features. • **A/B Testing:** Build variations of the MVP to test different features, designs or user flows and measure engagement, satisfaction, or conversion rates to determine which version performs better. • **Cohort Analysis:** Analyse user feedback and usage data to identify patterns and trends among different user groups. • **Customer Interviews:** Gather feedback on experiences to understand pain points and satisfaction levels and capture suggestions for improvement. • **Surveys:** Gather feedback on specific aspects such as features, user interface or overall satisfaction • **Iterative Development:** Continuously iterate and release new versions of the MVP and have a feedback loop to allow users to provide input and make suggestions to improve.	To assess if the MVP provides core functionality to users to prioritise future development.
Pre-order MVP	• **Landing Page Testing:** A landing page that describes the product with pre-order option and measure metrics such as click-through rates and number of pre-orders. • **Price Testing:** Experiment with different pricing options or tiers to assess willingness to pay. • **Exploratory Surveys:** Conduct surveys to understand their decision to pre-order and capture feedback and feature requests. • **Prototype Demos:** Develop a functional prototype to demonstrate its features, benefits and value and offer a demo to potential customers and gather feedback on reaction, interest, and suggestions for improvement. • **Limited Release Pre-Order:** Launch a limited release for pre-order to a select group of customers to gauge early adoption, gather feedback and test demand. • **Referral Programmes:** Incentivise existing pre-order customer to refer others and track referral rates and measure the effectiveness of word-of-mouth. • **Customer Interviews:** Interview customers that have expressed interest to understand their needs and use cases and likelihood of following through with the pre-order.	To evaluate the MVP as a pre-order before it is fully developed to understand pricing strategies, level of demand and requested features plus gain early traction before launch.

Type of MVP	Relevant Lean Experiments	Goals
Explainer MVP	• **Customer Interviews:** Gather feedback on the clarity and effectiveness of the explainer MVP in conveying the value proposition. • **Landing Page Testing:** Create a landing page with an overview of the concept and problem it solves and measure metrics such as click-through rates and engagement. • **Explainer Video Testing:** Develop an explainer video that presents the concept and value proposition and share with potential customers to collect feedback on comprehension, engagement, and interest levels. • **Concept Testing Surveys:** User surveys to gauge potential customers' understanding and perception of the problem and ask questions to assess comprehension, interest, and potential willingness to adopt the solution. • **Feedback Sessions:** To gather insights on areas that may need further clarification, additional information, or adjustments in messaging. • **Social Media Testing:** Share snippets or descriptions of the explainer MVP on social media channels or relevant online communities to analyse reactions, comments, and engagement levels. • **Landing Page Copy Iteration:** Continuously iterate and refine the messaging, copy, and value proposition presented on the landing page. A/B test different variations to optimise the communication of the concept and value proposition.	To assess a simplified version of a product or service that explains the concept and value proposition to potential users.

In addition to these Lean Experiments, other methods can be used to track user behaviour and assess the financial viability of a Minimum Viable Product on the market. These methods include analytics to measure engagement and conversion metrics such as user count, session duration, bounce rate, and conversion rates. Sales and revenue metrics can also be used to track sales, revenue, and customer acquisition costs. It is important to analyse customer retention and churn rates to identify Product-Market Fit and long-term viability. More information on these methods can be found in Chapter 14, which covers ongoing user and customer research when the product is in the market.

Usability testing for MVPs

Carrying out specific user tests on the MVP can be helpful to increase the likelihood of adoption. UX and usability testing can capture bugs, design problems, and even highlight opportunities for improvement that can be put into the product roadmap. The types of tests that could be conducted on an MVP are:

— **Comprehension Testing:** Tests and validates the UX copy. Different methods, such as Think Aloud and Cloze tests, can be used, where the user replaces missing language.
— **Desirability Studies:** To understand the emotional appeal of a product or service by having users rate its visual design, tone, and overall appeal.
— **User Journey Mapping:** To understand the user's experience of a product or service by mapping their interactions and emotions throughout their journey.
— **Tree-Testing or Tree-Jacking:** To evaluate the effectiveness of an Information Architecture (how information is organised) by having users navigate a text-based representation of the site or app's structure to complete specific tasks. Tree-testing aims to determine if users can find specific items within the site or app's hierarchical structure. During tree testing, users are provided with a simplified text version of the site or app structure without visual design elements. Users are then asked to complete tasks by navigating through the system, and their ability to find the correct items is assessed. This helps identify issues with content organisation, labelling, and navigation before investing in detailed design and development.
— **Cognitive Walkthrough:** To evaluate a product's or service's usability by having users walk through a task, providing feedback on the user's thought processes and interactions.
— **Heuristic Evaluation:** To evaluate the usability of a product or service by having experts assess it against a set of usability principles or heuristics.
— **A/B Testing:** To compare two or more versions of a product or service to determine which performs better, based on user behaviour and feedback.
— **Usability Testing:** To test a product or service's ease of use and efficiency. Users are given tasks to complete, and their interactions with the product or service are observed and recorded to identify usability issues. Usability testing is typically done either remotely or in-person. Usability tests can be moderated, which means a facilitator is there to observe the tests or the tests can be unmoderated, where testers complete tasks on their own. Usability testing can be explorative in the early stages or comparative in later stages using an A/B testing approach. Usability tests can use biometrics such as eye tracking to see how participants interact with the product, and first-click testing can uncover the first clicks to complete tasks.

- **Card Sorting:** A technique used to understand how people categorise the information architecture of a product or service.
- **Content Inventory:** A comprehensive list of all the content on a website or an application. The inventory typically includes information about each content item, such as its title, description, URL, file type, and metadata. A content inventory is often used during a website redesign or audit to identify outdated, irrelevant, or duplicate content that needs to be updated, removed, or consolidated. Content inventory helps provide a clear understanding of the existing content landscape, which is essential for effective content management and optimisation.
- **Task Analysis:** To study and understand the cognitive and physical processes involved in completing a task or activity. It involves breaking down a task into smaller subtasks and examining each subtask to determine the required knowledge, skills, abilities, and other resources for successful completion. Task analysis can help identify potential bottlenecks, inefficiencies, and areas for improvement in a process. It is often used in designing products, systems, and training programmes to ensure they are user-friendly and meet the intended user's needs and abilities.
- **Cognitive Task Analysis (CTA):** A specialised type of task analysis that focuses on understanding the mental processes, such as decision-making, problem-solving, and information processing, involved in completing a task. CTA aims to reveal the cognitive demands and challenges users face while performing a task, which can be difficult to observe directly. Methods used in CTA may include interviews, observations, think-aloud protocols, and other techniques to gather data on users' thought processes. The insights gained from CTA can help inform the design of user interfaces, training programmes, and support tools that better align with users' cognitive abilities and requirements.

The digital team of a UK charity wanted to understand how users interacted with their website and chatbots. The team felt it needed to be more straightforward for users to navigate their website. There were multiple ways for donors to give funding and interact with and between the website and chatbots. For this project, I did Task Analysis, setting tasks for the user to complete to understand how the website and chatbots were used. The participants used a think-aloud approach, telling me how they had completed the tasks. It was interesting to find that they all started in the same place and ended in the same place, but they used various paths. Also, this charity had older people as its primary user and donor demographic. We found that the website design, such as hamburger icons, which are three horizontal lines to access the main menu, was challenging to understand, so some donors didn't use them as they didn't know what they were for. This example highlights the importance of understanding how people interact with designs and products, but also how being inclusive by testing with a range of users can highlight usability issues that can, more broadly, make the product or service better designed for more people.

Feedback on Willingness to Pay and pricing strategies from MVPs

Determining the Willingness To Pay (WTP) is crucial for a product's pricing strategy, financial viability, and sales models, and forecasting. Exploring WTP during the MVP stage is advisable, which allows prospective customers and users to try a product close to market. This stage offers a better chance of testing WTP since the idea or solution is less mature, abstract, and hypothetical compared to the earlier stages of development.

The WTP is affected by several factors:

— State of the economy.
— How trendy the product is.
— Consumer's price points.
— Psychological approaches such as anchoring (offering a high and low price to make the middle cost the most attractive).
— Circumstantial needs in different customers.
— Availability and rareness of the product.
— Quality of the product.
— Competitive environment.
— Brand awareness and brand equity.
— Social proof.

There are two ways to test WTP: 1) Revealed Preference (RP) and 2) Stated Preference (SP). WTP is informed by customer and market research through testing the RP and SP. Pricing can be sensitive and be affected by factors that are dynamically shifting over time as conditions change. Revealed Preference is a way to infer a preference based on observations of choices, based on actual decisions. Stated Preference is a question used to establish a valuation and may be asked how much they would pay.

To validate the WTP using RP, you could test by taking pre-orders on a landing page or asking in interviews if they would buy it to identify their reaction and how much they would pay.

There are several ways to run experiments on different types of MVPs, the main goal being to evaluate feasibility, validity, and desirability to reach the goal of Product-Market Fit. We've mentioned continuous iterations and improvements in this section. Now we'll turn to Teresa Torres's book on *Continuous Discovery Habits* as a framework for continuous learning and experimenting to harness the insights to create products that customers and users need.

Continuous Discovery Habits

Teresa Torres's (2021) book, *Continuous Discovery Habits*, proposes a framework for building a continuous learning and experimentation culture within product development teams. The framework consists of four habits:

1. **Talk to customers:** This habit involves regularly speaking with customers to understand their problems, needs, and behaviours. This feedback helps inform product decisions and ensures the team builds something customers want.
2. **Test your ideas:** From testing product ideas through prototypes, experiments, and MVPs (Minimum Viable Products), the goal is to quickly validate assumptions and learn what works and what doesn't. Plus doing interviews to identify opportunities to do both generative and evaluative research.
3. **Prioritise learning:** Prioritising learning over-delivering features. Instead of simply focusing on shipping features, the team should focus on understanding what customers want and need and using that information to inform future product decisions.
4. **Cross-functional collaboration:** Building cross-functional teams and working collaboratively across different departments to ensure that everyone is aligned on the product vision and goals and that everyone is working together to achieve them.

Overall, the Continuous Discovery Habits framework is focused on building a culture of experimentation, learning, and collaboration within product development teams. By continuously talking to customers, testing ideas, prioritising knowledge, and collaborating across functions, teams can build better products that meet customer needs and drive business results.

It is being introduced at this point because project-based research may not suit your project, particularly if your team is at a starting point with existing products and services or a foundation of knowledge about the customer, market, and product.

> *"While there's nothing inherently wrong with project-based research, it's not sufficient for teams who continuously ship value to customers. The key idea is this simple: If we are continuously making decisions about what to build, we need to stay continuously connected to our customers, so that we can ensure that our product discovery decisions will work for our customers."* (Teresa Torres)

The main concept is that an output is a concrete item that can be delivered, such as a product or feature. Meanwhile, an outcome is a transformation that could lead to higher customer satisfaction; it is a change in state. Companies should prioritise outcomes by selecting the appropriate ones and allocating sufficient time to accomplish them. This entails concentrating on a small number of outcomes at the same time and avoiding jumping from one to another. Outputs are essential for achieving outcomes, so they should remain objective, businesses should ask, 'What impact will this change have?'.

Product teams use the Opportunity Solution Tree to determine the best opportunities for a product.

It's crucial to use questioning techniques when doing research to understand opportunities and solutions. For example, asking questions such as 'Can you describe the last time you purchased a product similar to X?' rather than 'What do you want from a product like this?'

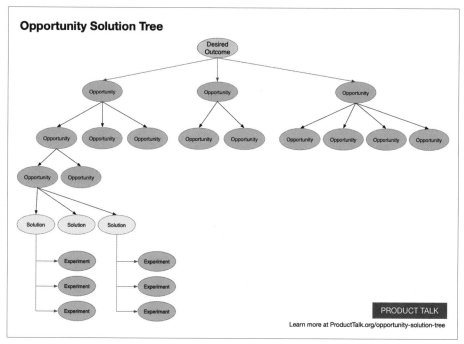

Torres, T. Opportunity Solution Trees: Visualize Your Thinking,
ProductTalk: https://www.producttalk.org/opportunity-solution-tree/

The Opportunity Solution Tree (OST) helps to evaluate opportunities found in the research, organise ideas for solutions and decide which experiments to do. To create the OST, you:

1. Identify the desired outcome.
2. Recognise opportunities that emerge from generative research, such as the needs and pain points of customers.
3. Remain open to solutions from everywhere.
4. Experiment to evaluate and evolve your solutions to test a single solution with sets of experiments.

The OST is useful for Product Discovery and conducting focused generative research to further understand the customer and user as well as have clear aims for experiments through evaluative research.

In this chapter, we explored the MVP and ways to test the MVP using methods from prototyping and usability testing. Pricing to identify the product's financial viability is critical to understanding profitability. We outlined the Willingness To Pay approach to explore this further to help set the right price for the product. The Opportunity Solution Tree was outlined, which sets us up for the next chapter. All the lessons learned from running experiments and testing the MVP mean we know the first release requirements. In the next chapter, we explore moving from MVP to deployment and testing phases here through to the final product ready for first release into the market.

13

How to Move from MVP to Beta to Final Product

Introduction

Before building the product, the developers or technical team will have a clear overview of user and technical requirements. Some of the previous work done, such as the user stories, personas, High-Fidelity Prototype or MVP designs, will inform the requirements. This chapter focuses on software however, the principles of non-technical testing such as Beta Testing and Pilots can apply to other technologies and products.

We start this chapter with the assumption that the user, technical and design requirements for the product have been outlined. An overview of technical testing and order of release is given to provide the context for non-technical testing such as beta testing and a pilot.

Overview Minimal Viable Product to Release

We've moved from **Proof of Concept**, where we've set out our assumptions and had these validated through research and experiments. We've further tested assumptions through the **Minimal Viable Product** (MVP) by gathering user feedback to validate the viability of the product concept. After this phase, we move on to the product release. The first phase is the **alpha release**. The alpha release is an early, unstable software version intended for internal testing and development. It often lacks complete features, has known issues, and is unsuitable for public use. Alpha releases help developers identify and fix problems early in the development process. The product is available to a limited group of internal testers or users to identify major bugs, usability issues and performance concerns.

The next phase is the **beta release**. A pre-release version of the software made available to a wider group of users for testing and feedback. Beta releases often include most of the features and functionality of the final product, but they may still contain minor bugs, performance issues, or unfinished features. Beta testing helps identify and address any remaining issues before releasing the software to the public.

Through the alpha and beta release phases, feedback from testers is collected and used to iterate and refine the product. After this iterative period ends as functionality, usability and performance issues are addressed, the product moves into the next phase where a **Release Candidate** (aka Delta/Gamma) version is created. A Release Candidate is a software version considered feature-complete and stable enough for final testing before the official release. It represents the final stage of testing, and any issues discovered at this stage are typically critical and must be fixed before the product can be released. It is made available to a larger audience for final testing and validation.

The **General Availability (GA) or Production Release** follows the Release Candidate. This marks the product's official launch to the wider market and customer base. The GA release signifies that the product has passed the testing phases and is considered stable and ready for public use.

At this point there are also the following types of releases:

— **Stable Release:** A software product that has undergone thorough testing and is deemed reliable and suitable for general use.
— **Production/Live Release (Gold):** The final version of a software product, deemed stable and feature-complete, ready for end users and the beginning of the end-of-life support phase.
— **First Release (or Version 1.0):** The first official, public release of a software product. This release marks the completion of the development phase and the beginning of the product's life in the market. The first release typically includes the core features and functionality the development team believes will provide value to users and address their needs.

Following this release, the product enters a phase of ongoing updates and support. Product teams and developers will need to consider a Release strategy that means that all key stakeholders can stay updated on the right timing, competition, customer needs, and market dynamics for the Release as to what makes sense for your product and business.

There are different Release strategies, including Phased Roll-Out, where a product is gradually made available to a broader audience, allowing for continuous feedback and improvements; Agile Release, based on iterative development, where software is developed and released in increments; Canary Release, when a new version of the software is deployed to a small subset of users, to monitor its performance and identify potential issues before rolling out to a larger audience; Waterfall Release, which takes a linear sequence of stages when all stages are completed, the product is released after thorough testing and planning; and Continuous Deployment, where software updates are released frequently and automatically as soon as they pass automated testing and validation for rapid delivery of new features, bug fixes, and improvements, but this requires robust testing and monitoring infrastructure to ensure the stability and quality of the software. Releases are known as 'Roll-Outs' or 'Service Launches' for services.

Introduction to software testing

During the First Release, the product should be feature-complete, stable, reliable, and optimised for user experience. To get there, here are different testing approaches to products:

— **White Box:** This process checks the internal components of a program, rather than its functionality for the end user, such as APIs and code coverage.
— **Black Box:** Testing the functionality of a system without knowing its internal workings is called use case testing.
— **Grey Box:** This is a testing approach that combines both white and black box testing methods. Testers possess only partial knowledge of an application's internal structure or code.

There are two main software testing types: functional and non-functional. As a non-technical product team member, you wouldn't be expected to do these tests, but it can be helpful to understand the testing process.

Functional Testing

Functional testing aims to test individual features and functions of a software product to ensure they work as intended.

Unit Testing	Testing individual components or units of code to ensure they function correctly in isolation.
Integration Testing	Testing the interaction between multiple software components to verify that they work correctly together.
System Testing	Testing an entire system or application to validate its overall functionality and performance.
User Acceptance Testing	Testing a software product with real users to ensure it meets their needs and expectations.
Pre-Alpha	An early development stage of a software product, before it's ready for alpha testing.
Alpha Testing	Early stage testing of a software product, usually done internally to identify and fix major bugs and issues.
Beta Testing (Closed/Open)	A later stage of testing, where a limited number of external users (closed) or the general public (open) test the software and provide feedback.

End-to-End Testing	Testing a complete application workflow or process to ensure it functions as expected from start to finish.
Smoke Testing	A basic test to ensure the critical functionalities of a software product work correctly before proceeding to more in-depth testing.
Sanity Testing	A quick, focused test to verify that a specific functionality or bug fix works as intended.
Happy Path Testing	Testing the most common and straightforward user scenarios to ensure basic functionality works as expected.
Monkey Testing	Random, unstructured testing to uncover unexpected bugs or issues in a software product.
Operational Acceptance Testing	Testing to ensure a software product is ready for deployment in a production environment, including factors like reliability, maintainability, and compatibility.

Non-Functional Testing: Usability, Performance and Reliability

There are two types of non-functional software testing: alpha and beta. Alpha testing is conducted in the early stages of development after the core features and functionalities have been completed. Its purpose is to identify and solve major issues before the software undergoes beta testing. The testing is done by either the development team or a dedicated quality assurance team, who have extensive knowledge of the software and its technical aspects. The testing environment is closely controlled to allow the development team to monitor and troubleshoot the software in a virtual environment.

After alpha testing and fixing any bugs, beta testing takes place to identify and resolve any remaining issues, such as minor bugs or usability. The testers are usually a diverse user or customer group representing the software's target audience. They provide feedback to improve the product and meet user needs. Beta testing is conducted in the real world, where testers use the software in typical scenarios to uncover issues that may not have arisen during alpha testing.

Beta Testing: User Acceptance Testing

In the beta phase, once alpha testing and quality checks have been done, User Acceptance Testing (UAT) can now be performed. UAT is critical in software development, where end users test the software to ensure it meets their needs, requirements, and expectations. The primary goal of UAT is to validate that the software is ready for deployment and use in real-world environments. It is the final testing stage before the software is released.

UAT can ensure that the software application is built according to the user requirements and can perform the tasks it was designed for. It can identify gaps, errors, or discrepancies in the software from a user's perspective. During UAT, test scenarios and test cases are designed to cover real-life use cases that the end users will encounter whilst using the software. These test cases are derived from the user requirements and focus on functionality, usability, and performance from a user perspective. End users or subject matter experts representing the target audience usually conduct the tests. These testers deeply understand business processes and requirements, enabling them to evaluate the software's effectiveness and suitability. Testers perform tasks and operations in the software as they would in real life. The results determine whether the software is ready for deployment or if further improvements and fixes are required. UAT concludes with a formal sign-off once the identified issues have been resolved and the software meets user requirements.

"The goal of User Acceptance Testing is to assess if the system can support day-to-day business and user scenarios and ensure the system is sufficient and correct for business usage." (Matthew Setter)

UAT has other types of acceptance testing, including Operational Acceptance Testing (OAT), which focuses on the operational readiness of a software application, ensuring that it is stable, reliable, and ready for deployment in the production environment. OAT involves evaluating various aspects of the software's operation, such as system performance, stability, security, and data integrity, verifying the necessary support infrastructure, procedures, and documentation. Contractual Regulatory Acceptance Testing (CRAT) verifies that the software complies with the contractual, regulatory, or legal requirements specified by the client, industry standards or governing bodies.

Additional testing in the beta stage may be:

— **Unit Testing:** Testing individual components or units to verify they function, and the code is working.
— **Functional Testing:** Check the functionality of the product.
— **Integration Testing:** Verify the interfaces between software components.
— **System Testing:** This verifies that the system meets its requirements and evaluates the software in that it meets specified requirements and functions correctly.
— **Regression Testing:** Ensure existing functionality remains intact after changes, bug fixes, or updates have been made.
— **Performance Testing:** Evaluates software's responsiveness, reliability, and scalability, such as high load or limited resources.
— **Security Testing:** Identifying potential vulnerabilities and weaknesses that could be exploited.

Technology Acceptance Model

The Technology Acceptance Model (TAM) is a framework for evaluating a particular product or service's User Interface, User Experience, and user behaviour in a 'real-world' environment.

TAM isn't associated with a particular release or product development stage. Organisations often use TAM to evaluate the likelihood of successful technology implementation. Companies can plan for proper training, support, and change management by understanding users' perceptions and attitudes towards new technology to ensure smooth adoption.

It can be used to understand users' adoption and use of emerging technologies. It explores the users' intent to use (acceptance of technology) and usage behaviour (actual use) of technology is predicated by the perception of the product's usefulness and ease of use. Users are more likely to adopt technology with good UX design.

The TAM explores perceptions of usefulness and ease of use as mediated by external factors such as individual differences, social influences, and system characteristics. TAM models are based on the premise that the actual use of a technology is determined by users' intentions, which are influenced by their attitudes, beliefs, and perceptions about the technology. Several widely recognised technology acceptance models exist, including the original Technology Acceptance Model (TAM), the Unified Theory of Acceptance and Use of Technology (UTAUT), and their subsequent iterations.

The TAM was proposed by Fred Davis in 1986. TAM is based on the Theory of Reasoned Action (TRA) and focuses on two key factors that influence user acceptance of technology: Perceived Usefulness (PU) and Perceived Ease of Use (PEOU). Perceived usefulness (PU) refers to the degree to which users believe using the technology will improve their job performance or provide value. Users who perceive technology as applicable are more likely to accept and adopt it. Perceived Ease of Use (PEOU) is whether users believe using the technology will be effort-free. Users are more likely to adopt a technology if they think it is easy to learn and use.

The TAM suggests that PU and PEOU influence users' attitudes toward using the technology, which affects their intention to use it. The will to use it can determine actual technology usage. The Unified Theory of Acceptance and Use of Technology (UTAUT) is an extension of TAM that integrates multiple models. It has four key determinants of technology that determine technology acceptance and usage.

1. **Performance Expectancy:** The degree to which users believe that using the technology will help them achieve gains in job performance.
2. **Effort Expectancy:** The extent to which users believe using the technology will be easy and free of effort.
3. **Social Influence:** Whether users perceive that essential people (e.g., peers, supervisors) believe they should use the technology. Social influence can affect users' intentions to use the technology.
4. **Facilitating Conditions:** To support users with learning and utilising technology by providing resources, training, and technical support when needed.

The moderating factors in UTAUT are gender, age, and experience. TAM and UTAUT are widely used in research to understand and predict technology acceptance, assess user needs, and inform the design and implementation of technology solutions to increase adoption rates.

Research methods to test TAM and UTAUT are surveys, interviews, experimental designs, and longitudinal studies (collecting data over a long period).

Closed Beta Testing

UAT is a crucial part of the beta phase. It involves real end-users testing the software in their own environment to ensure that it meets their needs and expectations. Users perform various tasks to validate the software's functionality, usability, and overall user experience. The primary goal of UAT is to identify any issues that could affect user satisfaction and to gain valuable feedback for further improvements.

However, Closed Beta Testing is conducted with a limited group of pre-selected users invited to participate in the testing phase. The software is made available to this group under controlled conditions, and they provide feedback to the development team. Closed Beta Testing allows for more targeted feedback from a specific user segment and is often used to test the software with early adopters or trusted customers.

A structured, Closed Beta Testing programme aims to identify the following:

— **Quality:** Do the features work as they are supposed to? Does the code work as expected?
— **Usability:** Is it a frictionless experience for users to navigate through the product to find what they need, and does it do what they expect? Is it easy to use?
— **Bug Identification:** Are there serious bugs? What are minor bugs?
— **Performance:** How do the device and operating system impact performance?

— **Marketing:** Will testers refer their friends? What are the benefits they are getting from the product?
— **Product-Market Fit:** Is there a product-market fit?
— **Technology Acceptance Model:** What are the facilitating conditions that need to be in place for the user to use this product? Are there any social influence factors impacting whether they'd use the product?

A structured beta programme may use the following structure:

— Recruitment of relevant testers.
— Clear onboarding process for testers.
— Collect real-time qualitative data and quantitative data through pop-up surveys.
— Pre-trial and post-trial surveys.
— Qualitative feedback sessions.
— Set up trial communication and support with testers and product teams for bug reporting and live chat.
— Synthesis and analysis of data.

On one project, I found that conducting 'clinics', which are online group calls, at the start of the process, helped save time answering queries and difficulties getting the set-up right. We ensured the live chat and bug reporting features were easy to use and could capture screenshots to describe the issues.

These task-level satisfaction questions could be used in the Closed Beta Testing in the surveys to assess the satisfaction and usability of specific tasks within a product or system and commonly in formative evaluations to identify issues and areas for improvement during the design and development process. The user needs to answer immediately after completing a task (whether the goal was completed or not) and how easy it was in a user test. Task-level satisfaction questions are as follows:

— **ASQ: After-Scenario Questionnaire (3Qs):** This is a short questionnaire used to assess user satisfaction with a specific task or scenario, focusing on ease of completion, time spent, and adequate support.
— **NASA-TLX: NASA's task load index (5Qs):** A widely used subjective workload assessment tool that measures perceived workload across six dimensions, such as mental demand, physical demand, and effort.
— **SMEQ: Subjective Mental Effort Questionnaire (1Q):** A single-item questionnaire designed to measure the subjective mental effort required to perform a task, allowing users to rate their perceived effort on a visual scale.
— **UME: Usability Magnitude Estimation (1Q):** A single-item questionnaire where users are asked to assign a numerical value to a product's usability based on their experience, allowing for a quick estimation of usability.
— **SEQ: Single Ease Question (1Q)** A simple, one-question survey that asks users to rate the ease of completing a specific task on a seven-point scale, providing a quick assessment of task-level usability.

Next, we will turn to Open Beta Testing. Open Beta Testing, in contrast to closed beta, is made available to the general public. Anyone interested can access and use the software during this phase. Open Beta Testing aims to gather a larger pool of testers and obtain feedback from a diverse user base. It helps identify a broader range of issues and provides insights into how the software performs under real-world conditions.

THE LEMONADE VAN

CLOSED BETA TESTING: THE DELIVERY AND SUBSCRIPTION VALUE PROPOSITION

Sam has developed a range of lemonade products and understands what customers want when making decisions to buy at events. She has developed working relationships with the event managers for key local events to create a calendar of events she'll be attending to sell her lemonade. She will be experimenting with different flavours, which will become a continuous development process. The Closed Beta Testing will evaluate the delivery app she's created.

Sam's objective for Closed Beta Testing is to evaluate the functionality, usability and user experience of the ordering, delivery and scheduling service and app. She will do this with support of a software development agency.

The participants will be recruited from both 'snowball sampling' (asking for recommendations for others to take part in the research) and visiting local gyms and sports venues to invite them to participate. There will be approximately 5–10 people in the closed Beta.

The app has been set up with easy ways to report bugs, issues, and suggestions and to provide live chat and tester support. In addition, Sam will track user engagement, website visits, and interactions. She has ensured there is enough stock and recruited one driver to help support her if she has many deliveries during this testing period. She has considered data policies to protect user data.

Sam has sent a series of emails, the first to introduce the testers to the testing, which will last two weeks, and what their role as testers is in the process, which is to provide feedback and complete tasks. The tasks that need to be completed:

1. Download and install the app
2. Register and create an account
3. Place an order for lemonade and customising the order
4. Schedule a delivery date and time
5. Choose a payment method and submit payment (a 50% discount has been given to testers) (payment details are produced to testers)
6. Track the delivery status of the order
7. Reschedule or cancel at least one order
8. Provide feedback on the app's performance, user interface and overall experience (this will be through a survey)

Testers are provided with guidelines as follows:

— Test the app on different devices and platforms to identify compatibility and consistent performance.
— Use different network connections (e.g., Wi-Fi or mobile data) to test the app's performance and responsiveness.
— Test the performance under different scenarios, such as low battery.
— Test the app's error handling and recovery capabilities by intentionally introducing errors or issues, such as incorrect input.

Feedback and reporting will be done through bug reports via designated channels such as an in-app form, email, or online survey. They testers need to provide detailed feedback, including their steps, the device and platform and any error messages or screenshots. Sam will support throughout the testing period and check in with testers' data to see their engagement level and how to keep them engaged and provide feedback.

Reflections on the completed Closed Beta Testing
Her findings showed that further development needs to be done, as many deliveries were scheduled at the same time and were far away from one another, which identified the need to iterate and develop the product further. Sam needed to evaluate a feasible way to service many deliveries when she may have the van at events. The testing also highlighted a number of performance issues and bugs that need to be fixed.

Open Beta Testing

Open Beta Testing aims to test the software with a larger audience. This type of testing provides valuable insights into how the software performs under real-world conditions and with a diverse user base. When approaching Open Beta Testing, consider the following for quick feedback from users:

— Have a clear research plan (see project based research plan).
— The beta version should be easily available to testers for a set time.
— Promote and market the beta testing opportunity.
— Provide clear instructions and guidelines for using the product, how to report bugs and submit feedback.
— Set up channels for communication and support.
— Monitor and collect the feedback, bug reports and usage data.
— Consider doing interviews for in-depth feedback.
— Analyse the data and feedback.

It's important to have feedback mechanisms available to users, but don't rely solely on methods like live chat or complaints. Product teams should be proactive in seeking continuous user feedback. As the product develops, it's a good time to update personas and segment customers with data. While qualitative research is a great way to engage with customers, it's also useful to use quantitative methods to track engagement, behaviour, and survey responses. Ultimately, nothing beats talking to your customers directly.

Pilot

A pilot is a test-run of a product or service by a customer on a small scale. It allows for exploration of whether the product works as planned in a real life environment. Piloting a product or service offers benefits such as identifying unexpected outcomes, testing market demand, and gaining valuable insights.

Like beta testing, pilots need significant planning, strong project management and stakeholder buy-in. The pilot typically measures user satisfaction, Return on Investment, success, and impact from a non-technical testing perspective. User satisfaction can be measured using the techniques outlined in Chapter 14. The Return on Investment (ROI) and impact could be calculated using the Logic Model or Theory of Change. The success criteria will depend on the purpose and aims of the pilot. The Theory of Change and Logic Model can be used for programme planning, evaluation, and social impact assessment. The Theory of Change is a comprehensive and systematic approach to understanding and articulating how and why a particular programme or intervention leads to desired outcomes or impact. A Logic Model is a diagram that illustrates the components and relationships of a programme or intervention and presents a logical sequence of how inputs, activities, outputs, and outcomes connect to achieve the desired impact.

The Theory of Change and Logic Model have similarities as they both show the inputs, such as expertise and funding, and the expected outputs and outcomes in the short, medium, and long term, such as a change in behaviour. The pilot can be seen as an 'intervention' where the product or service is expected to change the state of something because it is a solution that meets a challenge effectively. A pilot to evaluate ROI usually entails research such as pre-and post-surveys with interviews with key stakeholders in the pilot, to identify the states before and after to show the changes that your product or service made. The interviews and surveys can also measure success criteria such as satisfaction levels, how easy the product or service was to use, the nature of the user experience and if it added value as anticipated. Other measures for evaluating impact and Return on Investment are through measures such as:

— **Cost-Effectiveness Analysis (CEA) and Cost-Benefit Analysis (CBA):** These methods involve comparing the costs and benefits of different interventions to determine their relative efficiency in achieving desired outcomes. CEA measures the cost per unit of outcome achieved (e.g., cost per life saved), while CBA measures the net monetary value of the intervention (i.e., benefits minus costs).

— **Outcome Harvesting:** This method involves collecting evidence of outcomes that have occurred and then working backwards to determine the contribution of an intervention to those outcomes. It is beneficial for complex programmes or those operating in rapidly changing contexts.

— **Most Significant Change (MSC) Technique:** MSC is a participatory, qualitative method that collects and analyses stories of significant change resulting from an intervention. Stakeholders then engage in the process of selecting and discussing the most important stories to gain insights into the intervention's impact.

— **Contribution Analysis:** Seeks to establish plausible causal links between intervention and observed changes by examining the intervention's theory of change, the available evidence, and alternative explanations for the observed differences.

— **Social Network Analysis (SNA):** SNA analyses relationships and interactions between actors within a system, such as individuals, organisations, or communities. It can help to understand the extent to which an intervention has influenced the structure and dynamics of the network and the resulting impact on outcomes.

- **Social Return on Investment (SROI):** SROI is a framework that combines elements of CBA and stakeholder engagement to measure and monetise an intervention's social, environmental, and economic value.

In this chapter, we discussed the move from MVP to beta, where we've progressed from a basic product to test its viability and value to a full, complete product where we're testing for different aspects such as performance and usability. Now the product or service has been through stages of testing. The product, marketing and development teams need to consider the product or service's launch into the market. Each launch is different for each product or service. The next chapter will start from the assumption that the product is launched and readily available for public use in the market to demonstrate ways to test live products and services.

14

How to Test Products and Services in The Market

Introduction

This chapter will cover how to clearly explain the product or service to customers, particularly for marketing and branding the product to the target audience through the Value Proposition Canvas. We'll look at how the adoption of newly introduced products and services in the market works and how to continuously test products and learn about product and service sucesses post-launch.

Communicating clear value: Value Proposition Canvas

The Value Proposition Canvas is a strategic tool designed to help businesses identify and improve their value proposition to customers. Alexander Osterwalder and Yves Pigneur alongside Greg Bernada and Alan Smith (2014) outline the canvas in their book *Value Proposition Design* developed the canvas. The Value Proposition Canvas consists of two building blocks.

The first is **Customer Profile**. This canvas section outlines the customer's needs, wants, and desires. It includes information about the customer's jobs, pains, and gains.

The second is **Value Proposition**. This canvas section outlines the business's unique value to its customers. It includes information about the product or service features, benefits, and how it solves the customer's problems or fulfils their desires.

The steps for using the Value Proposition Canvas are as follows:

— **Customer Profile**: Start by identifying your target customer segment and understanding their needs, wants, and desires. This involves identifying their jobs (the tasks they are trying to accomplish), pains (the problems or challenges they are facing), and gains (the benefits they are seeking).
— **Value Proposition**: Once you clearly understand your customer segment, you can focus on developing your value proposition. This involves identifying the features, benefits, and unique value your product or service offers the

customer. This includes determining how your product or service solves customers' problems, fulfils their desires, and provides benefits that meet their needs.

— **Fit**: The final step is to assess the fit between the customer profile and the value proposition. This involves identifying whether the value proposition meets the customer's needs and whether there is a market for the product or service. If the fit is not strong, businesses can use the information gathered from the canvas to refine their value proposition and better meet the needs of their target customers.

This is a powerful tool for developing and refining the value proposition, focusing on meeting their target customers' needs and desires. By breaking down the customer's needs and the unique value offered by a product or service, businesses can comprehensively understand their customers and make informed decisions about its business strategy. Like the Lean Canvas, this can be continuously returned to once the customer is better understood through research and insights from rapid feedback loops.

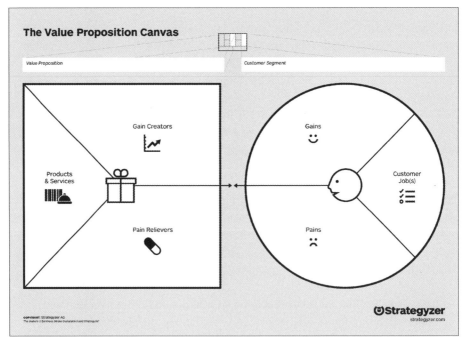

© Strategyzer AG, Value Proposition Canvas, Strategyzer: https://www.strategyzer.com/resources/canvas-tools-guides

THE LEMONADE VAN
VALUE PROPOSITION: EVENTS

Using the Value Proposition Canvas, Sam can analyse the customers' needs and the company's offerings to create a value proposition that meets their pain points while also providing a unique and compelling offering for fresh lemonade at local events. This is a separate value proposition to the fresh lemonade delivered through a subscription model.

Customer Profile
— **Jobs-To-Be-Done:** Finding a beverage at events, accessing high-quality lemonade conveniently and enjoying a memorable experience.
— **Pains:** Long wait times at events, high sugar content in other beverages, unavailability of lemonade in specific flavours, limited options for fresh, high-quality lemonade at events, inconvenience of making lemonade at home, inconsistency in taste and quality from other lemonade vendors.
— **Gains:** Access to fresh lemonade at events and unique flavour options.

Value Map
— **Products & Services**: The Lemonade Van serving freshly made lemonade at events and various lemonade flavours and options, including seasonal specials and customisable choices.
— **Pain Relievers**: Bringing lemonade directly to customers at events, ensuring consistent taste and quality through carefully crafted recipes and high-quality ingredients and saving customers time and effort sourcing their lemonade.
— **Gain Creators**: Unique flavours, building a loyal customer base through excellent customer experience, providing an enjoyable experience through unique branding, presentation, and customer engagement.

Adoption of new products

According to Everett Rogers' (1962) theory, outlined in the book the *Diffusion of Innovation* describes how users adopt new products. It analyses the factors that influence the rate of adoption of new ideas, products, and technology in different cultures and societies. Rogers was interested in why early adoption happens. In particular, understanding why a particular target market decides to adopt a specific product or service is critical to its success or failure for the business.

The adopter categories, based on the Diffusion of Innovations, are as follows:

— **Innovators:** This group is enthusiastic, with a tolerance for high-risk.
— **Early Adopters:** Customers and users have an appreciation of the potential to get a competitive advantage.
— **Early Majority:** The market uptakes the product after a long time and represents the majority of the market.
— **Late Majority:** This group is very cautious and wants to see results before buying.
— **Laggards:** Customers that are last to adopt as they are very sceptical and will buy if they must.

Innovators are high-risk takers. They are the first to try out new ideas and technologies. They are most likely to try out MVPs, as they are interested in exploring new concepts and can provide valuable early feedback. **Early Adopters** are opinion leaders who carefully evaluate any products before adopting them. They are influential within their social circles and help to spread the news of innovations to the broader community. Early adopters are more likely to use products in the initial release stage rather than MVPs, as they prefer to adopt innovations that have been refined and validated. The **Early Majority** are cautious and deliberate when adopting anything new; they will likely adopt products in the initial release or later. The **Late Majority** are sceptical of innovations and adopt them after most of society has already accepted them. They are likely to adopt products well after the initial release stage once the product has been widely accepted and adopted. **Laggards** are the last to adopt innovation and risk change and are likely to adopt the product only when necessary or unavoidable.

In his book, *Crossing the Chasm,* Moore (1991) suggested that the most challenging transition is from early adopters to early majority; the Early Market to the Mainstream Market.

> *"For companies to be able to cross the chasm, they need to find new ways to make their products more attractive to in the eyes of the early majority."* (Geoffrey Moore)

For product teams and entrepreneurs, it's vital to get continuous feedback to identify how the product moves through these adoption stages.

Continuous testing and learning for products in the market

Products and services can be continuously measured, tested, and assessed in the market. Incremental changes may be made by this point to refine the product and service using relevant metrics and quantitative data. Qualitative data can evaluate the user experience and the long-term viability of the product or service.

We'll now explore techniques and tools for continuously testing and measuring products in the market for several purposes. Continuous learning is key for understanding user satisfaction, keeping updated on market conditions, assessing growth strategies.

User Experience Satisfaction

When doing usability and UX testing on existing products, test-level satisfaction measures the user's overall impression of the usability and experience of the product or service. It is usually used at the end of the design and development process, after the product has been launched, as a form of summative evaluation to help determine if the product meets its intended goals, usability requirements and customer needs.

— **SUS: System Usability Scale (10Qs):** A widely used, reliable and valid ten-item questionnaire that provides a quick and easy assessment of the overall usability of a product, system, or interface, generating a score from 0-100.
— **SUPR-Q: Standardised User Experience Percentile Rank Questionnaire (13Qs):** A thirteen-item questionnaire that measures the quality of user experience on websites or digital products, providing scores for usability, trust, appearance, and loyalty as well as an overall percentile rank score comparing the product to a benchmark database.
— **UMUX (Usability Metric for User Experience) (4Qs):** Measures a product's or system's perceived usability and satisfaction. It is designed to be a shorter alternative to SUS.
— **PSSUQ (Post-Study System Usability Questionnaire) (16Qs):** Evaluates users' satisfaction with the overall system usability, such as information quality, interface quality and system usefulness.

Customer Satisfaction

Customer satisfaction can be measured to understand the overall experience.

— **CSAT:** The Customer Satisfaction Score is an average of how satisfied customers feel about their experience. They are usually asked a simple question with a rating scale of 1-3 (happy, neutral, unhappy) or 1-5 (star rating). This metric indicates the level of satisfaction customers have at a specific moment, and can be used after an interaction, purchase, or at regular intervals.

— **CES:** The Customer Effort Score (CES) measures how easy a customer's experience was. It is determined by asking, 'Overall, how easy was it to [perform a specific task] with [a particular product or service] today?' The response is rated on a five-point scale ranging from 'Very Easy' to 'Very Difficult.' The CES score is calculated by subtracting the percentage of customers who found the experience difficult from the percentage who found it easy. It is a more effective predictor of behaviour than the Net Promoter Score (NPS). The NPS is a customer loyalty metric that measures the likelihood of customers recommending a company's products or services to others. The CES is typically used to evaluate the user experience of a product or specific features, such as onboarding after customers have completed a task to ensure that it is easy to use.

Other sources of measuring customer satisfaction are live chat conversations, follow-up survey feedback left by customers, social media sentiment (emotional tone of online discussions), churn rate (how many customers stop using the product), and milestone surveys at critical moments in the customer journey.

Continuous Market Research

All the research should pay off at the late stages of product development and when the product is being marketed. As Justin Zidaru (2023), a market research consultant stated, doing this difficult research at the beginning will make marketing and communicating the product and services to customers and users easier later.

Once the product is in the market, we can continue to analyse the market conditions and competition to stay up-to-date with any changes.

— **Brand Perception:** Brand perception refers to how customers perceive and interpret a brand based on their experience, interactions, and overall impressions of a brand. Brand perception can be measured and refined through research and assist with messaging and communication for marketing purposes and overall customer experience. You can use the market research methods previously outlined with a steer toward exploring the brand. You can use surveys, interviews, and focus groups for brand perception research. It is

good to have brand assets available to present to participants after exploring the customer needs of the problem space in more detail.
— **Market Segmentation:** Assessing market segmentation helps you understand your customers better, refine your marketing strategies, and identify opportunities for growth and product improvements. Collect data from sales data, customer surveys, customer interviews and keep monitoring it.

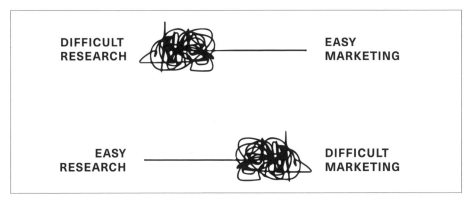

DIFFICULT RESEARCH — EASY MARKETING

EASY RESEARCH — DIFFICULT MARKETING

Zidaru, J. (2023) Difficult Research and Easy Marketing, LinkedIn

User Engagement and Behaviour

With a digital product, you can understand your customers and users more through platforms like Hotjar, Amplitude, Google Analytics and Segment. Engagement and behaviour can be measured with metrics and give a good insight into user behaviour, user interaction, and whether the product is being used as intended or designed.

— **Google Analytics** can measure engagement with your website, such as how long is spent on the page and page views.
— **Hotjar** has heatmaps to allow you to see the hot spots on your website, have recordings of how people use the website and may provide more insights around survey feedback.
— **Amplitude** allows marketers to get data from a 'behavioural layer' to understand more about users. This can be from how they interact with the application, cross-platform tracking and real-time analytics. It provides deep analytics for product development strategy.
— **Segment** is a customer data hub that collects data and has business tools to make using the data more accessible.
— **MixPanel** is an analytics platform for deeper analytics on site usage, to understand where customers are getting lost, and to run experiments to resolve the issues.

UX Audit and Benchmarking

The UX Audit is a comprehensive evaluation of a product and service's user experience with a review of the interface, interaction design, information architecture, content and visual design, analysis of usage data and usability metrics. The aim is to uncover pain points and friction in the user experience and provider recommendations. These can be conducted periodically to evaluate the UX.

"UX benchmarking is the evaluation of a product or service's user experience by using metrics to gauge its relative performance against a meaningful standard" (NN/g)

UX Benchmarking can evaluate the usability, effectiveness, and overall user experience by comparing it to predetermined standards, competitors, or previous product versions. Its purpose is to identify areas of improvement, track progress over time and inform any upgrades.

There are two types of UX benchmarking: 1) **Competitive benchmarking** to compare a product or service to a similar product or service offered by the competitor to identify industry standards and best practices and identify opportunities to differentiate and improve the user experience; 2) **Iterative benchmarking** involves comparing the previous versions to the current version to measure progress and identify if it's moving in the right direction for usability and user satisfaction.

Google's HEART is a framework used to measure and evaluate a digital product or service's user experience (UX). It stands for Happiness, Engagement, Adoption, Retention and Task Success. Each component of the HEART framework provides specific metrics and insights to assess different aspects of the user experience.

— **Happiness:** Users' overall satisfaction, enjoyment and subjective well-being, and is measured by surveys, feedback ratings or sentiment analysis to understand emotional response.
— **Engagement:** This measures user involvement, interaction and active participation with a product or service. The metrics measure time spent, frequency of visits or user actions (clicks, shared, comments) which can indicate the depth and quality of engagement.
— **Adoption:** Adoption evaluates the extent users are willing to adopt and use a product or feature. The metrics include user sign-ups, account creations or initial usage indicating the level of adoption and interest in the product.
— **Retention:** This assesses the ability of a product or service to retain users over time. Metrics such as user churn rate, active user rate, or repeated visits are measured to help understand user loyalty and long-term engagement.
— **Task Success:** Measures how well users can accomplish their goals and complete tasks within the product or service. Metrics to evaluate this include

task completion rate, error rates, or time to complete a task, as they provide insights into the usability and effectiveness of the user interface.

This framework enables product teams to assess and track the user experience across various dimensions. By monitoring and analysing these metrics, product teams can identify areas for improvement, prioritise design and functionality enhancements and make data-driven decisions to enhance the overall user experience.

Marketing Analytics

The marketing team is likely to have metrics and analytics in place to measure marketing activities such as:

— **Cost Per Acquisition (CPA):** Total cost of acquiring a new customer through a specific marketing channel or campaign, calculated by dividing the total marketing spend by the number of customers acquired.
— **Percentage of Market Share:** Market share represents the percentage of an industry's total sales that a particular company or product holds, calculated by dividing the company's or product's sales by the total sales in the industry.
— **Cost Per Lead (CPL):** Measures the cost of generating a potential customer or lead through a marketing campaign, calculated by dividing the total marketing spend by the number of leads generated. Quality of leads is essential to ensure the investment in marketing efforts results in actual conversions.
— **Conversion Rate:** The percentage of users who complete a desired action (e.g., purchase, sign-up, download) out of the total number of users who visit a website, app, or landing page.
— **Click Through Rate (CTR):** The percentage of users who click on a specific link or advertisement out of the total number of users who view the link or ad, typically used to measure the effectiveness of online marketing campaigns.
— **Page Views:** Total number of times users have viewed a specific web page, often used to measure the popularity or effectiveness of website content.
— **Bounce Rate:** Percentage of users who leave a website after viewing only one page, often used as an indicator of the quality or relevance of a website's content and user experience.
— **Share of Voice (SOV):** A metric that represents a brand's or product's visibility or presence in a given market or media channel, typically calculated by comparing the brand's or product's advertising or mentions to those of its competitors.
— **Email Metrics:** Open rate, conversion rate and churn rate
— **Search Engine Optimisation (SEO) metrics:** Keyword rankings, indexed pages and referring websites (backlinks).
— **Pay Per Click (PPC):** Cost Per Click (CPC), Impressions and Cost Per Sale (CPS).
— **Social Media Metrics:** Applause rate, Return on Engagement (ROE) and post reach.
— **Website metrics:** Traffic sources, time on site and unique visitors.

Proof Points For Growth And Traction

Investors may be seeking proof that there is traction in the market and may seek metrics to measure this in various ways:

— **Run Rate Total Revenue:** This is an annual projection of a company's current revenue, calculated by multiplying the current monthly or quarterly revenue by 12 or 4, respectively.
— **Run Rate Total Revenue Growth:** An annual projection of a company's revenue growth based on the current growth rate observed in monthly or quarterly revenue figures.
— **Average Order Size/Number Of Subscriptions:** Refers to the average value of each purchase or order made by customers, while the number of subscriptions represents the total count of active subscribers for a subscription-based product or service.
— **Run-Rate Total Annual Recurring Revenue (Arr):** An annual projection of a company's recurring revenue, typically calculated by multiplying the current monthly recurring revenue by 12.
— **Year on Year Revenue Growth:** The percentage change in a company's revenue from one year to the next, typically used to measure and compare financial performance over time.
— **Gross Margin:** A measure of a company's profitability, calculated as the difference between total revenue and the cost of goods sold (COGS), expressed as a percentage of total revenue.
— **Monthly Gross Churn:** The percentage of customers or subscribers who cancel or discontinue their subscription in a given month, typically used to measure customer retention and satisfaction.
— **Monthly Recurring Revenue (MRR) Net Retention:** A metric that measures the change in MRR from existing customers over time, accounting for both expansion revenue (upsells and upgrades) and revenue lost due to churn.
— **LTV:CAC:** A ratio is a measure of the return on investment for customer acquisition, calculated by dividing the average lifetime value of a customer (LTV) by the average cost of acquiring a new customer (CAC).

Metrics For The Growth Strategy

The chosen growth strategy will influence the metrics and tests needed to learn user and customer behaviour. Businesses may take a **Sales-Led Growth** (SLG), **Marketing-Led Growth** (MLG) and **Product-Led Growth** (PLG) approach. **Sales-Led Growth** relies on dedicated sales teams to generate leads, build relationships, and close deals. **Marketing-Led Growth** has marketing at the core of generating leads, creating brand awareness, and nurturing prospects through the sales funnel. For **Product-Led Growth** businesses, the focus is on the product itself for driving customer acquisition, retention, and expansion. The PLG approach identifies the product's value, user experience and ease of use as priorities, making it easier for customers to discover, try and adopt the product. A typical PLG approach includes offering a freemium model, focusing on user onboarding, and providing a self-service model.

The key metrics that PLG companies may track are:

— **Monthly Active Users (MAU):** A metric that represents the number of unique users who engage with a product or service at least once a month.
— **Net Promoters Score:** The Net Promoter Score (NPS) is a popular method for collecting customer feedback. The NPS has one question, 'How likely are you to recommend this (product or service) to a friend or colleague?' Then there is a scale of 0-10 where calculations are made to break responses into three areas: Promoters (9-10), Passives (7-8) unlikely to refer and Detractors (0-6). It keeps track of how well you do over a more extended period. However, the NPS has flaws (Spool, 2017), as the score doesn't mean much on its own and could be harmful if relied on too heavily.
— **Weekly Active Users (WAU):** Reflects the number of unique users who interact with a product or service at least once within a given week.
— **Daily Active Users (DAU):** Represents the number of unique users who engage with a product or service at least once within a given day.
— **Activation Point(s):** Specific actions or moments when users first experience the value of a product or service, leading to increased engagement and retention.
— **DAU/MAU Ratio:** A measure of user engagement calculated by dividing the number of daily active users by the number of monthly active users, with higher ratios indicating more frequent user engagement.
— **Features Scoring:** A method used to analyse and evaluate the importance of various features within a product or service.
— **Customer Lifetime Value:** Predicts the total value a customer will bring to a business over their lifetime, based on their interactions with specific product features.

This chapter has provided a broad overview of the questions to ask customers and users and metrics to use to assess whether a product in the market, whether newly in the market or established, is meeting customer and user needs. This chapter viewed the evaluation of meeting customer and user needs from different perspectives from the marketing team to the product team. The next chapter will focus on the product management aspect, where there is some cross-over with the continuous feedback and measures outlined here.

15

Continuous User Feedback

Introduction

Now that the product is available in the market, and we have feedback mechanisms in place we will provide a brief overview of Agile and product management from a research perspective. Ongoing research is an integral part of product management and development.

Agile and sprint planning

Agile is an iterative and flexible project management framework that delivers customer value through continuous improvement and collaboration. It emphasises adaptability, responsiveness to change, and close collaboration between cross-functional teams. Agile methodologies, such as Scrum, Kanban, and Lean, have gained popularity across various industries for their ability to handle complex and evolving projects effectively.

Sprint planning is a critical component of Agile, specifically in the Scrum framework. It is a time-boxed event where the Scrum team comes together to plan and prioritise the work to be completed in the upcoming sprint, which is a fixed period, typically ranging from one to four weeks. Sprint planning aims to define a clear sprint backlog, tasks for the current sprint a set of user stories or tasks the team commits to completing within the sprint.

Agile and sprint planning are integral components of product management, and they work together to support the successful development and delivery of a product.

Product management and continuous user feedback

Product management is crucial in establishing a clear product strategy, vision, and direction. This involves gathering requirements and continuous feedback and refinement. Various professionals can carry out these tasks, including entrepreneurs, product managers, UX designers, and UX researchers. It's important to note that the product team is responsible for ongoing discovery and research activities.

The product strategy helps product teams develop a clear vision for their product's long-term goals. This involves conducting ongoing research on the market and users, identifying opportunities for improvement, and getting continuous customer feedback. The product needs to align strategically with the company's Objectives and Key Results (OKRs) and overall vision.

A product roadmap is a plan that outlines the main milestones of product development, such as new features and updates. It helps prioritise initiatives, a specific project or action taken to achieve strategic goals related to a product, and manage stakeholder expectations.

Product managers continue to gather and analyse customer feedback, usage data and market trends to inform ongoing product improvements and enhancements. This means working with customer support and success teams to address issues and find opportunities for optimisation and tracking and analysing KPIs to measure the product's success to meet its goals using this as a data-driven approach to decision-making and prioritisation of future updates.

This feedback drives further requirements from stakeholders, research, and customers to refine and improve the product. This includes creating the outputs mentioned earlier, such as user stories, use cases, and functional specifications, to outline the features and capabilities for the development team.

Putting the requirements into action means working closely with the developers and designers so the product keeps improving from user feedback on the market. Product managers work with UX/UI designers to create wireframes, mock-ups and prototypes that illustrate the product's look, feel and functionality. During this phase, product teams can use iterative design and user testing to fine-tune and validate concepts. Product managers can collaborate with Quality Assurance teams to plan and execute product testing, identifying, and resolving any bugs to ensure the final product meets our high-quality standards before its release.

Product managers may be responsible for or work with the marketing and sales team for launch and go-to-market. They plan and execute product launches by coordinating with marketing, sales, and support teams to develop marketing materials, sales tools, and customer support capabilities. This includes pricing, distribution channels and marketing strategies.

There are also crucial soft skills which are stakeholder management and leadership skills. Ensuring all stakeholders, including sales, marketing, and engineering, are aligned with the product vision, strategy, and priorities. Effective communication and collaboration are essential. To create safe spaces, product managers create psychological safety. Edmondson's book *The Fearless Organisation* defines this as *"A shared belief held by members of a team that the team is safe for interpersonal risk-taking".* An organisation built on psychological safety where people feel safe to take risks, experiment, critique and ask questions provides an environment where innovation and development are more likely to occur and successful product management.

By integrating Agile and sprint planning with product management practices, teams can create a customer-centric approach to product development, ensure alignment with business goals, and maintain responsiveness to changing market conditions. This iterative process facilitates delivering valuable products to customers more frequently and ultimately contributes to overall product success.

The democratisation of research for product development

The democratisation of research for product development is an approach that means anyone in a business can deliver user or UX research, no matter their role. For product managers, it can have benefits such as having equal voices within organisations from multiple perspectives and increasing UX maturity as the user is the focus across the business. Product managers, UX Designers or User Researchers in the team that are experienced or qualified in doing research could coach and mentor others to conduct research.

However, there are some challenges with the democratisation of research with users, which is that there will be different skill levels, which may impact the quality of insights. NN/g is the Nielsen Norman Group, an American computer user interface and user experience consulting firm. It outlines that good research requires time and involves many aspects, including choosing the best method for the project's goals, keeping participants' information safe and turning observations into insights that shape design.

It's essential to upskill those that want to do research but have little experience, as there can be harmful by-products such as underestimating the value of research training and experience, poor research means poor design, a lack of accountability for research, misuse of resources and stunted growth in UX maturity. NN/g suggest using VISE: Viable, Influential, Sound and Efficient of user research.

Viable is where research is mature, ongoing, and part of the culture, meaning the research benefits are tracked, respected, and communicated. **Influential**

means that research insights drive ideas and changes with leader support, and researchers are referred to regularly for support. **Sound** refers to clear and purposeful research questions and the most appropriate research methods are used. The insights represent what was observed, and research participants are treated ethically and fairly. **Efficient** means there are systems and processes for planning, conducting, and analysing research and tracking insights. Project schedules include time for research and running multiple rounds on one design.

Even if the approach to UX research is democratised, it needs to be strategic. Jared Spool (2023) argues that UX Leaders need to drive strategic UX research, not for validation work, but for innovation-generating work. If businesses assume that UX research is for validation only, which implies checking or proving something, it means that research is bought in too late when design decisions have already been made. Investing in research means bringing in researchers early in the process to create products and services more likely to meet user needs for innovative products and services.

Avoid the 'Build Trap'

Melissa Perri (2018) wrote *Build Trap* in product development. The build trap is a common pitfall where a product development team becomes overly focused on continuously building and adding new product features without adequately considering customer needs, market feedback, or the product's overall strategy.

Characteristics of the build trap include a feature-centric approach where the team prioritises building new features based on internal preferences or assumptions rather than customer feedback or validated market needs. Features are added without properly validating whether they align with the product vision, solve real customer problems, or contribute to the product's success. The team does not gather user feedback or conduct iterative testing to learn from user behaviour and refine the product accordingly. The product becomes bloated with excessive features, which may overwhelm users and make the user experience less intuitive and user-friendly. Constantly adding new features without a clear strategy may lead to longer development cycles, delaying the product's time-to-market. Resources are consumed on building features that may not be relevant or add significant value to the product.

Product teams should prioritise customer needs and gather feedback to avoid falling into the build trap to ensure new features align with real user problems. Focus on value by concentrating on features that bring the most value to customers and the product's overall strategy. Then, continuously assess market trends, competition, and customer expectations to stay relevant and competitive. If product teams use data-driven decision-making, they rely on data and user insights to validate assumptions and make informed decisions about feature development. Product teams can benefit from embracing iterative development to conduct regular testing to receive user feedback for continuous improvement.

By avoiding the build trap and adopting a more strategic and customer-centric approach to product development, teams can create products that better meet customer needs, achieve higher user satisfaction, and stay competitive.

In this chapter, we explored Agile, sprint planning and product management and considered democratised research as an approach to receive feedback. To summarise the need for product teams to continue prioritising customer needs in building products and iterating existing products, we discussed the build trap so as not to focus too heavily on delivery. The next chapter will focus on stakeholder buy-in as product development is a team sport. Keeping stakeholders engaged is important, particularly if taking a data-driven, user-led, research-orientated approach.

16

Stakeholder Buy-In to Get Support to Do Research

"The most dangerous phrase in the English language: 'We've always done it this way.'" (Grace Hopper)

Introduction

In this chapter, we discuss the reasons why stakeholders can be opposed to research and want to focus on the build order we mentioned earlier in the book stakeholder buy-in can avoid customer feedback and testing occurring late in the product development process.

Show the benefits of research to stakeholders

If you work in an SME or larger organisation, you may face resistance from different organisational stakeholders to take a user-led, research-focused approach to product development. Common reasons for not wanting to do research are:

— **Assumption of knowledge**: Product teams may assume that they already understand the market and user needs and therefore feel that research is unnecessary. Another word for this is guessing.
— **Time constraints**: Product teams may be pressured to deliver a product quickly, making it challenging to allocate time for research.
— **Budget constraints**: Research can be expensive, especially if it involves hiring external consultants or conducting extensive user testing.
— **Lack of expertise**: Product teams may not have the necessary research skills and expertise to conduct effective research.
— **Fear of disrupting the creative process**: Some product teams may feel that research can stifle creativity and distract teams.
— **Lack of awareness**: Some product teams may not fully understand the value of research or be aware of the various available research methods.

Erika Hall (2013) outlines the main objections to doing research:

— *"There isn't enough time."*
— *"We know everything we need to know."*

— *"We'll find out what we need to once we launch the Beta version."*
— *"The CEO decides what we do."*
— *"We don't have the expertise or budget."*

What this means is:
— *"I can't be bothered to do research."*
— *"I'm worried I'll find out I'm wrong."*
— *"I don't want to talk to people about my product."*

Businesses and product teams not conducting research can lead to several issues during product development, including creating a product that does not meet user needs or does not have a market fit. In the long run, these issues can lead to wasted resources, lost revenue, and damage to the company's reputation. Problems can arise that show there has been some guesswork about customer or user needs. Failing to meet customer needs has consequences such as poor marketing, high number of complaints, low sales, high stock levels and low profits. Not understanding customer needs can have financial implications for a business.

— **Poor product-market fit:** A lack of understanding of the target and customer needs can lead to a weak solution being made that does not have a clear purpose or value proposition as the market need itself is unclear.
— **Poor sales:** If a business doesn't understand what its customers need and want, it may not offer desirable products or services. This can lead to poor sales and revenue.
— **Wasted resources:** If a business doesn't understand its customer needs, it may waste resources developing and marketing products that don't meet customer needs. This can result in wasted time, money, and effort.
— **Complaints:** The product may be challenging to use or understand due to poor product design or quality. This could lead to a high number of complaints.
— **High churn rate:** Customers are likelier to be loyal to businesses that meet their needs and provide excellent customer service. If a company doesn't understand its customer's needs, it may not be able to provide the level of service that customers expect, leading to a lack of loyalty.
— **Lack of innovation and differentiation:** Businesses that don't understand customer needs may miss opportunities to innovate and create new products or services that meet customer needs. This can make it challenging to stay competitive in the marketplace.

These symptoms of poor Product-Market Fit have negative consequences for businesses. Dr Ari Zelmanow (2023) explains how UX research can give companies what they want rather than what they need to hear, leading to effects such as mass layoffs and confusion about what UX Research does for a business.

Therefore, it is crucial for business to understand the benefits of research and to find ways to incorporate it into their product development process, even if it requires additional time and resources at the start.

The high ROI of good research

UX research can reduce the technical development time of a project from 50% to 33%, showing that there can be a tangible saving (U-Sentric, 2016). Forrester Research found that, on average, every dollar invested in UX brings $100 in return, which is an ROI of 9,900%. In addition, *"A rule of thumb is for every one dollar invested in User Experience research, you save $10 in development and $100 in post-release maintenance."* (Karat in Dam, 2021)

"A one-fourth delay in the amount of time it takes to bring a product to market results in a 50-per cent loss of that product's profit. In software, where about 5 per cent of features are used 95 per cent of the time, UX can enhance the focus on feature sets and dramatically improve the outcome" (Dam, 2021)

The research seeks to find unserved and unspoken needs to help create breakthrough ideas for innovation. Henry Ford said, *"If I'd ask customers what they wanted, they would've told me a faster horse."*

Research can provide a significant return on investment and ultimately help your business succeed in the long run. If you need to generate a business case for doing research internally, the benefits of doing research are as follows:

— **Identify customer needs:** Research can help you better understand your customers' needs, preferences, and pain points. By conducting market research and customer surveys, you can gain insights into what your customers want and need, which can help you create products and services that better meet their requirements.
— **Mitigate risk:** Developing a new product or service is always risky. Research can help you identify potential risks and opportunities before investing significant resources into development. This can help reduce the likelihood of developing products that do not have a market fit or face unexpected challenges during development.
— **Improve product development:** Research can provide valuable insights into product design, functionality, and usability. By conducting user testing and gathering feedback, you can improve your product development process and create products that better meet customer needs and preferences.
— **Competitor analysis:** Research can help you understand your competition,

including their strengths, weaknesses, and market positioning. This can help you identify opportunities for differentiation and create products that stand out from your competitors.

— **Increase revenue:** By creating products that better meet customer needs and preferences, you can increase your revenue and profitability. Additionally, you can expand your business and capture new revenue streams by identifying new product or service opportunities.

Research should not be something that stakeholders necessarily are asked about specifically, but it should be part of an established process such as Jobs-To-Be-Done, Design Thinking or Lean Start-up and done early on. Cindy Alvarez argues the research death cycle happens due to undervalued research that isn't impactful to the organisation.

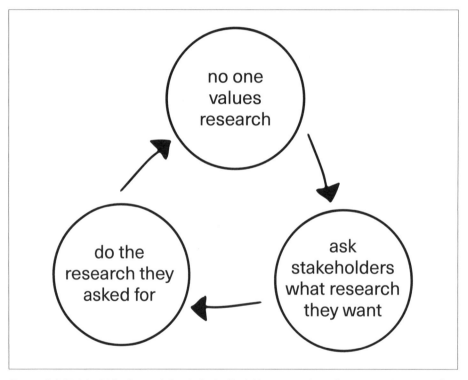

Alvarez, C. (2021) Avoid the Research Death Cycle, CindyAlvarez.com: https://www.cindyalvarez.com/avoid-the-research-death-cycle/

Stakeholder management in innovation and product development

Getting stakeholder buy-in to enable teams to undertake research and gather evidence before embarking on product development can be challenging. There is a stigma attached to research. Research can be viewed as expensive, time-consuming, and pointless. I like to challenge this and encourage directors and business owners to ask three simple questions to their customers and users: 'What is going well?', 'What's not going well?' and 'What could we improve?' and see what they get back. Those sceptical are often surprised by how insightful their customers are and how customers and users have needs key stakeholders such as directors or business owners never knew about and they typically learn something new that was useful to them.

Effective stakeholder management is crucial for ensuring buy-in for research, and maximising the chances of successful adoption and market acceptance.

The first step is to identify and map the relevant stakeholders. Stakeholders may include internal stakeholders such as executives, managers, and employees and external stakeholders such as customers, suppliers, and partners. Once stakeholders are identified, it's essential to understand their needs, expectations, and goals related to the product or innovation. This involves conducting interviews, surveys, focus groups, or other feedback mechanisms to gather insights and prioritise stakeholder requirements.

Regular and effective communication is essential for engaging stakeholders throughout innovation and product development. This includes sharing progress updates, insights from users, seeking feedback, and addressing concerns. Stakeholders may require tailored communication approaches like reports, presentations, workshops, or one-on-one meetings. Building positive and collaborative relationships with stakeholders helps establish trust, credibility, and a sense of shared ownership in the project. This can be achieved through open and transparent communication, active listening, and demonstrating responsiveness to stakeholder input.

Stakeholders have varying degrees of influence and impact on the success of an innovation or product. Assessing their level of power and influence helps prioritise engagement efforts and allocate resources accordingly. High-influence stakeholders may require more dedicated attention, while low-influence stakeholders may need periodic updates.

"Those tough conversations happen all the time. Product managers often have to say no to requests from customers and colleagues and even the big boss." (Ron Yang)

Inevitably, conflicts or disagreements may arise among stakeholders during the innovation and product development process. Address disputes promptly by facilitating open dialogue and finding mutually acceptable solutions. Mediation or negotiation techniques may be employed to resolve conflicts and maintain positive stakeholder relationships. Stakeholder management is an ongoing process that requires continuous engagement and proactive monitoring of stakeholder

dynamics. Regularly reassessing stakeholder needs and expectations and adapting communication strategies helps maintain stakeholder alignment and support throughout the product life cycle.

This chapter explored stakeholder management from a research buy-in perspective, as there is some reticence to wanting to talk to customers and users throughout the product development process. However, there is significant evidence that this approach works and can reduce risk product development if research is done correctly and be a good investment for the business.

17

The Business Case to Make a Strategically Aligned Product

Introduction

In this chapter, we will discuss the business side of creating products and services. Researching early-stage ideas can be risky, so it is important to justify the investment and have a plan for the return on investment and profitability. Understanding the company's strategy, assessing its capabilities to pursue an idea, and evaluating the business case can help product and business decisions align. This can also increase stakeholder buy-in, particularly if a Design Thinking approach is needed from the beginning.

Company Strategy

A company's mission, values and vision provide a clear direction and purpose for the business. They guide the business's and its employees' decision-making, actions, and behaviours. When a company has a clear understanding of its mission, values, and vision, these three elements can help to ensure that the business is focused on meeting the needs and wants of its customers. By aligning the company's goals with the needs and wants of its customers, a business can avoid having to guess what its customers want and instead create products and services that align with its mission, values, and vision. This can help the business to build a strong relationship with its customers and increase its chances of success in the long term.

Strategic roadmaps are visual tools that help organisations plan and communicate their strategic initiatives over time. They are a way to align the company's goals and objectives with its overall strategy, and they provide a high-level view of how the organisation plans to achieve those goals.

A strategic roadmap typically includes the following:

— **Objectives and Goals:** These are the high-level outcomes that the organisation hopes to achieve.
— **Initiatives**: These are the specific actions or projects the organisation plans to undertake to achieve its goals.

- **Timeline:** This is a visual representation of when each initiative will begin and end and could be over a one, three or five-year period.
- **Key Performance Indicators (KPIs)** will measure progress and success.
- **Resource Allocation:** This is an overview of the resources allocated to each initiative, including budget, staff, and other resources.

By providing a clear and concise overview of an organisation's strategic plan, a strategic roadmap can help align stakeholders, communicate progress, and provide a framework for decision-making. Aligning innovative projects with company objectives and principles is critical for prioritising and strategically choosing.

"Stay stubborn on vision, but flexible on the detail" (Jeff Bazos)

Strategic roadmaps and Objectives and Key Results (OKRs) are two complementary tools used in strategic planning and execution within organisations. They are interconnected and support each other in achieving the organisation's goals and objectives. Strategic roadmaps provide the overarching vision and direction for the organisation, while OKRs break down these strategic goals into specific, measurable, and time-bound objectives. Together, they provide a powerful framework for aligning efforts, tracking progress, and achieving success in pursuing the organisation's strategic vision.

Objective and Key Results (OKR) is a proven method developed by John Doerr for helping companies grow. It is a quarterly goal-setting method with two parts:

- **Objective:** A qualitative goal about what you want to achieve and improve
- **Key Results:** A quantitative measure to define how you'll know if you reach the Objective.

OKRs need momentum and leadership behind them. The OKRs encompass all business projects and plans that aim to achieve the Objectives, which determine what needs to be done, how to measure these through Key Results and what should be prioritised. To keep track of progress, weekly check-ins are conducted to identify what has been accomplished and what everyone will be working on next. All the OKRs are typically reviewed quarterly to identify if they are 'stretch goals', which means the objectives should be challenging the teams. The North Star goal is the crucial vision that the company is striving towards, and the OKRs developed are aligned with this objective.

THE LEMONADE VAN
STRATEGY

Sam wants to develop her business strategy and below the foundations of the strategy and reasons for starting the business through outlining her motivation, vision, mission, and values.

Motivation

I am very passionate about fresh lemonade, which reminds me of my childhood when my mother made lemonade in the summer. My mother had a secret recipe which she entrusted to me. The Lemonade Van is a personal journey for me. As a child, I used to run lemonade stands but want to make create a sustainable business from it.

Vision

To make fresh, homemade premium lemonade convenient in my local area and easily available at events and deliverable to customer homes.

Mission

We promote a healthy lifestyle by providing a natural, refreshing alternative to sugary drinks.

Values

Our values are:

— **Sustainability**: For our produce to be grown sustainably, which is kind to the planet, and to deliver products using the most eco-friendly vans available.
— **Ethical:** Our processes and systems support a fair, kind, and transparent way of working.
— **Quality:** The produce is grown in the best conditions possible, reducing the use of pesticides. We deliver a high level of customer service.
— **Innovation:** We stay innovative and keep pushing to stay ahead in our work practices, customer experience and sustainability.

Business Model Canvas for the validated business idea

The Business Model Canvas is a strategic tool entrepreneurs, start-ups, and established businesses use to create, refine, and communicate their business models. Alexander Osterwalder and Yves Pigneur (2010) developed the canvas in their book *Business Model Generation*.

The canvas consists of nine building blocks, which are used to describe, design, and evaluate a business model:

1. **Customer Segments:** The groups of people or organisations that a business aims to serve.
2. **Value Propositions:** The products or services that a business offers to its customers.
3. **Channels:** The methods through which a business delivers its value proposition to its customers.
4. **Customer Relationships:** The types of relationships that a business establishes and maintains with its customers.
5. **Revenue Streams:** The sources of revenue that a business generates from its customers.
6. **Key Resources:** The assets, skills, and capabilities that a business requires to create and deliver its value proposition.
7. **Key Activities:** The core activities that a business must perform to deliver its value proposition.
8. **Key Partners:** The external partners that a business relies on to deliver its value proposition.
9. **Cost Structure:** The costs that a business incurs to create and deliver its value proposition.

The steps for using the Business Model Canvas are as follows:

— **Define the problem or opportunity:** The first step is to identify the problem or opportunity that your business aims to address.
— **Identify customer segments:** Next, identify the groups of people or organisations that your business aims to serve.
— **Define value propositions:** Determine the products or services that your business will offer to its customers.
— **Design channels:** Identify the methods through which your business will deliver its value proposition to its customers.
— **Develop customer relationships:** Determine the types of relationships your business will establish and maintain with its customers.

— **Define revenue streams:** Identify the sources of revenue that your business will generate from its customers.
— **Identify essential resources:** Determine the assets, skills, and capabilities that your business will require to create and deliver its value proposition.
— **Determine key activities:** Identify the core activities that your business must perform to deliver its value proposition.
— **Identify key partners:** Determine the external partners that your business will rely on to deliver its value proposition.
— **Define cost structure**: Identify the costs that your business will incur to create and deliver its value proposition.

The Business Model Canvas can be used to provide an overview of your product idea by defining its business model and areas of improvement, understanding operations, and making informed decisions about strategy.

This exercise can be repeated once more insights about the customers, markets, and bigger picture come to light. Plus, it can be the basis of the business case and accessing the business model value propositions for its viability, feasiability and deliverability.

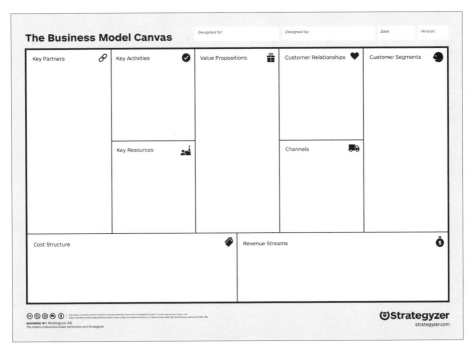

Strategyzer AG. The Business Model Canvas, Strategyzer: Licenced under the Creative Commons Attribution-Share Alike 3.0 Un-ported Licence: https://www.strategyzer.com/resources/canvas-tools-guides

THE LEMONADE VAN
BUSINESS MODEL CANVAS:
EVENTS VALUE PROPOSITION

Sam will use the Business Model Canvas, to understand the critical elements of The Lemonade Van's business model, including the customer segments, value proposition, channels, customer relationships, and revenue streams. The Business Model Canvas also helps identify the essential resources, activities, partners, and costs for the mobile lemonade van to succeed. Overall, the Business Model Canvas provides a comprehensive overview of the mobile lemonade van's business model and helps ensure that all critical aspects of the business are aligned with the company's overall strategy and goals.

— **Customer Segments:** Health-conscious individuals, parents with young children, event attendees.
— **Value Proposition:** Providing healthy and unique fresh lemonade conveniently.
— **Channels**: Social media, word of mouth, online ads, event sponsorships.
— **Customer Relationships:** Personalised service, high-quality organic ingredients for customers.
— **Revenue Streams:** Sales of lemonade at events.
— **Key Resources:** Organic fruit and ingredient suppliers, Electric Vehicle (food van), staff.
— **Key Activities:** Lemonade preparation, event planning and service delivery.
— **Key Partners**: Organic fruit and ingredient suppliers, event organisers.
— **Cost Structure:** Lemonade ingredients, van maintenance, marketing expenses, salary for Sam.
— **Revenue Streams:** Sales of lemonade at events.

McKinsey 7-S Model: Identify capabilities in the business

The McKinsey 7-S framework is a management framework developed by consulting firm McKinsey & Company. It provides a holistic view of an organisation and helps analyse and align various internal elements to achieve effective organisational performance. The 7-S framework can be used to identify critical capabilities available to support the development of the product or service.

Strategy	Build a solid market position and have a competitive advantage	· What is our strategy? · How do we intend to achieve our objectives? · How do we deal with competitive pressure? · How are changes in customer demands dealt with? · How is strategy adjusted for environmental issues?
Structure	How the business is organised and reporting structures	· How is the company/team divided? · What is the hierarchy? · How do the various departments coordinate activities? · How do the team members organise and align themselves? · Is decision-making centralised or decentralised? Is this as it should be, given what we're doing? · Where are the lines of communication? Explicit or implicit?
Systems	Activities and processes to complete tasks	· What are the main systems that run the organisation? Consider financial and HR systems, as well as communications and document storage. · Where are the controls, and how are they monitored and evaluated? · What internal rules and processes does the team use to keep on track?
Shared Values	Core values of the organisation	· What are the organisation's core values? · What is its corporate/team culture like? · How strong are the values? · What fundamental values was the company/team built on?
Skills	Employee and team skills and capabilities	· What are the most vital skills represented within the company/team? · Are there any skill gaps? · What is the company/team known for doing well? · Do the current employees/team members have the ability to do the job? · How are skills monitored and assessed?

Style	The leadership style of the organisation	· How participative is the management/leadership style? · How effective is that leadership? · Do employees/team members tend to be competitive or cooperative? · Are real teams functioning within the organisation or just nominal groups?
Staff	The employees and skills	· What positions or specialisations are represented within the team? · What positions need to be filled? · Are there gaps in required competencies?

Behind successful products are organisations built well, with these seven areas covered to ensure a clear vision, mission and strategy, strong leadership team, quality product, concise marketing messages, excellent financial understanding and management and an infrastructure for continuous learning.

The 7-S Model can be used to consider the product from a business perspective:

— **Strategy**: How does this product fit with the business strategy? How does it help to achieve business objectives? Is this idea original? Will it help the business to be competitively advantageous? Is it the right time for the market and business to develop the product? What are the customer needs? What exists already to solve the customer needs?
— **Structure:** Are there the processes, resources, and tools to invest in the product? Does the idea fit with the existing product/service range?
— **Systems:** Is it possible to develop this product? What data is available to understand customers?
— **Shared Values:** Does this product fit with the business values? Is there a culture to support investing in the product?
— **Style:** Will leaders support this product? What is the process to get backing for the product?
— **Staff:** Is there the skill to commercialise the product? Does the team have the experience to support the product? Are the team aligned? Can the team deal with unknowns and chaos?
— **Skills:** Are the right people or skills available to develop the product? Has the problem been defined in the right way?

Building a business case for executing the solution

You'll likely need to raise funding or justify the budget for the building or further development of the product. It may be a natural point to re-assess the strategic business fit.

The components of a business case are:

— **Strategic Case:** The strategic context and rationale behind the investment needed, how the project (or product development) aligns with organisational objectives, policies: 'Why is this investment needed?'
— **Economic Case:** To assess the project's value for money, to identify, evaluate and compare a wide range of options to determine the most cost-effective and beneficial solution and may include a Cost-Benefit Analysis based on research.
— **Commercial Case:** This is to assess the project's viability from a commercial perspective. This considers the procurement strategy, contracting arrangements, risk allocation and market conditions.
— **Financial Case:** This focuses on the affordability and funding requirements. It includes detailed cost estimates, financial modelling, financial forecasts, and an assessment of the financial risks associated with the project. It should show the affordability within the organisation's budget and the available required funding.
— **Management Case:** This outlines the project's governance, risk management and delivery arrangements. It should show that the organisation can deliver the project successfully and that robust management and control processes are in place.

This chapter considered the business perspective on product development, particularly the company strategy, capabilities, and business case, to consider whether the business can and should build the product or service. Having the company strategy and capabilities clear for product teams can help to ensure that strategically aligned decisions are made for early-stage ideas and developing products.

18

From Slow Research to Fast Research

Throughout the book, we have explored a broad spectrum of research methods. To summarise, slow research takes place at the beginning, as it aims to explore and evaluate abstract, immature ideas, empathise, and understand the user and market needs, and define the problem, to inform strategic decisions about developing a product.

As we move through the product development process, from in-depth, slow, project-based research into fast research, we see quick learning from faster feedback, as we test a more concrete solution that can be put in front of users. These learnings inform the iteration of the product to continuously improve it for it to meet user and business needs.

On the following four pages, there is a table that summarises the research methods and their outcomes across the whole product development process.

Speed and Depth	Product Development Process	Model	Research method	Main Outcome
Slow and steady In-depth research Early-stage ideas Many unknowns and assumptions Abstract	Develop the Idea	Design Thinking	Interviews with users and experts	Understand how users think about a topic and the wider context .
			Focus Groups with users	Get a broad view toward a problem.
			Observation (Ethnography) and field studies	Observe people in their natural settings to understand behaviours and the problem.
			Contextual Inquiry	Understand the thought process to tackling a problem in more detail.
			Secondary analysis of existing data	Insights from data such as key potential customers.
			Desk research for competition analysis and market analysis	Snapshot of the market and industry trends.
			Desk research for SWOT and PESTLE analysis	Wider analysis of internal and external factors influencing the business.
			Small-scale survey	Broad views on a topic without depth.
			Diary study and experience sampling	Understand what influences behaviours.
			Max Diff and Conjoint analysis	Analyse decision making processes and see differences between products.
			Concept testing a low-fidelity prototype test	A reaction to an early-stage idea to evaluate if it has problem-solution fit.
			Co-creation workshop and participatory design	Work with users to develop solutions and understand problems.
			Webscouting and social listening	Have an understanding of feelings and emotions about problems with existing products and services.

Validate the idea	Design Thinking and Open Innovation	Ideation workshops	Generate ideas for potential solutions based on insights.
		Hackathon, open-source development, crowdsourcing	Externally source ideas for solutions to a problem.
		Design Sprints	Quick process for validating ideas through prototypes and user feedback.
	Design Thinking: Low-fidelity prototyping	Five Act Interview	Test the prototype through tasks and understand the context of the problem.
		Mental Model interview	Understand why people do what they do.
		Usability testing	Specific tasks to identify fundamental usability issues.
		Concept testing	Overall value proposition to understand if it addresses the core problem.
		Paper prototype testing	Paper representation of the product to simulate user flows and find issues.
		Card sorting	Group and categorise elements to design the information architecture.
		Cognitive walkthrough	UX expert follows user flow and imitates user to identify usability issues.
		User flow testing	Identify issues with navigation paths.
	Mid-fidelity prototyping	Happy path testing	Understand perspectives on design and way flow is structured.
		Usability testing	Identify usability issues.
		Concept testing and card sorting	As above.
		Clickable prototype testing	Click through interface and navigate to identify task completion.
		Heuristic evaluation	UX expert reviews the prototype against usability principles.
	High-fidelity prototyping	A/B testing	Comparison of two versions to find which one performs best.
		User Acceptance Testing	Validate product features and functionalities.
		First click testing	Evaluate how intuitive the interface is.
		Task analysis	User tasks to be completed to identify gaps in user flow.
		Accessibility testing	Evaluate compliance and issues.
		Usability testing, cognitive walkthrough, heuristic evaluation	As above.

Speed and Depth	Product Development Process	Model	Research method	Main Outcome
Fast Multiple changes a day Concrete solution Data-driven business decisions	Build the product	Design Thinking/ Lean Start-up	Lean experiments on the MVP	Identify market reaction and willingness to pay.
			Closed Beta for the first release Task-level satisfaction scores	Identify bugs, performance issues and product-market fit and task-level satisfaction scores.
			Open Beta for the first release	Evaluate how the product operates in a real-life environment.
			Pilot for the first release	A wider experiment and testing of the product in a real-life setting.
		UX Research	Usability testing, A/B testing, cognitive walkthrough, heuristic evaluation, card-sorting	As above.
			Comprehension testing	Tests UX copy.
			Desirability study	Evaluate the emotional appeal of the product.
			Content inventory	Evaluate all the content on the website.
			Tree testing	Evaluate the effectiveness of the information architecture.
			Task analysis	Understand the cognitive processes involved in completing a task or activity.
			Cognitive Task Analysis	Understand the mental processes such as decision-making process in completing a task.
			Accessibility testing	Ensure the product complies with accessibility guidelines.
		Sprint Planning and Agile	User Acceptance Testing	Evaluate if the software is built to user requirements.
			Smoke tests	Sanity tests to rapidly test for bugs or critical defects.
			Technology Acceptance tests	Evaluate acceptance of the technology across users.

	Release the product	Lean Start-up	Test-level satisfaction for user experience	Evaluate UX of the product.
		Continuous Discovery Habits	Customer interviews Usability testing Lean experiments	Deep understanding of product-market fit and UX.
		UX Research	Customer satisfaction	Scores for evaluating customer experience and ease of use.
	Improve the product	Continuous Discovery Habits	Usability testing Customer interviews	Continuous evaluation where improvements can be made and where bigger innovation opportunities are.
		UX Research Agile/Lean Start-up	Market research and desk research Lean experiments	
		Open Innovation	Market analytics and user engagement and behaviour	Measure user engagement and identify success of sales and marketing.
			Proof points for traction and growth	Provide investors proof of market interest.
			Impact evaluation	Identify the influence the product or service has.

To see it all together again on the diagram we showed you at the start of the book, here is the summary of slow research to fast research.

Abstract — Problem-Solution Fit			Concrete — Product-Market Fit			
Slow research and in-depth feedback			Fast research, feedback and iterations			
Idea development	Explore problem and the context	Define the problem and ideate solutions	Test prototypes of solutions	Validate feasibility, validity and desirability of MVP	Deploy and launch product	Commercialise and continuously test
-Assess the risk -Create assumptions -Identify knowns and unknowns	-Collect data on users and customers to identify needs -Market and competition analysis	-Analysis and synthesis -Define problem -Generate ideas for solutions -Test concepts	-Create prototypes -Run experiments -Refine solution -Test usability -Prioritise core features	-Run experiments -Test usability -Validate the product and market -Identify business model	-Create final product -Test in real-life settings -Product vision and strategy -Product launch	-Continuous discovery -Metrics to measure engagement and uptake -Impact evaluation
Design Thinking			**Lean Start-Up**		**Agile**	

Slow Research to Fast Research, Sharp, C. (2023)

The future of research in product development

We've provided an overview of the research process, and now you may be able to identify where and how AI could assist and make your research processes efficient.

AI tools for doing research

The Artificial Intelligence (AI) industry is rapidly evolving, and ChatGPT4 was recently made available when writing this book. AI can help create ideas and can be used as a tool to help your research. Consider GDPR and data regulations regarding how the tool is used for personal and sensitive data. In addition, these are not research tools and cannot provide accurate persona profiles. They could give you some good ideas about the questions to write in the interview guide and the strategies to use for research design. However, AI is a tool that is not 100% reliable, and ideally, it should be validated with research rather than assuming that the AI output is correct. AI is not a replacement for research but can enhance some aspects of the research process. But be cautious as to which parts of the process you're automating.

At the time of writing, there are several AI tools available to assist us with research:

— **Scite.ai**: Help finds reliable citations.
— **Notably.ai**: Builds a research repository.
— **Looppanel**: Records and transcribes sessions.
— **Sprig**: Identifies common feedback themes for design decisions.
— **Grain**: Generates insights.
— **UserEvaluation**: Identifies key insights and suggests research questions.
— **Synthetic users**: Conducts user research without humans.
— **Kraftful**: Provides AI summaries of user feedback.
— **Checkmyidea-ia**: Validates your business idea.
— **VenturusAI**: Generates feedback on your business concept.
— **RhetorAI**: Helps you achieve product-market fit faster.
— **Validly**: Runs continuous user interviews for product teams.
— **Monterey.ai** – helps organise and action user feedback.

Low-code and no-code AI tools for prototypes and iteration

The rise of low-code and no-code AI tools that aim to simplify application development tasks may lead to the creation of AI solutions for non-technical people. This may not only make software development for some products easier and more accessible, but this could also change how prototyping is used in product development as products may become easier to build. How we run experiments may change and speed up as the way coding develops moving from hundreds of lines of code to a few lines only when we iterate products based on user feedback.

The future for the evolution of the product development process is one that may speed up in some phases, however, the need to understand customer and user needs will always be there to ensure that we make products that matter as they solve problems and make a difference to people's lives.

Thank you

Thank you for taking the time to read this book *Make Products That Matter*. Its purpose is to provide an overview of research in product development for innovative products and development and how to innovate to improve existing products and services. It's a book I wish I had about ten years ago, and I hope it was useful to you.

REFERENCES

References

Accenture (2010) Companies make innovation a priority for growth in aftermath of downturn but management shortcomings hinder results, Accenture

Agile Manifesto (nd), Principles behind the agile manifesto

Airfocus, What is an alpha test? Airfocus

AJ&Smart (nd) Lightning decision jam resource page, AJ&Smart

Alvarez, C. (2021) Avoid the research death cycle, Cindy Alvarez online

Anderson, N. (nd) 3 effective methods for content tests (beyond usability testing), DScout

Anderson, N. (nd) A researcher's guide to mental models (and how to use them wisely), DScout

Anderson, N. (nd) Generative research: A complete guide to running a successful study, DScout

Anderson, N. (nd) Spooky sample sizes: Choosing "The Right" number of research participants, DScout

Andreesen, M. (2007) The only thing that matters (cited Rachleff), PMArchive

Bland, D. (nd) 7 things I've learned about lean start-up, Precoil

Bland, D.J. (2015) 7 things I've learned about lean start-up, Medium

Bland, D.J. (2018) An introduction to experiment pairing, Medium

Blank, S. (2005) The four steps to the epiphany: Successful strategies for products that win, K&S Ranch

Blank, S. (nd) Customer Development, SteveBlank.com

Bradley, S. (2010) Designing for a hierarchy of needs, Smashing Magazine

Brown, T. (2009) Change by design: How design thinking transforms organisations and inspires innovation, HarperBusiness

Buley, L. (2013) The User Experience Team of One: A research and design survival guide, Rosenfield Media

Burghardt, J. (2022) Activating insights to overcome common barriers to product impact, Medium

Busch, C. (2022a) Connect the Dots: The Art and Science of Creating Good Luck, Penguin Life

Busch, C. (2022b) The Science of Good Luck, Nesta

ByteStart (nd) The power of the 'pilot' – 3 reasons you should test your business idea before launch, ByteStart

Cagan, M. (2011) Product discovery with live-data prototypes, svpg

Cagan, M. (2013) The power of reference customers, svpg

Cagan, M. (2015) Product Fail, svpg

Cagan, M. (2015) Root causes of failure, Mind the Product (San Francisco)

Cagan, M. (2017) INSPIRED: How to create tech products customers love, Wiley

Cagan, M. (2018) The root causes of product failure, Mind the Product

Cagan, M. (2019) Product is hard, Mind the Product

Capozucca, P. (2012) Sustainability 2.0: Using sustainability to drive business innovation and growth, Deloitte

Carayannis, E., Acikdilli, G. & Ziemnowicz, C. (2017) Strategic knowledge, serendipity, and arbitrage in action: Examples of new venture formation and growth by region and sector, Academy of International Business - Midwest Chapter Annual Meetings held in conjunction with the MBAA International Conference, Illinois, 31

Carter, J. (2020) How to manage an innovation portfolio, Viima

Carter, T. (2021) The true failure rate of small businesses, Entrepreneur

Cases, 7th Edition, UK: Prentice Hall

Catmull, E. (2014) Insight the Pixar brain trust, Fast Company: Inside The Pixar Braintrust

CB Insights (2021) The top 12 reasons startups fail, CB Insights

Chang, W. (2017) The build order every start-up should follow to become successful, Hackernoon

Chesbrough, H.W. (2003) Open innovation: The new imperative for creating and profiting from technology

Chi, T. (2015) Rapid prototyping and product management by Tom Chi, Mind the Product

Christensen, C.M. (1997) The Innovator's Dilemma: When New Technologies Cause Great Firms to Fail, Harvard Business School Press

Christensen, C.M. (2003) The Innovator's solution: Creating and sustaining successful growth, Harvard Business Review Press

Christensen, C.M., Hall, T., Dillon, K. & Duncan, D.S. (2016) Competing against luck: The story of innovation and customer choice, HarperBus

CIO (2017) Notorious project failures – Google Glass, CIO

Clegg, D., and Barker, R. (1994). Case Method Fast-Track: A RAD Approach. Addison-Wesley

Cohen, W. & Levinthal, D. (1990) Absorptive Capacity: A new perspective on learning and innovation, Administrative Science Quarterly, 35 (1), 128

Croll, A. & Yoskovitz, B. (2013) Lean analytics: Use data to build a better start-up up faster, O'Reilly

D.School (2012) Streamlined Design Thinking Process (Hasso Platnner, Institute of Design), Stanford University

Dam, R.F. (2021) Improve customer experience with UX investments that increase ROI, Interaction design foundation

Dam, R.F. and Siang, T.Y. (2021) What kind of prototype should you create? Interaction Design Foundation

Design Council, What is the framework for innovation?: What is the framework for innovation? Design Council's evolved Double Diamond, Design Council

Dingle, M. (2023) Why I am breaking up with design sprints, Reason

Dodgson, M., Gann, D.M. & Salter, A.M. (2008) The management of technological innovation: Strategy and Practice, Oxford University Press

Doerr, J. (2021) Measure what matters: OKRs – The simple idea that drives 10x growth, Portfolio Penguin

Dror, E. (2019) 9 reasons why we start projects with design sprints, Medium

Eberle, B. (2008) Scamper: Creative games and activities for imagination development, Routledge

Ellis, S. and GoPractice (nd) Product/market fit survey, pmfsurvey.com

Emmel, N. (2008) Toolkit 03: Participatory mapping: An innovative sociological method, Morgan Centre for research into everyday lives, The University of Manchester

Fisher, A. (2019) Adam Fisher on how to navigate the product-market fit journey, Bessemer Venture Partners

Fisher, R. A. (1935) *The Design of Experiments* (9th ed.). Macmillan

Fitzpatrick, R. (2013) The mom test: How to talk to customers and learn if your business is a good idea when everyone is lying to you, CreateSpace Independent Publishing Platform

Forrester Research (2019) The ROI of design thinking: Part 1, overview, Forrester

Franks, M. (2015) Prototyping, Austin Centre for Design: AC4D Design Library

Gartner (2016) Enterprise Architects Combine Design Thinking, Lean Startup and Agile to Drive Digital Innovation, Gartner: https://www.gartner.com/en/documents/3200917

Gochermann, J. and Nee, I. (2019) The idea maturity model – a dynamic approach to evaluate idea maturity, International Journal of Innovation and Technology Management, 16 (5)

Google IO (nd) Accessibility, Product Inclusion and Equity, Google IO

Gothelf, J. and Seiden, J. (2013) Lean UX: Applying lean principles to improve user experience, O'Reilly

Griffin, A., and Hauser, J.R. (1993) The voice of the customer, Marketing science 12(1), Winter

Hall, E. (2013) Just enough research, A Book Apart

Hamel, G. (1996) Strategy as Revolution, Harvard Business Review

Hamel, G. (2000), The search for a new strategic platform. Chartered Management Institute

Hamel, G. (2006) The why, what, and how of management innovation, Harvard Business Review, 84 (2): 72-84, 163

Hengsberger, A. (2019) What is innovation management? Lead Innovation: What is innovation management?

Herbig, T. (2023) Probing questions for navigating the solution space, herbig.co

Hinterhuber, A. and Liozu, S. (2012) Is it time to rethink your pricing strategy? MIT Sloan Management Review

Holliday, B. (2019) Hypotheses in user research and discovery, Leading Service Design,

Holliday, B. (2019) Hypotheses in user research and discovery, Medium

Houde, S., Hill, C., Helander, M.G., Landauer, T.K. & Prabhu, P.V. (1997) The Handbook of Human-Computer Interaction, Elsevier Science

Hubner, S. (2019a) How companies can innovate and scale, Itonics Innovation

Hubner, S. (2019b) 70:20:10 Rule of Innovation, Itonics Innovation

Hubner, S. (2019c) How Companies Can Innovate and Scale, Itonics Innovation

Humphreys, A. (2023) 'The concept of an MVP is crap, here's why', LinkedIn

IBM, Defining user groups, IBM

IBM, Hopes and Fears, IBM

IDEO (2015) Design Kit: The Human-Centred Design Toolkit, IDEO

IDEO (nd) Innovation accounting: What it is and how to get started, IDEO

IDEO, Design kit: Brainstorm rules: Seven little rules that unlock the creative power of a brainstorming session, IDEO

IKEA (2023) Co-creation – working with you to develop better products for life at home, IKEA

Interaction Design Foundation (2021) A simple introduction to Lean UX, Interaction Design Foundation

Interaction Design Foundation (nd) Prototyping, Interaction Design Foundation

Interaction Design Foundation (nd) User Centred Design, Interaction Design Foundation

Interaction Design Foundation (nd) What are Wicked Problems? Interaction Design Foundation

Intercom (nd) Intercom on Jobs-To-Be-Done, Intercom

Johnson, G., Scholes, K. and Whittington, R. (2006) Exploring Corporate Strategy: Text and

Johnson, S. (2011) Where good ideas come from: The seven patterns of innovation, Penguin

Jones, D. (2012) Design for a thriving UX ecosystem, UX Magazine

Jones, N. (2017) MVP Throwback: Airbnb, Fueed

Kano, N., Seraku, N., Takahashi, F. and Tsuji, S. (1984) Attractive quality and must-be quality, Journal of the Japanese Society for Quality Control (in Japanese). 14 (2): 39–48.

Kauffman, S. A. (2000). Investigations. Oxford: Oxford University Press

Kay, G. and Hartmans, A. (2021) Amazon trained Alexa in secret by hiring unsuspecting people to ask questions in a room with hidden prototypes, Business Insider

Keely, L. Ten Types of Innovation: The Discipline of Building Breakthroughs, Doblin

Knapp, J. (2016) How to test prototypes with customers: The five-act interview, Medium

Koçoğlu, I, Akgun, A.E. & Keskin, H. (2015) The Differential Relationship between Absorptive Capacity and Product Innovativeness: A Theoretically Derived Framework, International Business Research 8 (7)

Koller, R.H. (1988) On the source of entrepreneurial ideas, in B.A. Kirchoff, W. Long, W. McMullan, K.H. Vesper and W.E. Wetzel (eds)., Frontiers of Entrepreneurship Research, Wellesley, MA: Babson, pp. 194-207

Kowitz, B., Knapp, J. & Zeratsky, J. (2016) Sprint: How to solve big problems and test new ideas in just five days, Simon & Schuster

Kucheriavey, S. (2015) Good UX is good business: How to reap its benefits, Forbes

Kylliainen, J. (2018) Innovation Strategy – What is it and how to develop one? Viima:

Lafley, A.G. and Martin, R. (2013) Playing to win; How strategy really works, Harvard Business Review Press

Leal-Rodríguez, A.L., Roldán, J.L., Leal, A.G., & Ortega-Gutierrez, J. Knowledge management, relational learning, and the effectiveness of innovation outcomes. The Service Industries Journal, 33(13), 1294–1311, 2013

Lohenchuk, Y. (2019) How to find product/market fit: A practical guide, Medium

MacCarthy, O. (2018) A hypothesis-driven design canvas. For designers, Medium

Market Research Future (2022) Global Lemonade Market Overview, Market Research Future

Marmer, M., Herrmann, B.L., Dogrultan, E. & Berman, R. (2012) Startup Genome report: A new framework for understanding why startups succeed, Startup Genome

Martin, R. (2021) How to develop a strategy that wins in competitive markets, Youtube: Growth Manifesto Podcast

Maurya, A. (2012) Running Lean: Iterate from plan A to a plan that works, O'Reilly

May, M. (2017) The Play-To-Win Strategy Canvas v.3.0, LinkedIn

May, M. (2022) The new playing to win canvas (plus: framework and process!) LinkedIn

McKinsey (2011) Putting strategies to the test, McKinsey

McKinsey (2018) The Business Value of Design, McKinsey

Microsoft Design (nd) Microsoft Inclusive Design Manual, Microsoft

MindTools (nd) McKinsey 7-S Framework, MindTools

Miro (nd) Validation Research/MVP Experiment: Experiment Template, Miro

Monstarlab (nd) When to use the design sprint (and when not to) Monstarlab

Moore, G. (1991) Crossing the Chasm, Harper Business Essentials

Morales, J. (2020) A guide to experience mapping for UX Design, Adobe XD Ideas

Moran, K. (2020) Benchmarking UX: Tracking metrics, Nn/g

NASA (2010) Technology Readiness Levels Demystified, NASA

Neufeld, D. (2021) Long waves: The history of innovation cycles, Visual Capitalist

Newman, D. (nd) The Process of Design Squiggle, The Design Squiggle

NHS England (2021) NHS England: Ladder of engagement and participation, Patient Safety Learning

Nielsen, J. (2000) Why you only need to test with 5 Users, NN/g

Nieminen, J. (2019) Innovation maturity matrix – A model to successful innovation transformation, Viima

Ohr, R.C. (2021) Innovation habits of high-growth companies, LinkedIn

Osterwalder, A. (2015) Validate your ideas with the test card, Strategyzer: Strategyzer - Test card

Osterwalder, A., & Pigneur, Y. (2010). Business Model Generation: A Handbook for Visionaries, Game Changers, and Challengers, John Wiley & Sons.

Osterwalder, A., Pigneur, Y., Bernarda, G., Smith, A. & Papdakos, T. (2014) Value proposition design: How to create products and services customers want, Wiley

Pacheco, J. (2019) The history and nature of user-centred design, Medium

Pernice, K. (2022) Democratize user research in 5 steps, NN/g

Perri, M. (2018) Escaping the build trap: How effective product management creates real value, O'Reilly

Peters, T. J., & Waterman, R. H. (1982). In Search of Excellence: Lessons from America's Best-Run Companies. New York: Harper & Row.

Peterson, RT. (1988) An analysis of new product ideas in small business, Journal of Small Business Management, 26, 25-31

Pham, T. (2018) Brushing away the problem: The Gripper, Medium

Plano, C. (2023) The benefits of encouraging creativity and innovation in the workplace, Startup Nation

Polaine, A., Lølie, L. & Reason, B. (2013) Service Design: From insight to implementation, Rosenfeld Media

Polaine, L. and Reason (2013) Service Design: From insight to implementation. Rosenfeld Media

Porter, M.E. (1979) How competitive forces shape strategy, Harvard Business Review

Porumboiu, D. (2021) What is the 70-20-10 rule of innovation and how do we use it, Viima

Precoil (2023) Assumptions mapping, Precoil

ProductPlan (nd) Opportunity Solution Tree, ProductPlan

Public Health Quality Improvement Encyclopaedia (2012) Ideas Parking Lot Matrix

Qualtrics (nd) The complete guide to idea screening, Qualtrics

Raworth, K. (2017) Doughnut economics: secen ways to think like a 21st-Century economist, Random House Business

Reis, E. (2011) The lean start-up: How constant innovation creates radically successful businesses, Portfolio Penguin

Reynolds, P.D. (2005) Understanding business creation: Serendipity and scope in two decades of business creation studies, Small Business Economics, 24 (4), 359-364

Rittel, H. W., & Webber, M. M. (1973). "Dilemmas in a General Theory of Planning." Policy sciences, 4(2), 155-169

Rogers, E. (1962) Diffusion of Innovations, New York, Free Press of Glencoe

Rothwell, R. (1994), Towards the Fifth-generation Innovation Process, International Marketing Review, Vol. 11 No. 1, pp. 7-31.

Sattell, G. (2017) Here's why your innovation strategy will fail, Medium

Schneider, J. (2017) How to move your team closer to clarity, O'Reilly

Schoups, A. (2017) An introduction to assumptions mapping, Mural

Setter, M. (2023) User Acceptance Testing – How to do it right in 2023, UserSnap

Shanks, M. (nd) An introduction to design thinking: Process Guide, D.School: Institute of design at Stanford

Sharon, T. (2012) It's our research: Getting stakeholder buy-in for user experience research projects, Elsevier

Sharon, T. (2016) Validating product ideas: Through lean user research, Rosenfeld Media

Sharon, T. (2017) Democratizing UX, Polaris (Medium)

Sibbet, D. (nd) Five Bold Steps Vision Canvas, The Grove Consultants International

Sinek, S. (2011) Start with why: How great leaders inspire everyone to take action, Penguin

Skapyak, M. (2023) Qualitative smoke testing – a theoretical product research method, UX Collective - Medium

Spool, J. (2017) Net Promoter Score Considered Harmful (and what UX professionals can do about it), UIE Centre

Spool, J. (2023) LinkedIn, 23 June 2023

Spradlin, D. (2012) Are you solving the right problem? Harvard Business Review

Startup Genome (2019) The State of the global start-up economy, Startup Genome

Statistica (2023) Soft Drinks – United Kingdom, Statistica

Stevens, E. How to run an effective ideation workshop: A step-by-step guide, UX Planet,

Stobierski, T. (2020) 3 most common types of customer needs to be aware of, Harvard Business School

Strategyzer (nd) Building blocks of business model canvas, Stratagyzer

Strategyzer (nd) Learning Card, Stratgyzer

Strategyzer, Value Proposition Canvas, Strategyzer

Sullivan, C. (2023) Should we do UXR or product discovery? Userresearchstudio

The Build Network Staff (2013) Do you even have a pricing strategy? Inc: Do You Even Have a Pricing Strategy? | Inc.com

Theil, P. (2014) Zero to One: Notes on startups, or how to build the future, Currency

This is Service Design Doing, Method Library, This is Service Design Doing

This is Service Design Doing, Pre-Ideation, This is Service Design Doing

Tomitsch, M. (2022) The case for using non-human personas in design, Medium

Torres, T. (2021) Product Discovery, Product Talk

Torres, T. (2021a) Continuous discovery habits: Discover products that create customer and business value, Product Talk LLC

Torres, T. (2021b) Product Discovery, Product Talk

Traynor, D. (nd) Understanding direct and indirect competiton, Intercom

U-Sentric Blog (2016) 3 ways in which your company can greatly benefit from User Experience Research, Medium

Ulwick (2017) Outcome-Driven Innovation, Medium: Jobs-To-Be-Done, Medium

Ulwick, A. (2016) Why ideas don't solve problems, Anthonyulwick.com

Ulwick, T. (2016) Jobs to be Done: Theory to Practice, Idea Bite Press

UserPilot (2022) An overview on Teresa's Torres Continuous Discovery framework, UserPilot

UXPlanet (2019) How to run an effective ideation workshop: A step-by-step guide, Medium

ValTech, Design Thinking: An innovation journey in 6 phases, ValTech

Waterman, R.H. and Peters, T. (1982) In search of excellence, Harper, and Row

Wick, D.A. (2018) Strategy – What are your core capabilities? Play to your strengths, Strategic Discipline: Positioning Systems

Wicks, A. (2017) Enter the matrix – Lean prioritisation, Mind the Product

Y Combinator (2023) How to build an MVP: Startup School, Youtube

Yang, R. (2017) How good product managers deliver bad news, Aha!

Young, I. (2008) Mental models: Aligning design strategy with human behaviour, Rosenfeld Media

Zahara, S.A. & George, G.(2002) Absorptive capacity: A review, reconceptualization and extension, The Academy of Management Review, 27 (2)

Zelmanow, A. (2023) Let's blow up UX research, Medium

Zidaru, J. (2023) LinkedIn post, June 2023

Zwilling, M. 8 innovative pricing strategies every business should evaluate, Inc: 8 Innovative Pricing Strategies Every Business Should Evaluate | Inc.com

FURTHER READING

Further Reading

Acaroglu, L. (2017) Tools for systems thinkers: The 6 fundamental concepts of systems thinking, Medium

Blank, S. & Dorf, B. (2012) The start-up owner's manual: The step-by-step guide for building a great company, K&S Ranch

Boston Consulting Group, Business Model Innovation, Boston Consulting Group

Boysen, M. (2018) How to get results from jobs-to-be-done interviews, Medium

BrandGenetics (2017) Where good ideas come from – The natural history of innovation, BrandGenetics

Buley, L. (2013) A user experience team of one: A research and design survival guide, Rosenfeld Media

Carayannis, E., Provance, M. & Givens, N. (2011) Knowledge arbitrage, serendipity, and acquisition formality: Their effects on sustainable entrepreneurial activity in regions, IEEE Transactions on Engineering Management, 58 (3), 564-577

Chamorro-Premuzic, T. (2015) Why group brainstorming is a waste of time, Harvard Business Review

Conn, R. (nd) 6 rules of product design according to Maslow's hierarchy of needs, ProductPlan

Continuous Innovation (nd), Continuous Innovation Framework, Continuous Innovation

Denning, S. (2012) Gary Hamel on Innovating Innovation, Forbes

Emprechtinger, F. (2018) Identification of innovation potential - 6 important triggers for innovation, LEAD Innovation

Emprechtinger, G. (2018) What is the degree of innovation? Lead Innovation

Froes, H. (2019) Building a research repo when you don't know how, Medium

Funnell, S.C., and Rogers, P.J. (2011) Purposeful Program Theory: Effective use of theories of change and logical models: Jossey-Bass

Google (nd) People + AI Guidebook, Pair with Google

Gov. UK (2014) Policy paper: Government digital inclusion strategy, UK Government online

Green, N. (2017) Stop Guessing: The 9 behaviours of great problem solvers, Berrett-Koehler Publishers

Groschupf, S. (2022) The proven process for developing a go-to-market strategy, HubSpot

Hague, P. (2021) Market research in practice: An introduction to gaining greater market insight (4th edition), Kogan Page

IDEO (nd) Pilot, DesignKit

Interaction Design Foundation (nd) Information Radiators, Interaction Design Foundation

Johnson, G., Scholes, K. & Whittington, R. (2011) Exploring Corporate Strategy (Eighth Edition), Prentice Hall

Johnson, G., Scholes, K. & Whittington, R. (2011) Strategic Management - An Introduction: Analysis, Decision, and Execution

Kaplan, R.S. & Norton, D. P. (1992) The balanced scorecard - Measures that drive performance, Harvard Business Review

Kuratko, D. F., Goldsby, M. and Hornsby, J. (2018) Corporate Innovation: Disruptive thinking in organisations, Routledge

Lee, R. (2023) Building an integrated ResearchOps tool stack, User Interviews

Marinova, R. & Phillimore, J. (2003) Models of innovation. V. Shavinina (Ed.), International handbook on innovation, Elsevier, Amsterdam

McGivern, Y. (2013) The practice of market research: An introduction, Pearson

McKeown, M. (2014) The innovation book: How to manage ideas and execution for outstanding results, FT Publishing

Miro (nd) Template for non-human personas under creative commons license by designthinkmakebreakrepeat

MoreSteam (nd) Design of Experiments: Toolbox, MoreSteam

Mummby-Croft, B. & Chugh, H. (nd) Idea Canvas, Imperial Enterprise Lab

Parrish, S. (2017) The "0 to 1 trap" and seven other things I learned from Peter Thiel, Farnam Street (Shane Parrish), Medium

Pernice, K. (2020) Research repositories for tracking UX research and growing your researchops, NNGroup

Porumboiu, D. (2021) The complete guide to ideation, Viima

Predictable Innovation (2022) Go-To-Market Framework, Predictable Innovation

Rajaraman, S. (nd) Launching with stakeholders, Coda.io

Sattell, G. (2017) Mapping Innovation: A playbook for navigating a disruptive age, McGraw Hill

Schonthal, D. (2022) The key to successful innovation? Progress over product, Inc.com

Sharp, C. (2019) Why user research could be a gamechanger in sustainability, Medium

Shaywitz, D.A. (2020) "The Innovation Delusion" Review: Mistaking novelty for progress, The Wall Street Journal

The Decision Lab (nb) Why do we focus on trivial things? The Decision Lab

Ulwick, T. (2005) What customers want: Using outcome-driven innovation to create breakthrough products and services, McGraw Hill

W3 (nd) Web accessibility evaluation tools list, W3C

Waterman, R. H., Peters, T. J., & Phillips, J. R. (1980). Structure Is Not Organization. Business Horizons, 23(3), 14-26.

Zaltman, G. (1997) Rethinking market research: Putting people back in, Journal of marketing research, 34 (4), 424-437

Acknowledgements

Writing a book is a team sport and I would like to thank my husband, Simon Sharp for his undying patience and support over the past two years when I have been spending weekends and evenings on this book. My children Emma-Rae and Tom for being the reason why I work hard.

Thank you to Harm van Kessel and Soraya Clevers from BIS Publishers for all the support and making this book a reality. Thank you to Daniel Chehade from Studio Chehade who did the book cover and interior design and did an amazing job. Thank you to David Haviland for your wonderful copy editing. I greatly appreciate the feedback from my family and James, Frances, Bukky and Mike.

About the Author

Make Products That Matter joins the dots across UX research, new product development, product management and innovation and is a step-by-step guide for those new to the world of creating products. This book is on a mission to show the value of research in the development of products and services to grow successful businesses.

Dr Chloe Sharp stands as a seasoned expert in product, user, and market research, with extensive experience in translating insights and evidence into innovative, impactful products and services in the UK. She led an innovation consultancy, providing research and grant writing services to charities, start-ups, scale-ups, and SMEs, transforming their concepts into tangible realities.

Prior to her consultancy role, she worked with a research and development organisation specialising in customer experience, social research, and impact evaluation for transport technologies. Further sharpening her research acumen in an academic setting, she mastered her research skills to high standards. These diverse consultative experiences, along with her academic qualifications (BSc, MSc, and PhD), have informed the creation of this book.